Cognitive Processing in the Right Hemisphere

This is a volume in

PERSPECTIVES IN
NEUROLINGUISTICS, NEUROPSYCHOLOGY,
AND PSYCHOLINGUISTICS

A Series of Monographs and Treatises

A complete list of titles in this series appears at the end of this volume.

Cognitive Processing in the Right Hemisphere

Edited by

ELLEN PERECMAN

New York University Medical Center
New York, New York

 1983
ACADEMIC PRESS
A Subsidiary of Harcourt Brace Jovanovich, Publishers
New York   London
Paris   San Diego   San Francisco   São Paulo   Sydney   Tokyo   Toronto

ACADEMIC PRESS, INC.
111 Fifth Avenue, New York, New York 10003

United Kingdom Edition published by
ACADEMIC PRESS, INC. (LONDON) LTD.
24/28 Oval Road, London NW1   7DX

Library of Congress Cataloging in Publication Data
Main entry under title:

Cognitive processing in the right hemisphere.

(Perspectives in neurolinguistics, neuropsychology,
and psycholinguistics)
    Includes index.
    1. Cerebral dominance--Addresses, essays, lectures.
2. Cognition--Physiological aspects--Addresses, essays,
lectures.   3. Brain damage--Complications and sequelae--
Addresses, essays, lectures.   4. Aphasics--Rehabilitation
--Addresses, essays, lectures.   5. Neurolinguistics--
Addresses, essays, lectures.   I. Perecman, Ellen.
II. Title: Right hemisphere. III. Series. [DNLM:
1. Cognition--Physiology. 2. Brain--Physiology.
3. Brain mapping. WL 335 C676]
QP385.5.C63 1983   612'.825   83-2692
ISBN 0-12-550680-5

PRINTED IN THE UNITED STATES OF AMERICA

83 84 85 86   9 8 7 6 5 4 3 2 1

In memory of my dear cousin
ABRAHAM JACOB WEXLER

Contents

3
Rethinking the Right Hemisphere   41

JASON W. BROWN

PART II
STUDIES OF NORMAL SUBJECTS

4
The Linguistic and Emotional Functions
of the Normal Right Hemisphere   57

M. MOSCOVITCH

5
Right Hemispheric Specialization for the Expression
and Appreciation of Emotion: A Focus on the Face   83

JOAN C. BOROD, ELISSA KOFF, and HERBERT S. CARON

6

Right Hemispheric Involvement in Imagery and Affect   111

M. P. BRYDEN and ROBERT G. LEY

7

Hemispheric EEG Asymmetries Related to Cognitive Functioning in Children   125

R. W. THATCHER, R. McALASTER, M. L. LESTER,
R. L. HORST, and D. S. CANTOR

PART III
STUDIES OF BRAIN-DAMAGED SUBJECTS

8

Selective Impairment of Semantic-Lexical Discrimination in Right-Brain-Damaged Patients   149

GUIDO GAINOTTI, CARLO CALTAGIRONE, and GABRIELE MICELI

9

Missing the Point: The Role of the Right Hemisphere in the Processing of Complex Linguistic Materials   169

HOWARD GARDNER, HIRAM H. BROWNELL,
WENDY WAPNER, and DIANE MICHELOW

10

Negative Evidence for Language Capacity in the Right Hemisphere: Reversed Lateralization of Cerebral Function   193

MARGARET HAN and SUN-HOO FOO

PART IV
LANGUAGE REHABILITATION VIA THE RIGHT HEMISPHERE

11

Heightening Visual Imagery: A New Approach to Aphasia Therapy   215

JOYCE FITCH-WEST

12

Exploiting the Right Hemisphere for Language Rehabilitation: Melodic Intonation Therapy   229

NANCY HELM-ESTABROOKS

Contributors

Numbers in parentheses indicate the pages on which the authors' contributions begin.

T. G. **Bever** (19), Department of Psychology, Psycholinguistics Program, Columbia University, New York, New York 10027

Joan C. Borod[1] (83), Aphasia Research Center, Department of Neurology, Boston University School of Medicine, and Boston Veterans Administration Medical Center, Boston, Massachusetts 02130

Jason W. Brown (41), Department of Neurology, New York University Medical Center, New York, New York 10016

Hiram H. Brownell (169), Psychology Service, Boston Veterans Administration Medical Center, Boston, Massachusetts 02130

M. P. Bryden (111), Department of Psychology, University of Waterloo, Waterloo, Ontario N2L 3G1, Canada

Carlo Caltagirone (149), Clinica Neurologica, Università Cattolica del Sacro Cuore, 00168 Roma, Italy

---

[1] Present address: Department of Psychiatry, New York University Medical Center, New York, New York 10016.

D. S. Cantor (125), Applied Neuroscience Research Institute, University of Maryland Eastern Shore, Princess Anne, Maryland 21853, and University of Maryland School of Medicine, Baltimore, Maryland 21201

Herbert S. Caron (83), Department of Psychology, Case-Western Reserve University, Cleveland, Ohio 44106

Joyce Fitch-West (215), Speech Pathology and Audiology Department, Manhattan Veterans Administration Medical Center, New York, New York 10016

Sun-Hoo Foo (193), Department of Neurology, New York University Medical Center, New York, New York 10016

Guido Gainotti (149), Clinica Neurologica, Università Cattolica del Sacro Cuore, 00168 Roma, Italy

Howard Gardner (169), Psychology Service, Boston Veterans Administration Medical Center, Boston, Massachusetts 02130

Margaret Han[2] (193), Department of Rehabilitation, New York Infirmary—Beekman Downtown Hospital, New York, New York 10038

Nancy Helm-Estabrooks (229), Neurology Service, Veterans Administration Medical Center, Boston, Massachusetts 02130, and Boston University School of Medicine, Boston Massachusetts 02130

R. L. Horst (125), Applied Neuroscience Research Institute, University of Maryland Eastern Shore, Princess Anne, Maryland 21853

Elissa Koff (83), Department of Psychology, Wellesley College, Wellesley, Massachusetts 02181, and Aphasia Research Center, Department of Neurology, Boston University School of Medicine, Boston, Massachusetts 02130

M. L. Lester (125), Applied Neuroscience Research Institute, University of Maryland Eastern Shore, Princess Anne, Maryland 21853

Robert G. Ley (111), Department of Psychology, Simon Fraser University, Burnaby, British Columbia V5A 1S6, Canada

R. McAlaster (125), Neurotrauma—M.I.E.M.S.S., University of Maryland School of Medicine, Baltimore, Maryland 21201, and Applied Neuroscience Research Institute, University of Maryland Eastern Shore, Princess Anne, Maryland 21853

Gabriele Miceli (149), Clinica Neurologica, Università Cattolica del Sacro Cuore, 00168 Roma, Italy

Diane Michelow (169), Psychology Service, Boston Veterans Administration Medical Center, Boston, Massachusetts 02130

---

[2] Present address: Laguna Honda Hospital, San Francisco, California 94116.

M. Moscovitch (57), Department of Psychology, University of Toronto, Erindale Campus, Mississauga, Ontario L5L 1C6, Canada

Ellen Perecman (1), Department of Neurology, New York University Medical Center, New York, New York 10016

R. W. Thatcher (125), Applied Neuroscience Research Institute, University of Maryland Eastern Shore, Princess Anne, Maryland 21853

Wendy Wapner (169), Psychology Service, Boston Veterans Administration Medical Center, Boston, Massachusetts 02130

Preface

The right hemisphere was, until recently, an uncharted territory in cognitive neuropsychology. Only in the last 20 years have investigators begun to identify the various roles of the right hemisphere in cognition. Gardner, Brownell, Wapner, and Michelow (this volume) suggest that the right hemisphere had previously failed to interest neuropsychologists because it had been commonly assumed that "an individual's cognitive competence is closely linked to the intactness of his left hemisphere" and consequently, that "individuals with right hemisphere damage, their language apparently intact, are not seriously compromised in their ability to understand situations, solve problems, and make their way in the world [p. 171].'' More careful studies of right-brain-damaged individuals have proven otherwise. Chapters 8, 9, and 10 in this volume attest to the seriousness of the compromises in cognitive functioning that may be associated with right hemisphere damage.

The book is divided into four parts: I, Theoretical Issues in Right Hemisphere Neuropsychology; II, Studies of Normal Subjects; III, Studies of Brain-Damaged Subjects; and IV, Language Rehabilitation via the Right Hemisphere. Theoretical issues raised by the behavior of the intact right hemisphere and by symptoms of right hemisphere pathology are given a refreshingly controversial treatment in Chapters 2 and 3. In the former, Bever calls into question the very notion that the right hemisphere is specialized for particular cognitive functions. In the latter, Brown argues that the so-called "specialized" right hemisphere cognition is in fact indistinguishable from left hemisphere cognition at preliminary cognitive levels.

Chapters 4, 5, 6, and 7 address the question of right hemisphere capacity as indicated in studies of normal populations. Moscovitch, in Chapter 4, takes the position that the functional asymmetry of the normal brain is seen primarily at higher levels of cognitive functioning. In Chapter 5, Borod, Koff, and Caron examine the role of the normal as well as the damaged right hemisphere in processing emotion, paying particular attention to the face as the principal expressor of emotion. In Chapter 6 Bryden and Ley present evidence on the lexical semantic capacity of the right hemisphere. Concluding this section on normals is a chapter by Thatcher, McAlaster, Lester, Horst, and Cantor that relates measures of cognitive abilities of the two hemispheres to electroencephalographic (EEG) data.

Inferences regarding right hemisphere capacity based on brain-damaged populations are presented in Chapters 5, 8, 9, and 10. Gainotti, Caltagirone, and Miceli concern themselves with the lexical semantic abilities of right-brain-damaged subjects in Chapter 8. In Chapter 9, Gardner, Brownell, Wapner, and Michelow address the paralinguistic aspect of language function in such patients. A case report describing a left hemisphere lesion in a right-hander, which gives rise to symptoms typical of right hemisphere damage, *but no aphasia,* is presented in Chapter 10 by Han and Foo.

Finally, Chapters 11 and 12 offer the views of language pathologists on how certain assumptions about the capabilities of the right hemisphere can lead to innovative approaches to the treatment of aphasic individuals. In Chapter 11, Fitch-West describes a therapy based on visual imagery, while Helm-Estabrooks discusses Melodic Intonation Therapy (MIT), which uses melodic and intonation contours to facilitate language, in Chapter 12.

In October 1980, the Institute for Research in Behavioral Neuroscience (IRBN) began a tradition of sponsoring annual conferences on topics in neuropsychology. The first conference, entitled "Cognitive Processing in the Right Hemisphere," was the catalyst for this book. Many of the participants in that conference contributed to the present volume. This volume was prepared under the auspices of the Institute for Research in Behavioral Neuroscience.

I would like to express my appreciation to Jason W. Brown for encouraging me to undertake the task of editing this volume and for allowing me to benefit from his knowledge and experience. To the contributing authors, I offer thanks for making my task so worthwhile.

1

Introduction:
Discovering Buried Treasure—
A Look at the Cognitive Potential
of the Right Hemisphere

ELLEN PERECMAN

ON THE NOTIONS DOMINANCE AND CAPACITY
IN NEUROPSYCHOLOGY

A schematic representation of the respective roles of the right and left cerebral hemispheres in cognitive processes, as portrayed in the literature on hemispheric asymmetries, calls to mind a socioeconomic map of the world. The left hemisphere is the industrialized, economically developed sector. It dominates the world of the brain, taking control not only in situations in which it is in fact better equipped to do so, but also in situations in which the right hemisphere might have performed quite adequately albeit by different and perhaps less sophisticated methods. The right hemisphere, in this analogy, is the underdeveloped, Third World sector of the brain, defined by more or less diffuse organizational principles and possessing crude but nonetheless valuable resources which often go untapped or underutilized.

As an illustration of the appropriateness of this analogy consider the following anecdote. Jerre Levy asked students at Cal Tech to describe the cognitive methods they used in performing a task in which they were asked to

COGNITIVE PROCESSING IN
THE RIGHT HEMISPHERE

Copyright © 1983 by Academic Press, Inc.
All rights of reproduction in any form reserved.
ISBN   0-12-550680-5

match a tactile stimulus with a visual one. She found that all of her subjects were surprised to learn that mental imaging, which is associated with the right hemisphere, could have been used as a strategy. Rather, they all reported using a presumed left hemisphere, analytic method. "One gets the suspicion," mused Levy, "that 18 or so years of schooling in the sciences may functionally ablate the right hemisphere [Levy, 1974]."

Moskovitch (Chapter 4, this volume) points out that as a rule hemispheric asymmetries are more robust in clinical populations than in normals. Moreover, he takes the normal literature to suggest that regardless of the right hemisphere's proven capacity to process verbal information semantically, in normals there is a strong tendency for the left hemisphere's semantic abilities to dominate the semantic abilities of the right hemisphere, assuming full control of semantic operations.

Consider also a dichotic study of split-brain patients by Gordon (1980). Results showed that although subjects responded more often to verbal commands given in the right ear (left hemisphere) and performed with the right hand, they did, on occasion, respond with the left hand (right hemisphere). Gordon suggests that these left hand responses reflect instances in which the left hemisphere was "caught 'off guard' allowing uninhibited expression by the right hemisphere [p.79]."

In each case we are reminded that there is a crucial distinction to be made between *Dominance* and *Capacity* (cf. Levy, 1974). Consider the following as a first approximation of that distinction:

> DOMINANCE is the *tendency* for one hemisphere to process a particular type of information and to control response behavior based on that information.

> CAPACITY refers to the *potential* of a hemisphere to process a particular type of information, where that potential may manifest itself in an overt response by the nondominant hemisphere when the dominant hemisphere is otherwise engaged.

Demonstrating the dominance of one hemisphere over another, for a given aspect of cognition, is a more straightforward task than demonstrating that a cognitive capacity is present in a hemisphere. Indeed, the very definition of dominance reveals why this should be the case. Thus, among investigators mapping cognitive functions onto the brain, it is quite commonly held that in 90–99% of right-handers, and in 50–70% of non-right-handers, the left hemisphere is dominant for speech and linguistic functions and the right hemisphere is dominant for nonverbal, visuospatial operations (Searleman, 1977).

A characterization of the cognitive capacities of the respective hemispheres apart from the question of dominance has been less forthcoming for several reasons. One reason, already hinted at in the preface, is that until recently the role of the left hemisphere in cognition has been investigated much more thoroughly than that of the right hemisphere. Another is that a disproportionately great focus has been placed on the phenomenon of cerebral dominance and its corollary cerebral asymmetry.

The following chapters represent a shift away from the traditional perspective in which interest in the right hemisphere is simply a by-product of a primary concern with the left, to a view in which the relational pejoratives "minor," "nondominant," and "speechless" recede into the background and the role of the right hemisphere in cognitive processing becomes the focal issue.

In Chapter 2, Bever calls into question the very notion of hemispheric dominance, on the premise that laterality for a particular task depends on the specific experience and acquired skills of the subject as well as the particular cognitive demands of the task. He thus points out that a figure-matching task can be performed either analytically or holistically, and that in a tracking task, meaningless syllables are recognized more quickly in the right hemisphere (left ear), but initial phonemes, equally meaningless, are recognized more quickly in the left hemisphere (right ear).

Bever argues that apparent cerebral asymmetries in cognitive function can have one of three sources: the physiology of the brain, experience in the world, and choice of cognitive strategy. He argues further that a failure to distinguish among these sources in conjunction with the failure to control for several subject variables has caused the existing literature to be uninterpretable. Regarding the importance of subject variables, he cites evidence of a distinctive hemispheric organization in familial sinistrals in relation to right-handers and nonfamilial sinistrals. In addition to the individual differences in genetic background and experience, Bever suggests that there are developmental changes in mode of cognition, and infers from this, changes over time in the relative contribution of the hemispheres to various cognitive processes. He introduces support for these developmental changes from work in language, music, and facial recognition.

Bever's thesis is that the right hemisphere is quantitatively and not qualitatively distinct from the left. He suggests that once the necessary variables have been controlled for, studies of cognitive operations in normals will be found to support the view that the left hemisphere is computationally advanced over the right from childhood onward, thereby encouraging more complex relational activities to be represented and executed in the left hemisphere. This discrepancy in computational ability would then account for the quantitative difference between the hemispheres.

Brown (Chapter 3) also sees the difference between the hemispheres as a quantitative one. Indeed, although more neurological in its orientation, Brown's characterization of this difference is quite consistent with Bever's view. For Brown, the left hemisphere is computationally advanced over the right in the sense that preliminary cognitive processes are mediated by brain levels shared by the right and left hemispheres, whereas end stage processing is mediated only by the left hemisphere.

Brown argues that the parietal lobes of the right and left hemispheres form a unitary cognitive system and that terminology used to suggest differences in the processing styles of the two hemispheres (e.g., holistic and analytic) rather capture differences at successive moments in a single processing continuum. He is explicit in his claim that cognitive processes carried out by the right hemisphere are also carried out by the left hemisphere and that the reverse cannot be the case since these processes constitute cognitive end points in the right hemisphere but are submerged in subsequent processing stages in the left hemisphere. Apparent hemispheric specialization, Brown maintains, is in fact a spurious phenomenon, an artifact of the organization of processing levels across the two hemispheres. Indeed, it is as a result of this organization that experiments which are actually tapping early cognitive stages in a single processing continuum yield what appears to be an effect attributable to some idiosyncratic property of the right hemisphere.

The evidence that right hemisphere functions deteriorate more rapidly than those in the left as people age (Albert and Kaplan, 1980) supports Brown's contention that functions common to both hemispheres are ontogenetically prior to the specialized functions of the left hemisphere. For it seems entirely plausible that those functions which are most recently developed will be better preserved and preserved longer in the course of aging. His theoretical position that right hemisphere processes are preliminary and subconscious in relation to later stage left hemisphere processes, is strengthened by evidence from Bryden and Ley (Chapter 6, this volume) that word recognition need not be at a conscious level for right hemisphere processes to be activated and that conscious recognition of a word, in fact, prevents a right hemisphere effect for highly imageable words in a priming paradigm.

Thus, both Brown and Bever take issue with the traditional theoretical position that the role of the right hemisphere in cognitive processing is qualitatively, as opposed to quantitatively, different from that of the left. Yet, even for those who argue in favor of a qualitative difference, the precise characterization of that qualitative difference is open to question. Historically, linguistic functions have been attributed to the left hemisphere, and nonlinguistic, visuospatial functions have been attributed to the right hemisphere. The last two decades have produced evidence that within the context of nonlinguistic behavior, the right hemisphere is important in the processing of emotion and humor, with the anosagnosic (denial) symptoms of right hemisphere damage possibly reflecting an abnormal emotional response. A right hemisphere component in language processing has also been indicated.

In the present volume, the chapters that pose the greatest challenges to the historical dichotomy between a language hemisphere on the left and a nonlanguage hemisphere on the right are those by Gainotti, Caltagirone, and Miceli (Chapter 8) and Bryden and Ley (Chapter 6), both of which provide evidence for linguistic-semantic capacity in the right hemisphere. Gainotti *et al.* infer semantic capacity from its disruption in right-hemisphere-damaged patients, whereas Ley and Bryden base their evidence on a normal population.

Gainotti *et al.* present a series of experiments designed to determine whether the apparent lexical-semantic impairment in right-brain-damaged patients is indeed linguistic in origin or whether nonlinguistic factors such as general mental deterioration, spatial neglect, or visuoperceptual difficulties can account for what appear as linguistic symptoms. Using discrimination, comprehension, and confrontation naming techniques, Gainotti *et al.* found that although spatial neglect could be ruled out as a factor, most of the semantic errors of their subjects were due to the influence of general mental deterioration. The authors' concern, however, is with the remaining errors, which indicate to them that there is a genuine lexical-semantic deficit in right-brain-damaged patients. The results from the confrontation naming task suggest that one cannot claim a purely visuoperceptual basis for semantic naming errors.

Bryden and Ley describe two experiments which support the hypothesis that, in normal populations, emotionally laden, imageable language is mediated by the right hemisphere. The studies reported use a semantic priming technique to address the question of whether emotionally laden versus neutral words, and high imagery versus low imagery words, lead to distinct priming effects by causing shifts of attention to either one hemisphere or the other. Finding evidence that there is indeed a shift to the left following presentation of affectively loaded or high imagery words, these authors suggest that the lexical representation of these types of words has a component that is represented in the right hemisphere. They account for the obtained priming effect by postulating that the presentation of high imagery or emotional words activates components of the lexical representation in the right as well as left hemisphere and that the priming effect is the result of persistent activation of the right hemisphere.

Gardner, Brownell, Wapner, and Michelow (Chapter 9) also claim that the role of the right hemisphere in language is greater than has traditionally been conceded. They argue that the right hemisphere is pivotal in processing extralinguistic parameters of language such as narrative and discourse functions. The experiments reported here by Gardner *et al.* are from a program of research formulated explicitly to delineate the role of the right hemisphere in processing linguistic material. These experiments test subjects' abilities to understand, integrate, and recall connected discourse in the form of narratives, jokes, puns, and linguistic puzzles.

Results from these experiments indicate that right-hemisphere-damaged patients have difficulty with linguistically complex materials. In trying to account for their results, Gardner *et al.* point out that there are two alternative and almost contradictory interpretations: (1) that the difficulty is a linguistic one and (2) that the difficulty is ideational in origin. Gardner *et al.* favor the interpretation that the problem is a linguistic one, drawing a distinction between linguistically complex functions and functions involving the canonical aspects of language. They note, however, that one might be justified in arguing from the same results that their subjects had problems handling ideationally complex material. They remark that the choice of interpretation is contingent upon one's definition of language and that although one might conceivably consider paralinguistic factors to fall outside of the domain of language, there is stronger motivation to include such factors among the linguistically complex functions of language.

In Chapter 4, Moscovitch takes the position that the important role of the right hemisphere in processing extra- or paralinguistic properties of language may be integrally bound up with the right hemisphere's superiority in mediating emotion. In this regard, he reviews the rather inconsistent results of recent research on lateralization of emotion, cautioning that clinical data are always suspect and that a number of methodological shortcomings are apparent in the literature on normals. Among such shortcomings is the possibility that artificially constructed laboratory studies are not, in fact, investigating true emotional expression. As far as Moscovitch is concerned, the problem is not with the hypothesis that the right hemisphere mediates emotion, but rather with the ingenuity of investigators in coming up with innovative experiments which ask the right questions.

Turning to the lateralization of properly linguistic functions, Moscovitch argues that it is primarily the higher order stages of information processing which are represented asymmetrically across hemispheres. He maintains that the processing of semantic information yields small hemispheric differences because both hemispheres contribute (in different ways) to semantic processing, the evidence of right hemisphere processing for concrete words reflecting submerged semantic abilities in that hemisphere. In the case of phonological and syntactic processing, on the other hand, the hemispheric differences are greater, indicating a clear left hemisphere superiority, because "the inferior hemisphere's capacities are simply inadequate or inappropriate for the task."

Although Moscovitch never explicitly makes the claim that semantic processing is an earlier stage of information processing than phonological (or syntactic) processing, a claim explicitly made (in this volume), by Brown, his argument is consistent with that position insofar as he contends that semantic processing is linked to smaller asymmetries than phonological processing and that the greater the asymmetry the later the linguistic stage.

In Chapter 5, Borod, Koff, and Caron present a review of the literature on emotion, in which they point out some of the confusion between the issues of facial recognition and recognition of an emotion on a face. [Cf. Bryden and Ley (Chapter 6, this volume), who consider the processing of emotion to be independent of the more general right hemisphere superiority for recognizing faces.] Making the assumption, on the basis of this review, that the right hemisphere is dominant for the expression and appreciation of emotion and that the face is a central communicator of emotion, these investigators ask whether asymmetries in the extent of movement, intensity of expression, and quantity of emotion on the face are systematic and, if so, how they are to be related to other lateralized functions of mental life.

Borod *et al.* believe that volitional emotional expression involves cortical control and might therefore provide an indication of underlying neuroanatomical processes. They address the problem of volitional (posed), as opposed to spontaneous, emotional expression, in terms of the question, Which side of the face is more involved in posed emotional expression? Obtaining results indicating that the left side of the face is the more involved, they try to reconcile the fact that the face and arm areas are adjacent in motor cortex, with evidence that the right hemisphere is more involved in the control of facial movement whereas the left is dominant for arm and hand movement. They conclude by proposing that facial movement may have developed phylogenetically in functional proximity with the human emotional system and may have become lateralized along with emotion by virtue of its association with emotion.

For the most part, evidence presented in this volume regarding the nature of right hemisphere cognitive capacity is inferred from the more or less overt behavior of subjects on various psychological tasks. In Chapter 7, Thatcher, McAlaster, Lester, Horst, and Cantor discuss electroencephalography (EEG) as a technique that provides a more direct source of information on this question. The focus of their chapter is on the extent to which measures of coherence and amplitude asymmetry in the resting EEG of children whose eyes are closed, are related to measures of cognitive ability. Results suggest that the greater the amplitude asymmetry for a particular child (the higher amplitude being on the left), the greater the full scale IQ of that child. Assuming that a state of maximal coherence and minimal amplitude asymmetry between the two hemispheres represents a state of minimal differentiation of brain activity from one area to another, these investigators interpret their data to support the notion that increased dissimilarity in EEG activity between pairs of scalp sites is positively correlated with mental capacity for processing information.

Another source of evidence on right hemisphere capacity for language processing is a small literature on crossed aphasia and an even smaller literature on the counterpart of crossed aphasia, namely, the absence of expected aphasia. Reports of such cases signal the possibility that language processing may be bilateral or even, in some cases, primarily a right hemisphere function. In Chapter 10, Han and Foo review these literatures and present a report on one of the very few published cases of absence of expected aphasia. Han and Foo observe that the deficits seen in their case of left hemisphere damage are typical of right-brain-damaged patients. They conclude that their case demonstrates an unusual reversal of cerebral organization in which the right hemisphere is dominant for linguistic, analytic processing and the left is dominant for visuospatial, holistic processing.

A more precise characterization of the cognitive capacity of the right hemisphere, to which the chapters in this volume contribute, is vital to research on rehabilitation techniques in aphasia, where one of the central questions is whether the right hemisphere takes on responsibility for language processing after left hemisphere damage. Delimiting the capacity of the right hemisphere constitutes a major stride in the resolution of that question, insofar as such a delimitation will provide an evaluation metric for judging the plausibility of a right hemisphere role in language rehabilitation. In the final chapters of this volume, Fitch-West and Helm-Estabrooks assume that the right hemisphere takes over the responsibility for language processing and advocate language rehabilitation programs designed to use intact nonlanguage capabilities of the right hemisphere in the service of language processing.

In Chapter 11, West proposes that, because the left hemisphere damage in an aphasia at the very least dampens the analytic mode of cognition, while leaving the synthetic or holistic mode of the right hemisphere unimpaired, an aphasia therapy should be designed to train patients to use the cognitive mode of the intact right hemisphere in processing language. Such a therapeutic program, she argues, would be more productive than one in which patients must rely on the impaired cognitive mode of the damaged left hemisphere and which requires rehabilitation of impaired function. West suggests instead that patients be trained to shift to a dependence on intact right hemisphere functions for the purpose of processing language.

The program of therapy which West proposes is motivated principally by work which indicates that two codes are available for processing linguistic information, a visual code and a verbal code, and that imagery can serve to facilitate the coding, storage, and retrieval of verbal information. As visual imagery is presumed to be a right hemisphere operation, West feels that left-damaged aphasic patients can be taught to use visual imagery to mediate verbal processes.

The therapy described by Helm-Estabrooks in Chapter 12 focuses on the motoric aspects of language. Having shown elsewhere that melodic intonation therapy (MIT) has had positive effects in the rehabilitation of language in aphasia, in the present chapter Helm-Estabrooks explains why the therapy has been successful in some cases but unsuccessful in others. She presents evidence that the MIT method has proven effective in facilitating motor aspects of speech production in nonfluent aphasias and that the success of the therapy depends on whether or not the brain lesion is restricted exclusively to the left hemisphere.

The MIT method takes advantage of the right hemisphere's capacity to process melody and intonation as well as its capacity to process slowly presented auditory stimuli. The training program begins with an exaggeration of the rhythmic structure of an utterance and the imposition on it of a musical intonation. If this proves effective, patients are trained to simply emphasize prosodic contours. Helm-Estabrooks suggests that this training should eventually facilitate the production of normally intoned speech and that, at the same time, the slow rate of presentation and musical intonation of the stimuli used in the therapy will maximize the potential of the right hemisphere to comprehend language as well.

The content of this volume, as reflected in the chapter summaries just presented, contributes to a definition of the right hemisphere's potential for cognitive processing and for the language processing in particular, upon which success of therapeutic programs such as MIT depends. We have seen that the right hemisphere plays a role in the processing of emotionally laden information. Presumably, this role is related to the role of the right hemisphere in processing paralinguistic aspects of language, as the paralinguistic aspects of language carry the emotional information in an utterance. Similarly, the ability of the right hemisphere to process lexical-semantic information is obviously related to that hemisphere's ability to process highly imageable language. As a final example of how the various roles of the right hemisphere in cognitive processes form a coherent set, consider that highly imageable language is more likely to be emotionally driven, and that there is thus a relation between the role of the right hemisphere in processing highly imageable language and its role in processing emotionally laden information in general.

The chapters in this volume that bear upon the role of the right hemisphere in language processing focus on lexical-semantic processes. The role of the right hemisphere in processing phonological information is not specifically addressed as it is a common assumption that the right hemisphere's role in language is restricted to the level of lexical semantics. Indeed, an overview of language studies in hemispherectomized, commissurotomized, and right-brain-damaged subjects reveals that the question of right hemisphere mediation of phonological processes has not been a frequent topic of investigation.

PHONOLOGICAL PROCESSING
IN THE RIGHT HEMISPHERE

Data from Hemispherectomy

Reports on language in left-hemispherectomized subjects present either conclusions about the status of general language capacity without any supporting data, or unsystematic observations on the status of language functioning, made during routine neurological evaluations (Zollinger, 1935; Krynauw, 1950; Crockett & Estridge, 1951; Hillier, 1954; French, Johnson, Brown, & Van Bergen, 1955; Gardner, Karnosh, McClure, & Gardner, 1955; McFie, 1961; Obrador, 1964, Smith; 1966, 1972; Smith & Burklund, 1966).

Gott (1973) provides the single truly comprehensive language evaluation performed following hemispherectomy. Her data on judgment of rhyme and her error analyses on reading constitute the only objective data bearing specifically on phonological capacity of the single right hemisphere. It is important to note, however, that early damage to the left hemisphere is thought to cause transference of language function to the right hemisphere. Thus, cases such as Gott's, involving patients whose left hemispheres were damaged during infancy or adolescence, may be of limited theoretical interest, as the more typical or "natural" role of the right hemisphere in the intact brain will have been obscured.

Gott describes the language of a 12-year-old right-handed girl (R.S.) whose left hemisphere was removed for a tumor at age 10. Gott notes that immediately upon awakening from surgery the patient had been able to sing and speak in single words. Gott reports that her patient was 100% correct in determining whether a list of words presented auditorily rhymed with *mat*. Similarly, the patient was 80% correct in determining whether a list of written words rhymed with the written word *son*. The list included 20 words, 10 of which rhymed with *son* but in many cases were visually different (e.g., *sun*, *bun*) and 10 of which did not rhyme with *son* but had some letters in common (e.g., *sin* and *sow*). Gott notes that whereas the patient could perform the rhyming task quite well, her ability to identify words in the list was limited to *sun* and *boy*. Although this result might suggest that the single right hemisphere can process a word in terms of its sound structure alone, independent of its meaning structure, such a conclusion is weakened by the fact that all stimuli on the rhyming task appear to have been real words, posing a question as to the extent to which sound structure alone was the basis for the patient's judgments.

Nonetheless, intact phonological processing capacity is also indicated by the fact that an error analysis of the reading aloud of single words revealed no phonemic errors, but 20% semantic errors. Comprehension in this patient was reasonably good; she could follow simple commands and understand propositional speech of up to three statements. Repetition was quite good even on sentences of 6–7 words. Her speech was nonfluent, with utterances limited to single words and short phrases.

Data from Commissurotomy

Experimental studies of commissurotomized patients that bear directly on the nature of the right hemisphere's phonological capacity are also uncommon. And, although the techniques employed in studying these patients are impressive, we must keep in mind that these studies are based on

very small and unusual subject populations. Studies carried out by Levy and Trevarthen (1977) included a series of rhyming tasks. Five commissurotomized patients served as subjects. The procedure was the following: After attending to a fixation point and receiving a double stimulus, one in each hemisphere, subjects either select and then point to a matching stimulus in an array or report what they have seen. The assumption in using such a paradigm is that the laterality of choice indicates which hemisphere assumes dominant control of the particular form of response or the mental processes on which it depends. Stimuli were constructed by combining the right half of one picture with the left half of another to form a single (chimeric) stimulus, whose left half would be projected to the right hemisphere and whose right half would project to the left hemisphere.

Subjects were asked to choose from among three chimeric stimuli by pointing to the picture whose name rhymed with the target stimulus. In order to avoid visual image matching, rhyming pairs consisted of pictures whose names included vowel sounds that were spelled differently. Of the five subjects, there was one (C.C.) who showed a tendency to be able to rhyme with the *right* hemisphere, scoring above chance when presented with whole stimuli confined to the left field and choosing the rhyming object with the left hand. This same subject (C.C.) performed with some degree of success (14/24) on a condition of the task in which whole pictures were presented to the right hemisphere (left field) and subjects were required to point with the left hand to a picture of the rhyming object. In a task involving judgment of rhyme between a spoken word and the mental sound image corresponding to a picture of an object, subject C.C. also performed well.

It is difficult to know exactly how much importance to place on these results, given that the remaining four subjects could not perform these tasks with the right hemisphere. Moreover, caution is suggested by the fact that C.C. is the only subject noted by Levy and Trevarthen to have extensive left hemisphere damage. However, it is also the case that C.C. was operated upon and tested at the same age as two of the other subjects (L.B. and A.A.) who did not demonstrate an ability to perform phonological tasks with the right hemisphere. And, in one subject (N.G.), results on the rhyming test were not entirely unambiguous, suggesting that the right hemisphere may have been performing the rhyming task with some measure of success.

Zaidel (1978), using a specially designed contact lense which provides for free ocular scanning of complex visual arrays, studied two commissurotomized patients and two hemispherectomized patients with respect to their performance on a series of phonological tasks. (The two commissurotomized

subjects, N.G. and L.B., were also among the subjects studied by Levy and Trevarthen, 1977.) In the first of these tasks, subjects were presented with dichotic pairs of stop consonant + vowel syllables followed by a consonant flashed briefly to one hemifield. Using the hand homolateral to the stimulated half field, the subjects were asked to respond to the question "Was this the sound heard?" by pointing to the word *yes* or *no*. Results showed massive left ear suppression in the left hemisphere, giving a large right ear advantage in correct responses. The right hemisphere performed at chance in either ear and in the dichotic as well as a monotic condition.

In another phonetic coding experiment, Zaidel presented a stimulus word binaurally and asked subjects to point to one of four pictures which were presented to a single visual half field. Foils differed from the target in one to three phonetic features—voice, place, and/or manner—and stimulus words were presented under two noise conditions—quiet background and conversational noise background. In the quiet background, no statistically significant difference emerged between the performances of the left and right hemispheres. In the noise condition, the difference was significant. Zaidel interprets these results to indicate that "the noise, lacking specific phonetic information, interferes with auditory analysis by the right hemisphere, which depends on general acoustic cues, much more than it interferes with phonetic analysis by the left hemisphere [p. 185]."

Zaidel's study also included a homonym test in which subjects were asked to match "pictures that sound alike but mean different things" from a choice card of four pictures. This test was administered to two commissurotomized patients, L.B. and N.G. Only L.B. could perform the task with the right hemisphere. Zaidel notes that no learning effects could be found with preliminary exposure to the exemplars.

Subject L.B. was also given a rhyming test in which he was instructed to "match two pictures whose names rhyme with each other." Again, L.B. was found to be able to perform this task with the right hemisphere. That hemisphere was, however, unable to match an orthographic representation of a word with a picture whose name rhymed with it, in spite of the ability to match the orthographic word with its pictorial referent.

It is of interest that both the right and left hemispheres of all subjects scored perfectly on the Spreen-Benton Sound Recognition Test. This is a standardized test in which subjects are presented binaurally with familiar environmental sounds (birds singing, piano music, etc.) and are asked to choose from an array of four pictures or words (depending upon the form of the test used) the corresponding picture or word. Zaidel presumably used the picture response mode.

Data from Right Brain Damage

Those investigations of language that bear on the issue of phonological ability in right-brain-damaged populations tend to show no deviation from the performance of normals on so-called phonological tasks (Lesser, 1974; Miceli, Caltagirone, Gainotti, & Payer-Rigo, 1978; Perecman & Kellar, 1981; Gainotti, Caltagirone, & Miceli, Chapter 8, this volume). Lesser (1974) reports normal performance on an auditory discrimination task in which subjects chose a target from a set of four pictures where foils were words that were found to be most commonly mistaken for the target when presented in a background of simulated airplane noise. Similarly, Miceli *et al.* (1978) found phoneme discrimination in right-brain-damaged subjects to be not significantly different from normal, and Perecman and Kellar (1981) found that right-brain-damaged subjects did not perform differently from normals in judging phonemic similarity in pairs of nonsense syllables. In both studies, judgments were made on the basis of a voice and/or place contrast in the initial consonant of a nonsense syllable.

From the point of view of production, however, deficient phonological capacity subsequent to right brain damage has been documented. Marcie, Hécaen, Dubois, and Angelergues (1965) describe the productions—particularly in repetition behavior, but also in sentence generation—of 28 right-brain-damaged subjects as evincing the following characteristics: (*a*) better preservation of vowels than consonants; (*b*) presence of voicing errors but not manner errors in consonants; and (*c*) omission of final consonants and, to a lesser extent, vowels. Marcie *et al.* also note inappropriate repetition of the initial syllable, for example [tati] → [tatati], and rare occurrences of augmentation, for example, (C)VC→(C)VCC. These authors remark that in terms of suprasegmental properties of language, their right-brain-damaged subjects speak slowly, often in monotone, and tend toward dysprosody.

CONCLUDING REMARKS

What might all of this mean? Perhaps that the left hemisphere is not the exclusive domain of phonological processing capacity, as some authors suggest. For we have seen evidence that the right hemisphere of some commissurotomized subjects can make judgments on the basis of a phonological parameter, namely, rhyme, and that damage to the right hemisphere can impair language production at the phonological level. Specification of lesion sites in right-brain-damaged subjects, comparable to standard prac-

tice in reports on left-hemisphere-damaged subjects, may prove useful in clarifying the role of the right hemisphere in phonological processing. In brief, what all of this may mean is that investigators should be looking more carefully at the performance of the right hemisphere on phonological tasks.

REFERENCES

Albert, M., & Kaplan, E. In L. W. Poon (Ed.), *New directions in memory and aging.* Hillsdale, N. J.: Lawrence Erlbaum Associates, 1980.

Crockett, H. G., & Estridge, N. M. Cerebral hemispherectomy: A clinical, surgical and pathologic study of four cases. *Bulletin of the Los Angeles Neurological Society*, 1951, *16*, 71–87.

French, L. A., Johnson, D. R., Brown, I. A., & Van Bergen, F. B. Cerebral hemispherectomy for control of intractable convulsive seizures. *Journal of Neurosurgery*, 1955, *12*, 154–164.

Gardner, W. J., Karnosh, L. J., McClure, C. C., & Gardner, A. K. Residual function following hemispherectomy for tumor and for infantile hemiplegia. *Brain*, 1955, *78*, 487–502.

Gordon, H. Right hemisphere comprehension of verbs in patients with complete forebrain commissurotomy: Use of the dichotic method and manual performance. *Brain and Language*, 1980, *11*, 76–86.

Gott, P. Language after dominant hemispherectomy. *Journal of Neurology, Neurosurgery and Psychiatry*, 1973, *36*, 1082–1088.

Hillier, W. F. Total left cerebral hemispherectomy for malignant glioma. *Neurology*, 1954, *4*, 718–721.

Krynauw, R. A. Surgical treatment of infantile hemiplegia. *Journal of Neurology, Neurosurgery and Psychiatry*, 1950, *13*, 243–267.

Lesser, R. Verbal comprehension in aphasia: An English version of three Italian tests. *Cortex*, 1974, *10*, 247–263.

Levy, J. Psychobiological implications of bilateral asymmetry. In S. J. Dimond & J. G. Beaumont (Eds.), *Hemisphere function in the human brain.* London: Elek Science, 1974.

Levy, J., & Trevarthen, C. Perceptual, semantic and phonetic aspects of elementary language processes in split-brain patients. *Brain*, 1977, *100*, 105–118.

Marcie, P., Hécaen, H., Dubois, J., & Angelergues, R. Les realizations du langage chez les malades atteints de lesions de l'hemisphere droit. *Neuropsychologia*, 1965, *3*, 217–247.

McFie, J. The effects of hemispherectomy on intellectual functioning in cases of infantile hemiplegia. *Journal of Neurology, Neurosurgery and Psychiatry*, 1961, *24*, 240–249.

Miceli, G., Caltagirone, C., Gainotti, G., & Payer-Rigo, R. Discrimination of voice versus place contrasts in aphasia. *Brain and Language*, 1978, *6*, 47–51.

Obrador, S. Nervous integration after hemispherectomy in man. In G. Schaltenbrand & C. Woolsey (Eds.), *Cerebral localization and organization.* Madison: University of Wisconsin Press, 1964.

Perecman, E., & Kellar, L. The effect of voice and place among aphasic, non-aphasic right-damaged and normal subjects on a metalinguistic task. *Brain and Language*, 1981, *12*, 213–223.

Searleman, A. A review of right hemisphere linguistic capabilities. *Psychological Bulletin*, 1977, *84*, 503–528.

Smith, A. Speech and other functions after left (dominant) hemispherectomy. *Journal of Neurology, Neurosurgery and Psychiatry*, 1966, *29*, 467–471.

Smith, A. Dominant and non-dominant hemispherectomy. In W. L. Smith (Ed.), *Drugs, development and cerebral function*. Springfield, Ill.: Charles Thomas, 1972.

Smith, A., & Burklund, C. W. Dominant hemispherectomy: Preliminary report on neuropsychological sequelae. *Science*, 1966, *153*, 1280–1282.

Zaidel, E. Lexical organization in the right hemisphere. In P. Buser & A. Rougeul-Buser (Eds.), *Cerebral correlates of conscious experience*. Amsterdam: Elsevier, 1978.

Zollinger, R. Removal of left cerebral hemisphere: Report of a case. *Archives of Neurology and Psychiatry*, 1935, *34*, 1055–1064.

PART I

THEORETICAL ISSUES IN RIGHT HEMISPHERE NEUROPSYCHOLOGY

2

Cerebral Lateralization, Cognitive Asymmetry, and Human Consciousness

T. G. BEVER

The study of cerebral asymmetries in humans has been a major area of growth in psychology for the past several decades. This is in part a result of the emergence of sophisticated experimental techniques that can be used with normal populations, and in part a result of medical technology which has provided spectacular cases of disconnected or absent hemispheres. Cerebral asymmetries are important because they are typically human and because they constitute an example of localization of function—crude as that localization may be. By studying simple asymmetries, one hopes, we will understand our own biology better, as well as gain insight into general laws governing the relation between brain and behavior.

Unfortunately, such hopes have been slow to be fulfilled, and our understanding of the phenomena recedes exactly as fast as new investigative techniques develop, or slightly faster. This chapter reviews some devastating problems that riddle the field, leaving us uncertain as to how to interpret most of the existing literature on normal subjects. These problems involve (*a*) subject variables, (*b*) task variables, and (*c*) the need for an independently motivated theory of congnitive behavior to test against functional asymmetries.

COGNITIVE PROCESSING IN
THE RIGHT HEMISPHERE

Cerebral asymmetries, in fact, constitute one of the most complex problems we could choose as an example of the relation between brain and behavior. Since, in fact, we have little choice, we must find ways to make the best of a nearly impossible situation. In this chapter I attempt to sharpen the empirical issues by embedding cerebral asymmetries in the context of a theory of cognitive activity and development. The main emphasis is that there are multiple sources for lateral asymmetries as they manifest themselves in normal and pathological behavior. I distinguish three sources of asymmetries—physiological, experiential, and cognitive. This clarifies a number of current controversies and alleviates some confusions in the field. Most important is that modern cognitive psychology affords a theory of consciousness that satisfies the intuition that consciousness depends on relational processes. This motivates the prediction that the left hemisphere, the seat of relational activity, is the usual seat of consciousness in normal people; we have confirmed this prediction experimentally by research on the interaction of levels of consciousness and cerebral asymmetries.

SUBJECT VARIABLES

Individual Genotype and Asymmetries

The brain is an extremely flexible organ, which produces similar behaviors in different ways. Yet, general references to so-called left-hemisphere and right-hemisphere activities presupposes that there is uniformity of the distribution of mental functions. The grossness of this neuro-geographical distinction lends confidence that there is relative constancy of the difference between hemispheres even if there is some variability in within-hemisphere organization. This confidence reflects the view that these differences must result from deep biological properties and therefore are genetically stable.

Nevertheless, we know of cases that demonstrate astounding resilience of behavioral organization in the face of major neurological differences: behaviorally normal people with one hemisphere damaged during childhood, or with a cortex that is virtually a thin layer lining the inside of the skull (Lewin, 1980). Given such evidence from extreme cases, why do we not expect a multiplicity of organizational differences among all people?

Variability in lateral organization has been studied to some extent. It is well documented that left-handed individuals can exhibit cerebral asymmetries that are different from those of right-handed people, if not the reverse. A recent burst of papers has suggested that adult men and women have different asymmetries, though the literature has not settled on which sex is more lateralized for what.

Explicit handedness and sex are unambiguous variables, although it is not obvious why sex should interact with neurological organization in particular. There are also more subtle variables that effect behavioral asymmetries. In our work, we have systematically studied the different kinds of behavioral asymmetries that are revealed by right-handed people with and without left-handers in their genetic background. We have found that people with left-handers among their parents, siblings, or grandparents show a systematic reversal of asymmetries on certain kinds of tasks.

For example, the recognition of musical two-note intervals is traditionally viewed as a right-hemisphere-dominant task, which it is when averaged across subjects. Lucia Kellar and I found, however, that the average superiority for the left ear is actually produced by a very strong left ear superiority for people without familial left-handedness and a weak *right* ear superiority for people with familial left-handedness (Kellar, 1976, Kellar & Bever, 1981; see Table 2.1).

Simple visual identification is also a traditional right hemisphere task. For example, recognition that two briefly presented figures are identical should be faster in the left visual field than in the right visual field. In our lab, Leonard Huber found that, when people are first confronted with the task, this is strongly the case for people without familial left-handedness and weakly the reverse for those with familial left-handedness (Huber, 1981; see Table 2.2).

Relating words and pictures can also be a right-hemisphere-dominant task. For example, choice of which of two pictures goes with a simple sen-

Table 2.1

SUBJECTS' REPEATED CATEGORIZATION OF CONTINUOUSLY VARYING INTERVALS INTO THREE TARGET CATEGORIES: FIFTH, TRITONE, OR FOURTH[a, b]

	Left ear	Right ear	Right ear advantage
Pure	1.2	1.3	− .1
Mixed	1.4	1.2	+ .2

[a]From Kellar, 1976.

[b]The measure was the variability of the categorization assigned to each interval.

Table 2.2
LATENCY FOR SUBJECTS TO DECIDE WHETHER THE SECOND OF
TWO SIMPLE GEOMETRIC FIGURES WAS THE SAME AS THE FIRST[a]

	Left visual field	Right visual field	Right field advantage
Pure	1213	1281	− 68
Mixed	1318	1330	− 12

[a]From Huber 1981.

tence might be faster when the sentence is pesented to the left ear. Claudia
Leslie, Chava Casper, and I found that this is strongly the case for people
with no familial left-handers, but weakly the reverse for people with familial
left-handedness (Leslie, Casper, & Bever, 1983; see Table 2.3).

Identification of simple nonsense syllabic sounds might also be better in
the left ear. Huber and I found this to be true for people with no familial
left-handers and the reverse for people with familial left-handedness (Huber
& Bever, 1983; see Table 2.4).

By now, the reader must grasp the pattern: On many tasks that are generally assumed to be right hemisphere dominant, a weak reversal of that
effect occurs among subjects with familial left-handedness. I return later to
why this may be so, but for the moment it is clear how devastating this
finding is for the interpretation of the existing literature. Most studies still
do not control for handedness background—those that are worth interpreting at all will simply have to be redone.

Another implication of the effect of familial handedness is that neurophysiological variability in the organization of behavior is under individual
genetic control. That is, there are physiologically determined asymmetry

Table 2.3
LATENCY FOR SUBJECTS TO DECIDE WHICH PICTURE IS
APPROPRIATE FOR A SENTENCE[a]

	Left ear	Right ear	Right ear advantage
Pure	1614	1692	− 78
Mixed	1618	1494	124

[a]From Leslie, Casper, and Bever 1983.

Table 2.4
LATENCY TO RECOGNIZE A TARGET NONSENSE SYLLABLE IN
A SEQUENCE OF NONSENSE SYLLABLES (TWO PER SECOND)[a]

	Left ear	Right ear	Right ear advantage
Pure	669	705	− 36
Mixed	689	648	+ 41

[a]From Huber and Bever, 1983.

patterns that may have the same magnitude of sensitivity to genotype as eye color.

Individual Experience and Asymmetries

Subject-induced variability can also depend on a person's individual experience. For example, a number of studies contrast the ear asymmetries of musicians and nonmusicians. The traditional result from other laboratories is that nonmusicians process music better in the left ear. We have consistently replicated this and also found that musicians recognize melodies better when presented in the *right* ear. This finding has been replicated by numerous other researchers (for a review, see Bever, 1980, Appendix 1). In fact, one study reports that musicians show patterns of electrical activity on the scalp indicating left hemisphere processing of melodies compared with nonmusicians, who show evidence of right hemisphere processing (Hirshkowitz, Earle, & Paley, 1978). We have also found the right ear superiority in children who are regular choir singers. Our interpretation has been that musicians have learned to listen to music in an analytic way, which stimulates the kind of processing natural to the left hemisphere (see Table 2.5).

Whatever the reason, should we not expect that other kinds of special experience and training interact with asymmetries? For example, might not commercial artists and architects recognize geometric figures better in the right visual field? Might not members of the Audubon Society recognize bird calls better in the right ear? What visual field should be dominant for postage recognition in philatelists?

Again, the point should be clear. We know that subjects' laterality differs as a function of specific experiences and acquired skills. How are we to interpret a literature that does not control for such variables? Very cautiously.

Table 2.5

PROCESSING OF MELODIES BY MUSICIANS AS COMPARED TO
NONMUSICIANS[a, b]

Study	Left ear	Right ear	Right ear advantage
Johnson[c]			
Musicians	16.0	19.8	+ 3.8
Nonmusicians	15.7	13.7	− 2.0
Musicians' advantage	0.3	6.1	
Johnson *et al.*[d]			
Musicians	4.9	4.5	+ 0.4
Nonmusicians	6.5	6.7	− 0.2
Musicians' advantage	1.6	2.2	
Gaede *et al.*[e]			
Musicians	10.87	10.00	+ 0.88
Nonmusicians	12.19	11.48	+ 0.71
Musicians' advantage	1.32	1.48	
Gates and Bradshaw[f]			
Musicians	0.83	1.10	+ 0.27
Nonmusicians	0.14	0.35	+ 0.21
Musicians' advantage	0.69	0.75	
Gordon[g]			
Musicians	15.3	17.6	+ 2.3
Nonmusicians	14.7	16.7	+ 2.0
Musicians' advantage	0.6	0.9	
Bever and Chiarello[h]			
Musicians	44	57	+ 13
Nonmusicians	54	36	− 18
Musicians' advantage	− 10	21	

[a]From Bever, 1980. Sources: Johnson (1977, table 1); Johnson, Bowers, Gamble, Lyons, Presbrey, and Vetter (1977, table 1); Gaede, Parsons, and Bertera (1978, table 1); Gates and Bradshaw (1977, table 2); Gordon (1978, table 1); Bever and Chiarello (1974, table 10.3).

[b]Note: Advantage scores compensate for whether the raw scores are based on correct responses or errors.

[c]Scores are the mean numbers of correct positive responses.

[d]Musicians are their groups 1 and 2; nonmusicians are their group 4. Scores are the mean number of errors.

[e]Groups are means of their high-aptitude and low-aptitude subjects. Scores are the mean number of errors.

[f]Groups the means of male and female subjects, responding to long and short excerpts, from their unfamiliar melodies. The scores are means of presented *d*'s.

[g]Excludes subjects performing at chance level. Scores are number correct (out of possible 24) on dichotic melodies differing in rhythm.

[h]Percentage correct, corrected for guessing.

RELATIONAL AND UNITARY PROCESSES IN TASKS

The dominant theories about the differences between the two hemispheres have evolved in several stages during recent decades. First it was thought that the difference between the hemispheres depended on the modality of behavior: The left hemisphere was viewed as normally specialized for language and reasoning, the right as specialized for such modalities as music and vision. (Kimura, 1973; Scheid & Eccles, 1975). This view became generalized into the distinction between a calculatingly "rational" or "analytic" hemisphere on the left and a creatively "intuitive" or "holistic" one on the right (Bever, 1971; Levy, 1969). On this view, language is left-hemisphered because it is analytic and vision is right-hemisphered because it is holistic, and so on. Specific modalities were viewed as asymmetric, but this in turn was viewed as the result of the kind of activity each modality involves.

The literature reveals considerable confusion about how to distinguish analytic and holistic processing, independent of observing facts about lateralization—some studies even use the lateralization pattern to differentiate the processing style. We can avoid this circularity by referring to a technical definition of the two kinds of activities from theoretical cognitive psychology (Bever, 1975, 1980).

It is a generally accepted notion that mental activity involves the processing of information. This point of view is espoused by researchers who agree on little else: Human thought involves the transformation of represented information in one form into another form. Of course, there are controversies about the forms of mental representation and the mechanisms of its transformation. Even on the latter question, though, there is general agreement that there are two types of processors: special purpose ones which carry out habitual functions and a "central" one that utilizes general problem-solving mechanisms (Anderson, 1980; Chomsky, 1980; Norman & Rumelhart, 1975; Pylyshyn, 1981; Simon, 1979).

The relative importance and the source of the special purpose processors are not constant. In some theories, special purpose processors play a minor role and are basically task dependent (Simon, 1979); in other theories, they account for almost all rational activity and are genetically prestructured (Chomsky, 1980; see Carroll, 1981, for a general discussion of these issues). Whatever the resolution of such controversies, it is generally claimed that the human mind operates, at least in part, in semiautonomous "faculties" or "modules," which carry out complex processes (Bever, 1975; Fodor, 1975; Pylyshyn; 1981). The mechanism for speech perception is one such module, that for visual object recognition another. The output of a module is relatively simple, and is expressed in units that are relatively accessible. In speech, it provides us with a meaning that corresponds to the sound, in vision with an object that corresponds to the visual array.

Whether general purpose or specific purpose, each module is an information-processing system—it performs operations on one form of representation that pair it with other forms. These operations can be complex internally, compared with their input or output. This contrasts the inner workings of a representational module with the result of relating those units into integrated schemata that present the accessible output of the module. For example, the computations involved in visual recognition of a square may require sensitivity to separate angles and lines, whereas the output of those computations is the gestalt of a square. Similarly, recognition of a word may involve considerable manipulation of acoustic and phonological features, but the accessed output is the percept of the word as a whole.

In this way, the modular concept provides technical definitions that can be used as the basis for explaining the difference between "holistic" and "analytic" processing. To avoid confusion with previous literature, I use the terms *unitary* and *relational*. Unitary processing accesses the output or input of a module; relational processing accesses the computational language normally intrinsic to a module. Another way of putting this is that relational processing involves the interrelation of more than one output of a module. For example, conscious recognition of a square is unitary, recognition that a line is part of the square is relational; intended production of a whole syllable is unitary, intended production of the same syllable as an ordered sequence of phonetic sounds is relational. This theoretical differentiation reformulates the concept of "analytic" processing as a special case of "relational" processing, the case in which the relation is that between a part and a whole. Other relational activities may not have this property—for example, the relations of actor to action and action to object do not involve inclusion.

The contrast between unitary and relational processing rests on differentiating the kind of output of a module. This formulation resolves a conundrum that we would otherwise face. Clearly, recognition of a square requires computation of equal sides and angles, itself a relational activity; therefore, we might argue that *no* activity is unitary. What is at issue in our definition, however, is the units and processes that are *accessed* in a cognitive domain— a unitary activity accesses only single units, a relational activity accesses units that bear some relation to each other.

In brief, cognitive theory offers a motivated differentiation of two kinds of processes, unitary and relational; we can postulate that this distinction is reflected in the difference between the activities that each hemisphere is most adapted to. This distinction is now formulated in terms provided by a cognitive theory, rather than by a generalization across observed hemispheric differences. It is not the case that speech is univocally lateralized to the left because it is analytic, nor is vision immovably lateralized to the right because it is holistic. Rather, we can show that even behavioral modalities can shift their lateral pattern if we shift the kind of cognitive processing that is required.

We can test the correctness of this distinction by showing that behaviors are not lateralized as modality defined kinds, as was previously thought. One demonstration of this is the fact that the same kind of material is processed preferably on the left or right as a function of the kind of task, not the modality. For example, Huber's figure-matching task would be classified as unitary, on the grounds that no internal analysis of the figures was required. Indeed, he found an overall superiority for left visual field presentations. He then paired the same kind of figures in such a way that the first member of each pair either was or was not a component part of the second figure. On this task, people performed better to stimuli presented in the right visual field (Huber, 1981; a similar finding is independently reported by Hurtig, 1982). We can intuitively recognize that the part–whole matching task is "analytic" in the sense that the whole figure must be recognized as made up of component parts.

We can demonstrate a similar effect on lateralization as a function of the way acoustic stimuli are processed. For example, Huber and I showed that overall there is a bias to respond more quickly to target nonsense syllables presented to the left ear than to the right ear. But the same stimuli elicit a right ear superiority if subjects are only told to recognize the first phoneme of the syllable. When a syllable is identified metonymously, in terms of its first component sound, then the processing is relational and better performed in the left hemisphere (see Table 2.6).

If the same stimuli can be processed in different ways, with opposite resulting lateralization patterns, we now have two possible explanations of the laterality patterns that differ according to such subject variables as handedness background and special training. Subjects might have differing neurological organization, as a function of, for example, familial sinistrality. Alternatively, at least in the case of subjects with special training, subjects might have different ways of approaching a stimulus; for example, musicians may listen to melodies relationally, and thereby perform better on stimuli presented to the right ear. Evidence for the latter interpretation

Table 2.6
LATENCY TO RECOGNIZE THE FIRST PHONEME OF A TARGET
SYLLABLE IN A SEQUENCE[a]

	Left ear	Right ear	Right ear advantage
Pure	760	716	44
Mixed	759	736	23

[a]From Huber and Bever, 1983.

comes from the fact that the difference between musicians' and nonmusicians' performance lies almost entirely in the relative superiority of the right ear performance in musicians, rather than in a decrease in their left ear performance (see Table 2.5). That is, they have learned to listen to music relationally, rather than actually shifting their overall neurological organization of music from the right to the left hemisphere.

But we remain in doubt about the basis of the behavioral effects on manifest asymmetries of such variables as sex and familial handedness. It could be the case that different sexes approach problems differently, which is then reflected in different patterns of manifest laterality. It could even be that familial left-handedness has its reversing effects indirectly, through a genetically controlled change in the ease of accessing different processing strategies rather than direct reversal in asymmetries. For example, familial left-handedness may underlie a more diffuse asymmetric organization, which makes all tasks easier to approach relationally. This would lead to the observed right-side advantage for people with familial left-handedness, without meaning that they actually perform unitary tasks better in the left hemisphere.[1]

Developmental Shifts in Asymmetries

The preceding discussions emphasize the importance of individual differences in genetic background and experiences. There are also general developmental patterns that are related to cerebral asymmetries. Three stages occur in a typical sequence in the development of a capacity: an initial "syncretic" stage, a later "analytic" stage, and a final "integrative" stage. The

[1]Such a speculation can be tested, for example by specifically studying relational and unitary processing styles in different groups of subjects. We have begun to do this but the preliminary results are downright terrifying: It seems that handedness background and processing style interact with lateral asymmetries in opposite ways in men and women.

terms for these stages differ widely according to the connotative desire of different theorists. Nevertheless, there is general agreement that the first stage is one in which a skill is carried out "globally," "holistically," or, in the terms of the current discussion, "unitarily." That is, the skill is based on fixed schemata or action patterns. The second stage is typically characterized as "analytic" or "relational"; the skill is broken down into component parts, typically resulting in a temporary regression in the manifest capacity. The third stage involves a new integrated balance between unitary and relational processes. (See Bever, 1982, for a general discussion of such sequences at various ages.)

Intuitively, one can see how such stages might result from a quantitative development of the complexity of individual cognitive modules—at first, they act unitarily, then they are assembled (interrelated) into more complex modules, which in turn act unitarily, and so on. Despite the appeal of such a model, I do not see how one can derive this pattern from formal considerations alone; most attempts to derive developmental phenomena in this way have failed, albeit nobly (the most noble being that of Piaget, see Piatelli-Palmerini, 1980). We must accept the fact that, like evolution, development is an empirical accident, constrained by certain boundary conditions, the result of happenstance and current history.

Consider the development of sentence perception with special reference to the assignment of the semantic relations, such as agent, action, and patient (see Slobin & Bever, 1982, for a full discussion). At an early age (around 2 years), children interpret sentences by way of a unitary schema. This schema accommodates to the unambiguous properties of the native language. In English, this schema is "Noun Verb. . ." = "agent, action. . ."; in Turkish, it is ". . .Noun + Suffix. . ." (i.e., an inflected noun, whatever it precedes) = "patient"; in Serbo-Croatian, it is "Noun + Suffix Verb . . ." = "patient + verb." Sentences that do not conform to the schema are simply not understood, in one way or another. At a later age (around 4 years), children show a sensitivity to word order (in those languages where it is relevant, e.g., English and Serbo-Croatian); they interpret the first noun as the agent. This leads to a temporary regression in performance on those sentences in which this is not the case (e.g., the passive in English, and the object-first constructions in Serbo-Croatian).

The emergence of the relational word-order strategy is associated with an emergence of cerebral lateralization. In English, children who show a relative dependence on the word order strategy are also those who are relatively lateralized for dichotic word recognition (see Table 2.7; a large difference between actives and passives indicates sensitivity to word order; the original

Table 2.7

CHILDREN ACTED OUT SIMPLE SENTENCES, ACTIVE (*THE DOG KISSES THE PIG*) AND PASSIVE (*THE PIG IS KISSED BY THE DOG*), AND RESPONDED TO A "DICHOTIC ANIMALS" TEST TO ASSESS EAR PREFERENCE

Percentage of correct-reversible actives	79	96	94	90	95	87	86	97	90	91	90
Percentage of correct-reversible passives	70	63	48	61	76	78	73	72	55	35	62
Difference	9	33	46	29	19	9	13	25	15	56	28
N	11	9	5	7	6	24	20	12	13	12	20
Ear preference	All left				No preference					All right	

experimental details are presented in Bever, 1971). This is consistent with the view that the word order dependence reflects the emergence of relational processing of language, which in turn is lateralized.

We do not have any collateral evidence, or counterevidence, that the younger children, who use the unitary comprehension strategy, are right-hemisphered for language. It is extremely difficult to obtain laterality measures with children at this age. There are, however, suggestions in the literature on older children that an early stage of learning a second language involves relative dependence on the right hemisphere (Obler, 1981). This is consistent with the view that the unitary stategies themselves are right-hemisphered. Children at the third stage (by age 6) appear to remain left-hemisphered for language, rather than switching back to the right hemisphere. As most language tasks involve comprehension, typically a cross-modal problem which requires relational processing, we can expect that left hemisphere dominance will remain.

Music does not ordinarily involve cross-modal activity. Accordingly, we might expect that musicians would reveal an increase in the extent to which they use the right hemisphere for unitary musical tasks. The fact that musicians are more strongly right-hemisphered for unitary musical tasks supports this prediction (Table 2.8). We might expect that with increased musical experience, musicians and nonmusicians would build up a balanced representation of musical function—more complex musical motives would be treated in a unitary fashion, while relational processes bind them together. Some evidence for this has been found by Wagner and Hannon (1981); they replicated our results contrasting late adolescent musicians and nonmusicians, but found that 40-year-old adults—"musicians" and "nonmusicians" alike—do not have an asymmetry for monaural melody recog-

Table 2.8

UNITARY MUSICAL TASKS AS PERFORMED BY MUSICIANS VERSUS NONMUSICIANS[a,b]

Study	Left ear	Right ear	Right ear advantage
Gordon[a]			
Musicians	16.9	14.6	− 2.3
Nonmusicians	15.1	14.3	− 0.8
Musicians' advantage	1.8	0.3	
Gaede et al.[b]			
Musicians	8.21	9.00	− 0.79
Nonmusicians	9.94	10.08	− 0.14
Musicians' advantage	1.73	1.8	
Gates and Bradshaw[c]			
Musicians	1.88	1.56	− 0.32
Nonmusicians	0.61	0.65	+ 0.04
Musicians' advantage	1.27	0.91	
Johnson et al.[d]			
Musicians	4.6	5.7	− 1.1
Nonmusicians	6.7	7.0	− 0.3
Musicians' advantage	2.1	1.3	
Zatorre[e]			
Musicians	73	67	− 6
Nonmusicians	63	59	− 4
Musicians' advantage	10	8	

[a]From Bever, 1980. Sources: Gordon (1978, table 3); Gaede *et al.* (1978, table 1); Gates and Bradshaw (1977, table 2); Johnson *et al.* (1977, table 1); Zatorre (1978, figure 2).

[b]Note: Studies and subjects are the same as in the corresponding studies in Table 2.5 except where noted.

[c]Scores are number correct on chord recognition.

[d]Scores are mean errors on note discrimination in chords.

[e]Scores on familiar melodies.

[f]Errors on short random-pitch sequences.

[g]Scores are the percentage correct recognition of short, repeatedly presented dichotic melodies.

nition (Table 2.9).[2] This is one of those results that must be replicated with explicit attention to subject variables: If it holds up, it may demonstrate

[2]A word about their adult subjects is in order. All were college professors; the musicians were taken from a department of music, the nonmusicians from other academic departments. As Table 2.9 shows, the overall performance of the nonmusical adults was similar to that of the musicians. This suggests that on this task *all* artistically aware adults develop an integrated ability to recognize tonal melodies.

Table 2.9
PROPORTIONAL EAR DIFFERENCES IN MELODY
RECOGNITION[a]

	Left − Right
College	
Musician	− .07
Nonmusician	+ .10
Adult	
Musician	+ .02
Nonmusician	+ .01

[a]From Wagner and Hannon, 1981.

the gradual reintegration in all musically aware adults of a coherent single cognitive module for melody perception, thus eradicating ear differences.

I am presenting a picture in which at various points in development the left hemisphere can act as a construction of unitary schemata and action patterns, building up relational representational systems of increasing complexity; as some of these systems become modules in their own right, they can create unitary processes of corresponding complexity. It may be difficult to bring this out in language (because of its habitual cross-modal involvements), and we have not yet studied it in music. There is, however, some evidence for a lateral shift back and forth in facial recognition that may reflect the alternation between relational and unitary processing, with the latter becoming more complex at each stage (see Bever, 1980, for discussion). The salient facts are that at the ages of entering primary and secondary school, American children actually show a temporary drop in the ability to recognize new faces, and (at the latter age) show a loss of the usual right hemisphere dominance for the task (this has not been tested at the younger age). On the present view, the temporary changes occur at points when the child is attempting to master a new and larger set of faces; he or she reorganizes a new canonical set of unitary facial schemata—the period of reorganization is associated with a drop in the growth of the skill, and a relative left hemisphere superiority, since the reorganizational activity itself is relational. Carey (1980) and Diamond, Carey, and Back (in press) have presented some evidence showing that the onset of puberty is a critical factor in the temporary loss of right hemisphere dominance. This is consistent with the view that when the child becomes particularly interested in mastering new faces and new kinds of facial features (on Carey's data, because of puberty), a period of relative left-hemisphered reorganization occurs.

CONSCIOUSNESS AND THEORIES
OF COGNITIVE ACTION

I have outlined current cognitive theory, in which different capacities are represented in relatively distinct cognitive systems, or "modules." The modular concept provides a technical basis for differentiating relational and unitary processing. Unitary processing normally accesses the output or input of one module; relational processing normally accesses the input or output of several modules.

Modular cognitive theory also offers a technical description of consciousness, and therefore a theory of why consciousness exists. Suppose that during ordinary wakefulness a number of modules operate simultaneously on their appropriate intero- and extero-receptor inputs. Different modules can provide different representations, which are either orthogonal to each other or in conflict. For example, the visual representation of a dog is of a different kind than the representation of a bark. But the two representations are properly unified, under simple circumstances in which they both have the appropriate magnitude and direction. In such cases the information is orthogonal; there are also cases in which it might conflict—for example, if the dog appeared retinally small, and to one side of the apparent location of the bark. One resolution of this relative disparity is that the dog is distant and the bark is being partially reflected. Such a percept might be immediate when presented with these two kinds of information. That is, we can reconcile apparently conflicting information by way of "inferences" about a possible world. These inferences occur so rapidly and automatically that one is tempted, like Helmholtz, to refer to them as "unconscious."

It is also tempting to suggest at this point that there is a central mental "executive" which actively mediates all representational conflicts by way of inferences. Clearly, some decision must be made at each moment as to which module to attend, and how to integrate it with other outputs. The result of such decisions appears to be what we think of as consciousness. Accordingly, it would be further tempting to call this executive "consciousness." In fact, I will succumb to this temptation, with one important exception—consciousness is not itself an independent mental module. Rather, it is an inner representation of reality that mediates conflicting information yielded by different modules. In this sense, consciousness is an automatic consequence, which resolves conflicting computational output of modules. It is the inference of reality. It is *automatic,* not autonomous, for without that property it would merely have the status of a junior executive modular homunculus.

The reader will recognize that this sort of view resonates with proposals by Piaget and others about the development of models of reality in general. The child builds up internal representations that mediate conflicts in individual systems of perception and knowledge. For example, the child builds up a theory of immutable quantity, which establishes a reconciliation between conflicting kinds of information about quantities. The child builds up a theory of the structure of the language that reconciles disparities created by habits of talking and listening. Just so for consciousness itself. It offers an internal representation of reality which carries us through representations of otherwise incoherent objects and events in relation to each other. Consciousness *must* exist in a complex computational system with many independent sources of representational information.

If we turn to traditional investigations of consciousness, we find that this treatment resonates loudly with what has been observed since Hippocrates. Virtually everybody argues, albeit in unique ways, that consciousness involves relating one kind of information to another. That is, the sensing of oneself or ones' something requires a setting-in-relation of more than one entity.

This requirement does find a reflex in the technical characterization of cerebral asymmetries. The processes underlying the empirical phenomena that distinguish the hemispheres are either unitary or relational. The effect of that difference is that the left hemisphere is more relational and hence more conscious, in the technical sense discussed here. This offers a theoretically motivated prediction for a claim that has already been made on the basis of clinical facts (Sperry, 1974; Gazzaniga, 1970) or anthropological speculation (Jaynes, 1977): The right hemisphere (as a complex organ) has some consciousness but in a physiologically integrated brain the left hemisphere is the seat of consciousness.

I do not wish to dwell on the philosophy of consciousness because I would like to believe that it is an empirical phenomenon. But it is difficult to know to get an empirical handle on it. We cannot compare directly beings whom we know have consciousness, like us, and beings whom we know not to have it. First, we cannot be sure that other animals do not have it; indeed, the cognitive theory of consciousness suggests they do have it to some degree. Second, their general intelligence may differ, thereby confounding any experimental comparisons. But we can manipulate a person's level of self-awareness (i.e., his self-consciousness) and examine the effects of that manipulation. In what follows I discuss a few effects of that manipulation on cerebral asymmetries.

Social psychologists have noticed that the way to increase a person's self-consciousness is to put him in front of a mirror (Duval & Wicklund, 1972). A variety of measures show that in such circumstances people think of themselves more as social entities, as others see them. For example, when people are in front of mirrors, they conform more to norms describing the behavior of others. This can be shown by having a subject rate the performance of somebody else on a task, such as digit recall, after telling the subject how other people rated that individual's performance of the task. When subjects are in front of a mirror, their judgment is much more influenced by what they are told other people thought than when they are not in front of a mirror.

An undergraduate colleague at Columbia, T. Engelmann, suggested that we examine the impact of this technique on cerebral asymmetries. We started with the view that has been outlined here, that consciousness is an automatic conflict-resolving representation of reality. We predicted several results. First, on a task that simply involves individual performance, such as recall of digit strings, we expected that the mirror would reduce any cerebral asymmetries. Our reasoning was that if the behavioral superiority of the right ear is related to the role of automatic processes in the left hemisphere, then increasing a person's total self-awareness would reduce the isolated operation of that hemisphere and thereby reduce behavioral asymmetries.

This prediction was borne out by our study, the results of which are given in Table 2.10. Subjects (who, of course, were controlled for all the variables mentioned in the previous section, and more), performed better in the right ear than the left on ordered recall of digit strings. However, when they were in front of a mirror, they performed equally on the two ears—primarily due to a relative increase in their left ear performance.

A second prediction is that in a socially interactive task the left hemisphere is more influenced than the right. To test this we used a social influence paradigm. Experimental subjects were presented with a recording

Table 2.10
PERCENTAGE CORRECT ON RECALL OF ELEVEN
DIGIT SEQUENCES[a]

	Left ear	Right ear	Right ear advantage
No-mirror	57.0	60.0	− 3.0
Mirror	58.8	57.5	+ 1.2

[a]From Engelmann and Bever, 1983.

of another subject attempting to recall strings of digits. After each trial, the experimental subjects had to rate how well the recalling subject had done. Experimental subjects were informed on each trial as to how other people had rated the recalling subject—though the ratings were, in fact, constructed by us. Experimental subjects heard the recalling subject in either the right or left ear. As predicted by the view that the left hemisphere is the seat of relational consciousness, we found significantly more conformity to the social standard when they heard the recalling subject in the right ear (see Table 2.11). This increase interacted with the effect of the mirror: The degree of social conformity was very strongly increased by the mirror when the recalling subject was heard in the right ear, but not when he was heard in the left. This is further evidence that the effect of thinking of oneself in relation to society is primarily a left hemisphere activity.

These experiments are preliminary, and I stipulate that they are somewhat outlandish. But they do demonstrate that levels of self-consciousness interact systematically with cerebral asymmetries.

CONCLUSION: THE BASES OF ASYMMETRIES

I have argued that an assiduous application of cognitive theory can guide us through the maze of subject and task variables that permeate research on asymmetries in normal people. It also motivates specific predictions about the interaction of asymmetries and consciousness, which we have tested. The view of the basis of cerebral asymmetries has become more general. I have outlined examples of three factors that govern the appearance of asymmetries—genetic, experiential, and cognitive.

Researchers who theorize about cerebral asymmetry always end up theorizing about its evolutionary basis. If we are constrained to believe that

Table 2.11

MEAN ABSOLUTE DISTANCE OF RATED PERFORMANCE FROM SOCIAL STANDARD[a]

	Left ear	Right ear	Right ear advantage
No-mirror	.23	.14	+ .09
Mirror	.20	.07	+ .12
No mirror advantage	.03	.07	

[a]From Engelmann and Bever 1983.

everything that evolved did so because it was good for us at the time, then I wish to bow out of the game, since it is exquisitely circular. It would be more encouraging to be able to look at our behavioral phylogenesis and conclude that we are like our ancestors only slightly more so, so far as fundamental capacities are concerned. I am not suggesting that one animal's brain is like another, only bigger or smaller; among other things, size of an organ rarely changes without some structural implications. But I do think that we can frame a nonapocalyptic view of what might have happened, a view that leaves intact the notions that evolution proceeds slowly and that small increments can have drastic implications for morphology and behavior (see Bever, 1975, 1980, for fuller presentations).

Many animals have the capacity to learn symbols. Many seem to have some relational capacities, even in the technical sense defined here. Suppose humans simply have more of each. Suppose, further, that the left hemisphere is usually computationally advanced over the right in the young child. The result will be that relational activities—the relatively more complex—end up being represented and executed in the more capable hemisphere. The epigenetic implications of this result we can only guess at. But it does allow us to understand the difference between the hemispheres as rooted in an early quantitative difference in a general capacity. The result for adults is the sharp differences in the ordinary activities of the two sides of the brain, ranging from the performance of special tasks, to language and consciousness itself.

REFERENCES

Anderson, J. R. *Cognitive psychology and its implications.* San Francisco: W. H. Freeman and Co., 1980.

Bever, T. G. The dominant hemisphere is the locus for perceptual learning in speech behavior. In E. Ingram & R. Huxley (Eds.), *Mechanisms of language development.* New York: Academic Press, 1971.

Bever, T. G. Cerebral asymmetries in humans are due to the differentiation of two incompatible processing mechanisms: Holistic and analytic. In D. Aaronson & R. Rieber (Eds.), *Developmental psycholinguistics and communications disorders.* New York: New York Academy of Sciences, 1975.

Bever, T. G. Broca and Lashley were right: Cerebral dominance is an accident of growth. In D. Kaplan & N. Chomsky (Eds.), *Biology and language.* Cambridge, Mass.: MIT Press, 1980.

Bever, T. G. Regression in the service of development. In T. G. Bever (Ed.), *Regressions in child development: Basic processes and mechanisms.* New York: LEA, 1982.

Bever, T. G., & Chiarello, R. J. Cerebral dominance in musicians and nonmusicians. *Science,* 1974, 137–139.

Carey, S. A case study: Face recognition. In D. Kaplan & N. Chomsky (Eds.), *Biology and language*. Cambridge, Mass.: MIT Press, 1980.

Carroll, J. Modularity and naturalness in cognitive science. IBM Research Report, RC 9015.

Chomsky, N. *Rules and representations*. New York: Columbia University Press, 1980.

Diamond, R., Carey, S., & Back, K. Genetic influences on the development of spatial skills during early adolescence. *Cognition,* in press.

Duval, S., & Wicklund, R. A. *A theory of objective self awareness*. New York: Academic Press, 1972.

Engelmann, T., & Bever, T. G. Cerebral asymmetries and mechanisms of consciousness, in preparation, 1983.

Fodor, J. *The language of thought*. New York: Crowell, 1975.

Gaede, S. E., Parsons, O. A., & Bertera, J. H. Note: Hemispheric differences in music perception: Aptitude vs. experience. *Neuropsychologia* 1978, *3,* 369–373.

Gates, A., & Bradshaw, J. L. The role of the cerebral hemisphere in music. *Brain and Language* 1977, *4,* 403–431.

Gazzaniga, M. S. *The bisected brain*. New York: Appleton-Century-Crofts, 1970.

Gordon, H. Left hemisphere dominance for rhythmic elements in dichotically-presented melodies. *Cortex* 1978, *14* (1), 58–70.

Hirshkowitz, M., Earle, J., & Paley, B. EGG alpha asymmetry in musicians and non-musicians: A study of hemispheric specialization. *Neuropsychologia,* 1978, *16,* 125–128.

Huber, L. Task, subject, and modality factors influencing cerebral dominance. Unpublished dissertation, Columbia University, 1981.

Huber, L., & Bever, T. G. Cerebral asymmetry debends on family handedness background. Unpublished manuscript, Columbia University, 1983.

Hurtig, R. R. Cerebral asymmetry in the strategies used in processing random line stimuli. *Cortex,* 1982, *18,* 337–344.

Jaynes, J. *The origin of consciousness in the breakdown of the bicameral mind*. Boston: Houghton Mifflin, 1977.

Johnson, P. R. Dichotically-stimulated ear differences in musicians and non-musicians. *Cortex,* 1977, *13,* 385–389.

Johnson, P. R., Bowers, J. K., Gamble, M., Lyons, F. W., Presbrey, T. W., & Vetter, R. R. Ability to transcribe music and ear superiority for tone sequences. *Cortex,* 1977, *13,* 295–299.

Kellar, L. Hemispheric asymmetries in the perception of musical intervals as a function of musical experience and family handedness background. Unpublished dissertation, Columbia University, 1976.

Kellar, L., & Bever, T. G. Hemispheric asymmetries in perception of musical intervals as a function of musical experience and family handedness background. *Brain and Language,* 1981, *10,* 24–38.

Kimura, D. The asymmetry of the human brain. *Scientific American,* 1973, *228,* 70–78.

Leslie, C., Casper, C., & Bever, T. G. Sentence picture matching: Performance of normal and brain-damaged subjects. Unpublished manuscript, Columbia University, 1983.

Levy, J. Possible basis for the evolution of lateral specialization of the human brain. *Nature,* 1969, *224,* 614–615.

Lewin, R. Is your brain really necessary? *Science,* 1980, 210.

Norman, D. A., & Rumelhart, D. E. *Explorations in cognition*. San Francisco: W. H. Freeman and Co., 1975.

Obler, L. K. Right hemisphere participation in second language acquisition. In K. C. Diller

(Ed.), *Individual differences and universals in language learning aptitude*. Rowley, Mass.: Newbury House Publishers, 1981.

Piatelli-Palmerini, M. *Language and learning*. Cambridge, Mass.: Harvard University Press, 1980.

Pylyshyn, Z. W. The mental imagery debate: Analogue versus tacit knowledge. *Psychological Review*, 1981, *87*, 16–45.

Scheid, P. & Eccles, J. C. Music and speech: Artistic functions of the human brain. *Psychology of Music*, 1975, *3*, 21–35.

Simon, H. A. *Models of thought*. New Haven: Yale University Press, 1979.

Slobin, D. & Bever, T. G. Children use canonical sentence schemas: A crosslinguistic study of word order and inflections. *Cognition*, 1982, *12*, 229–265.

Sperry, R. W. Lateral specialization in the surgically seperated hemispheres. In F. O. Schmidt & F. G. Worden (Eds.), *Neurosciences: Third study program*. Cambridge, Mass.: MIT Press, 1974.

Wagner, M. T., & Hannon, R. Hemispheric asymmetries in faculty and student musicians and nonmusicians during melody recognition tasks. *Brain and Language*, 1981, *13*, 379–388.

Zatorre, R. J. Recognition of dichotic melodies by musicians and nonmusicians. *Proceeding of the Acoustical Society of America*, 1978.

3

Rethinking the Right Hemisphere

JASON W. BROWN

Clinical and behavioral investigations of cognition have demonstrated an apparent right hemisphere bias or specialization on a variety of visuospatial or "holistic" tasks. Although the relationship between visuospatial capacity and the right hemisphere has been documented by numerous studies, its basis is still poorly understood. This chapter argues that the right hemisphere has neither a special role or function in cognition, nor a different style of cognition, but that the terms *holistic* and *analytic* capture differences at successive moments in a processing continuum, not parallel operations. It will be shown that symptoms of right hemisphere damage, especially to the temporoparietal region, as well as right hemisphere effects on various behavioral measures, and right–left differences in commissurotomy cases, can all be explained by a theory of perception in which the parietal lobe of the right and left hemispheres forms a *unitary* system mediating a preliminary stage in perception.

INTRODUCTION

Current accounts of visual perception assume that each visual half field is independent of the other at initial stages of perceptual processing and

COGNITIVE PROCESSING IN
THE RIGHT HEMISPHERE

that the visual half fields eventually fuse into a unitary visual space. These accounts posit in-processing of stimuli over the geniculocortical system. Form perception is mediated by visual cortex, and object construction occurs as a secondary process after registration in the striate area. The object is constructed out of its sensory elements and then mapped onto spatial coordinates in relation to the position of the body. According to this view, the parietal region has a control function in the interaction between object and viewer, and provides a continual update of the perception in relation to the body surround.

On an alternative model of perception which has been developed elsewhere (Brown, 1977, 1983b), the half fields do not fuse as a secondary process, but rather differentiate out of a unitary space. On this model, a perception develops as an autonomous series of representations over levels in brain structure, a series that unfolds in a direction conforming to growth patterns in the evolution of the forebrain. Sensations enter at successive levels in this system, tectal, limbic neocortical, and constrain its forward development. Sensations have a shaping effect on object development. They do not go into the object reconstruction but lead to a cognitive representation which models the world up to a certain point.

This approach differs from the classical account in that sensation does not supply the raw material of perception—the object is not constructed out of sensory elements—but rather sensation acts to modulate an endogenous process of object representation. This process begins with a two-dimensional map of body space arising in upper brainstem and leads to an egocentric or viewer-centered space elaborated at the limbic level. This is a stage of dream and symbolic transformation. Space is unitary, fluid, and lacking in depth. Subsequently, this construct is derived to a three-dimensional, object-centered space through mechanisms in parietal neocortex. This involves a selection of a target through a memory organized about relations of conceptual or, in the domain of language perception, semantic proximity (see Brown, 1981) to a stage where the target is constrained by its morphological or spatial properties. This is also a stage of limb action on proximate objects. The hemifield begins to differentiate out of a background unitary space. Finally, through striate and prestriate mechanisms an object-centered space is fully articulated, exteriorized, and "detached" as an independent world around the viewer.

This "bottom-up" view of object formation clearly turns the traditional account upside down. No longer are images interpreted as perceptual memories deposited *after* the object is perceived, but as objects that are truncated in their development. Thus, a dream is a preliminary object. On this view, object relations precede isolated objects and meaning is apprehended prior to form.

Of particular interest in the context of this chapter is the position that the half fields of visual space differentiate out of a unitary preobject space. A lesion of the right hemisphere involves and so exposes the parietal segment of the object formative process. This segment, the forming left hemifield, is normally submerged within the object as a "preprocessing" stage. According to this view, the symptoms of parietal damage do not reflect disruptions of "higher order" computations subsequent to the (conscious) perception of an object but are disruptions at a point where an object is first selected out of the egocentric space of mental imagery into a three-dimensional space of objects and object relations.

The prominence of parietal mechanisms in behavior involving an interaction between viewer and object points to the transitional nature of this phase in object formation. The "interaction" reflects the incomplete separation of internal space. Both viewer and object are part of the same space field. The use of the hand on the object in reaching or constructional tasks draws upon this space in a more explicit manner. This is also true for tests of spatial relations. The space elaborated by parietal mechanisms is closer to the perceiver than the independent space of "real" objects. When the perceiver is asked to cognize spatial relations, it is this more preliminary phase that is being challenged.

It is in this sense that parietal lesions involve a preprocessing stage. They interfere with perception at the stage of interaction between the viewer and the object field, a stage in object formation prior to the complete exteriorization of perceptual space. Preprocessing is linked to object relations and conceptual mechanisms. In language perception, preprocessing is bound up with a lexical-semantic operation. End stage processing in visual perception is linked to an analysis of features defining the form of an object. The same stage in language perception involves phonological processing or the analysis of properties defining the sound form of an utterance.

The experimental procedures used to investigate object perception challenge cognition in different ways. Those which engage early stages in perception give a spurious right hemisphere effect because preliminary cognition represents a ceiling on cognitive unfolding in the right hemisphere. However, the same cognitive level which is preliminary in the right hemisphere undergoes further analysis in the left hemisphere. This is why tasks that involve late or end stage processing yield a left hemisphere effect. The right hemisphere bias for preliminary processing is an artifact due to the relative sequestration of phonological processing, and with it a feature analytic stage in perception, to the left hemisphere.

This level of perceptual processing in the left hemisphere constitutes a new stage in perception and a new level in consciousness and behavior. Specifically, the advent of phonological analysis in language perception brings with it the possibility of a finer differentiation of features in a nonverbal perceptual array. In fact, the selection of the features of a visual perception is comparable to the selection of phonemes to "fill in" the abstract frames of lexical representations. When this occurs, conceptual or object relations (semantic relations in language processing) recede into the background, and the features of the percept, whether visuospatial or linguistic, become more salient. Accordingly, the phonological level of language processing elaborates a level of cognition that is continuous with the feature analytic stage of other perceptual systems.

A by-product of this process is that the left hemisphere becomes disadvantaged in access to early cognition. Conversely, preliminary processing in right hemisphere is close to the cognitive end point of that hemisphere. A right or left hemisphere advantage arises when a task favors early or late processing. Specifically, right–left asymmetries reflect differential access to preliminary processing in a unitary cognitive system.

There is a wealth of clinical evidence for this new account of perception, coming especially from the study of hallucinatory and agnosic states (Brown, 1983a,b). In the following section, the model is considered in relation to perceptual asymmetries, beginning with the problem of constructional disability in brain-damaged patients.

CONSTRUCTIONAL (DIS)ABILITY IS EQUALLY REPRESENTED IN RIGHT AND LEFT HEMISPHERE

A disorder of visuospatial cognition was first described by Kleist (1934) as a disturbance "in formative activities (arranging, building, drawing), where the spatial part of the task is lacking although there is no apraxia of single movements." Kleist used the term *optic apraxia* since he thought that perception and praxis were intact but that there was an interruption of an association between the visual and the motor image. Later the term *constructional apraxia* came into use, to indicate a relationship to other complex motor disorders with lesions of the *left* hemisphere.

However, there was evidence of a perceptual impairment. Pick noted that patients had difficulty understanding drawings. He claimed that there was an impairment in the composition of the parts of the figure into a whole, that it was a type of perceptual disturbance. Other workers proposed a regression in the analysis of spatial relationships (see Lange, 1936), a loss in spatial structure such that objects failed to achieve a clear perceptual organization. Disorders in localization and attention were present. Mayer-Gross (1936) found inability to analyze a real or imaginary pattern as a whole. His concept of "activity space" (*Wirkraum*), in which the disorder is bound up with the space of the arm's reach, is relevant to modern studies of optic grasping and spatial localization.

Visuospatial impairment was first linked to the *right* hemisphere by Dide (1938). Duensing (1953) distinguished between a perceptually based defect with right hemisphere lesions (visuospatial *agnosia*) and a motor executive defect with left hemisphere lesions (constructional *apraxia*). Subsequently, there were many attempts to document right–left differences in constructional impairment.

The drawings of left-sided cases were said to show more hesitation and greater simplification, and to be facilitated by copying from a model (Nielson, 1975) whereas those of right-damaged cases were characterized as comparable in complexity to the model, though disorganized (Piercy, Hécaen, & Ajuriaguerra, 1960). Right-sided cases had difficulty in representing perspective, and tended to orient the drawing on a diagonal (see Mendilaharsu, Miglionico, Mendilaharsu, Budelli, & DeSouto, 1968). It was thought that constructional disability in right-sided cases predicted a parietal lesion, whereas in left cases the lesion could be frontal or parietal. These descriptive studies gradually gave way to experimental investigations, and as this occurred the right–left differences became increasingly more difficult to substantiate.

Some hints of this were reported in the paper of Arrigoni and DeRenzi (1964). This study confirmed the greater frequency and severity of constructional disability with right brain damage, but attributed this to an unequal lesion size in the two groups. When left and right cases were matched for reaction time (i.e., presumably for lesion size), the differences were no longer significant. Despite some methodological shortcomings, the main conclusions of this study have been confirmed by subsequent research. The right–left difference is due to the presence of hemispatial neglect in right-damaged cases, and to the exclusion of severe aphasics from the left-damaged group. When allowance is made for these factors, the difference between left and right cases is no longer present.

Thus, *from an initial association with left, then right brain damage, the disorder is now regarded as comparable in left-and right-lesioned cases.* This conclusion is consistent with the idea that the elaboration of object space is bihemispherically mediated, and that both hemispheres participate about equally in this process. It leaves unexplained the right hemisphere bias with nonverbal measures, and the evidence in commissurotomy cases of superior right hemisphere spatial ability. The explanation of these phenomena, however, will become clearer after a consideration of the one perceptual symptom for which there is a clear right hemisphere predilection.

LEFT HEMISPATIAL NEGLECT

The terms *hemispatial neglect, inattention,* and *agnosia* refer to an altered awareness for half of perceptual or bodily space. The disorder is chiefly associated with lesions of the parietal area of the right hemisphere. In Gloning, Gloning, and Hoff's (1968) study, a right-sided lesion was even more common among left-handers. Constructional impairment and hemispatial "agnosia" may occur independently. Patients may show marked inattention with good constructional performance and the reverse. Patients with anterior lesions may also show inattention, so-called frontal neglect, probably a mild form of the parietal disorder (Chedru, 1976). A visual field defect is common but not obligatory. The patient can "see" on the affected side but does not attend to that side. There is probably defective imagery on the impaired side (Bisiach, 1980). The deficit in right parietal cases is not material specific; both verbal and nonverbal stimuli are ignored. This may not be true in left-damaged cases.

Neglect is usually most apparent in the periphery of the field (see Zihl & von Cramon, 1979), though it often involves the entire field into the parafoveal region, and may "spill over" into the intact field. Kinsbourne and Warrington (1962) found that right hemispheric cases may neglect the left side of words presented in the "intact" right hemifield. Bisiach, Capitani, Luzzatti, and Perani (1981) have shown that the extent of neglect changes with the orientation of the body. Such cases indicate that neglect is a dynamic alteration not easily accounted for by a cortical retinal map. These observations are also consistent with the idea that the *visual half field differentiates out of a unitary space.*

Left hemispatial neglect can be interpreted in the following way. The clinicopathological data, reviewed in the preceding paragraphs, indicate bilateral processing of visuospatial information. Space perception is symmetrically organized in animals. However, in man bilateral symmetry of spatial representation is obscured by the elaboration of a phonological component. The preferential involvement of right hemisphere lesions in hemispatial neglect occurs as a result of this left hemisphere specialization. The lesion of right hemisphere involves, and so exposes, the parietal segment of the object formative process. This segment—the forming left hemifield—is normally submerged within the object as a "preprocessing" stage. The neglect occurs because the end point of cognitive processing is centered about a feature analytic level which cannot access into analytic cognition the more preliminary stage disrupted by the lesion. The neglect or inattention is the sign of the unaccessed void in the forming left hemifield (Figure 3.1); the access problem *is* the inattention.

Neglect is uncommon with left hemisphere lesions but it does occur. For either left- or right-sided neglect, a large lesion is ordinarily required. However, such a lesion in the left hemisphere will tend to involve adjacent regions in the posterior superior temporal area mediating phonological representation. The involvement of these regions obviates the access problem. This does not imply that the right half of space is not disrupted, only

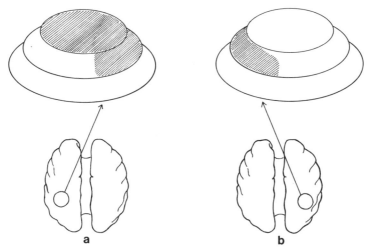

a   b

Figure 3.1. Hemispatial agnosia reflects a lack of access from a "surface" level to a more preliminary disruption. It is more common with right-sided lesions (b) because these do not disturb the surface level. The association is with lesions of generalized neocortex. The disorder may occur with left hemisphere lesions (a) when the pathology is interposed between levels. However, a smaller, more selective lesion is required. As illustrated here, the lesion will tend to involve adjacent structures mediating phonological realization, and thus obviate the access problem. Since the disorder requires a large lesion, it will be much less common with left hemisphere pathology.

that the disruption is not submerged within an intact subsequent level. Nor is neglect simply obscured in left-damaged cases by a concomitant aphasia. It is not the presence of aphasia but the rarity of a lesion intersecting the parietal cortex without involving neighboring regions underlying phonological representation that accounts for the infrequency of right hemispatial neglect. Aphasia alone does not invalidate tests for spatial neglect. It is common to see global aphasics point out or hold up their hemiplegic right arm when asked about their difficulty, though this is unusual in left hemiplegics. An implicit, nonverbal, or tacit neglect of the hemiplegic right side is rare. This is because neglect points to an interlevel access limitation which is not present in patients with phonological disruption.

It should be pointed out that according to this view spatial neglect is not a disturbance of attention. The term *inattention* used for this disorder implies incorrectly that there is damage to an attentional mechanism. Some workers have looked for lateral asymmetries in such a mechanism, others an attentional "circuit" in the brain. These simplistic interpretations betray a lack of ingenuity on the part of the clinician. The first question that should be asked is, what is attention?

One can say that attention is not extrinsic to perception but is part of the perceptual process. Disorders of attention and perception do not dissociate. The state of attention reflects the state of perceptual processing at a given moment. A focused attention is the same as an articulated perception. These are different ways of describing the same state. Put differently, to cognize an object in an analytic mode requires a discrete or selective type of attention. The perception is built up around object features. Conversely, holistic or global perception accompanies a more diffuse attention which is distributed over the object field (Brown, 1983a).

The attentional state of the left hemisphere can be characterized as focused, and that of the right as diffuse, but in what sense is attention impaired in hemispatial neglect except that the right hemisphere (holistic) mode is not consistently derived to an (analytic) end stage? The situation is similar to that in the split-brain patient (discussed in what follows). However, in the split, although the limitation in access to a left hemisphere mode is more pronounced, the perception that is realized by the right hemisphere is more developed. In the case of left spatial neglect, the access limitation is incomplete but, because of the pathological lesion, there is a more preliminary object. The failure of the right hemisphere to attend to objects on the left side indicates a lack of full differentiation of its object field. The incomplete resolution of the object is accompanied by a more diffuse attention. Objects differentiate fully into the right visual field. The focal attention (perception) for the right field and the diffuse attention (perception) for the left account for much of the clinical behavior of such patients. From time to time, left field objects do complete their development, giving the mistaken impression of normal or potentially normal perceptions.

Thus, hemispatial neglect involves two symptoms: first, a disruption of contralateral space, which occurs perhaps equally with lesions of either hemisphere; second, a lack of awareness for the disrupted level, which occurs chiefly with right hemisphere lesions and reflects the inability of one cognitive mode to access another that is more preliminary. The failure to derive left visual field (right hemisphere) contents to a left hemisphere end stage is comparable to the inability in the waking state to retrieve the submerged cognition of a dream.

BEHAVIORAL EVIDENCE FOR
COGNITIVE ASYMMETRIES

Behavioral studies of laterality in normal subjects using dichotic or hemifield presentations have consistently demonstrated a right hemisphere preference for nonverbal stimuli of various sorts (e.g., faces, dots, shapes) and a left hemisphere bias for most types of verbal material. However, the right–left difference is not a difference between verbal and visual stimuli. Left hemisphere effects are observed for feature or component detection on various perceptual tasks, while a right hemisphere effect occurs for verbal stimuli when the task involves early processing (e.g., script, semantic priming). Changing laterality occurs for some material (faces, music, etc.) depending on the degree to which it is analyzed. The relation to skill or familiarity is also a relection of degree of analysis. Such observations indicate that it is not the material but the operation applied to this material which determines laterality. Another way of putting this is that lateral asymmetries arise according to whether the operation challenged in an experiment involves an early or late stage in cognitive processing.

Set in this light, the behavioral data can be interpreted in the same way as the lesion cases. Specifically, a right hemisphere advantage appears when the task involves initial stages of processing, a left hemisphere advantage when the task involves end stage processing. The relative proximity to end stage processing determines hemisphere bias on a particular task.

THE MEANING OF THE CALLOSAL SYNDROME

The study of callosal patients provides what seems to be solid evidence for right–left differences in spatial capacity. However, the interpretation of these findings is not altogether clear. For one thing, the work relies chiefly on hemifield presentations and the assumption that input is restricted to a single hemisphere, an assumption which may be incorrect. Thus, Trevarthen (1970) found integration across the vertical meridian in splits, and Holtzman, Sidtis, Volpe, and Gazzaniga (1980) have demonstrated between-field spatial priming. These findings indicate that each hemisphere has access to a unitary visual field at a preliminary stage, certainly at upper brainstem, probably at even higher levels. Lesion studies in monkey have been interpreted to show that midbrain tegmental mechanisms construct a unified percept of the two half fields (Denny-Brown & Fischer, 1976). Comparable findings have been reported in humans with upper brainstem lesions (Brown, 1983). Cases with midbrain or limbic hallucination may not show a hemianopic tendency. The visual field is replaced by a scenic, two-dimensional, at times even cycloramic hallucination. Presumably, the elaboration of a deep level, unitary space, occurs through the retinotectal system which comprises as much as 20–30% of optic tract fibers (Bernheimer, 1899).

In other studies, left field presentations in some commissurotomy cases have elicited verbal and affective responses which suggest interhemispheric transfer. Nebes (1978) has described verbalizations in splits which are semantically related to left field verbal stimuli. Interhemispheric "transfer" of affect has been reported. Gazzaniga and colleagues (1980) have demonstrated cross-field semantic priming. One interpretation of these effects is that of transfer over the anterior commissure, but the phenomenon has been described in cases with section of this pathway (Zaidel, 1980). The idea that left hemisphere verbalization, semantically or affectively linked to right hemisphere stimuli, reflects cross-cueing or right hemisphere speech directly, is an ad hoc interpretation without much experimental support. It is comparable to the invocation of ipsilateral motor pathways to account for correct responses to verbal commands with the left hand, a phenomenon which might suggest that there is also a shared deep motor organization.

In my view, these findings can be explained by assuming a unified semantic representation prior to a representation of object form. Conceivably, cross-field semantic effects point to the degree to which a target can differentiate—or the degree to which it is selected—through this unified field. This is consistent with observations in aphasia which indicate that the representation of word meaning proceeds from an early stage organized about symbolic, affective, and experiential relations to a later conceptual stage (Brown, 1979). The verbalization to the left field stimulus would reflect the degree to which the content has "come up" in this system. This interpretation of lexical-semantic phenomena in the split is identical to that for visuospatial material. Specifically, semantic or symbolic transformation, or a stage of object relations, reflects early processing; phonological or form analysis reflects end stage processing.

A second point to be emphasized is that studies of spatial capacity in splits have not consistently demonstrated right–left differences on perceptual tasks. For example, right and left field performance on block design patterns is comparable when the response involves matching to a choice card. The asymmetry appears when a manual reconstruction of the pattern is required. In fact, most studies that show lateral asymmetries for spatial ability rely on differences in copying, constructional activity, or writing. Gazzaniga has stressed the role of limb behavior in this effect. It is the constructional activity of the right or left hand which introduces the asymmetry. Assuming that spatial capacity is equally represented between the hemispheres—an assumption that has not been disconfirmed by the experimental work—how does the response mode, that of vocal or limb movement, influence or determine hemispheric differences on spatial tasks?

As hand response in the split reflects the cognitive level in the contralateral hemisphere, the right hand–left hemisphere will be at a disadvantage in access to spatial cognition. This accounts for a left hand superiority on drawing tasks. Conversely, the left hand–right hemisphere will be relatively unable to analyze a lexical-semantic representation in right hemisphere into its constituent sounds or letters. This gives rise to a left-sided agraphia. In this view, writing or drawing are comparable to speech, in that they are motor performances that make underlying representations explicit, that is, they involve analysis of underlying configurations through sequential or kinetic patterns of movement.

Some recent findings in patients with right hemiplegia and severe aphasia support this conclusion (Brown, Leader, & Blum, 1983). Such patients have been found to write fairly well words to dictation using the hemiplegic right arm with the aid of a prosthesis, though they are profoundly agraphic with the intact left hand. Moreover, the ability to write words to dictation with the hemiplegic limb may be superior to the ability to produce the same words in speech. The phenomenon of hemiplegic writing is interpreted as reflecting access to preliminary lexical representations through the use of older proximal motor systems in the right arm.

Finally, the view that right and left hemisphere elaborate a unitary cognition which undergoes further processing in left hemisphere explains many other normal and pathological phenomena. For example, the underlying unity of consciousness in the split, though there is an appearance of isolated minds, cannot be explained by independent or parallel channels but can be understood through a single hierarchic system of levels. Separate consciousness does not arise from each hemisphere but reflects state-specific behavior at multiple levels in a "vertical" hierarchy. Similarly, the association between right hemisphere pathology and euphoria, or heightened affect, does not signal a difference between the hemispheres in the organization of emotion. Rather, lesions of the (posterior) left hemisphere which disrupt that level of cognition which is continuous with the cognition of the right hemisphere (i.e., a lexical semantic level in language) also give euphoria (Brown, 1982). The affect change is specific to cognitive level, not hemisphere.

REFERENCES

Arrigoni, G., & DeRenzi, E. Constructional apraxia and hemispheric locus of lesion. *Cortex*, 1964, *1*, 170–197.

Bernheimer, S. Die Wurzelgebiete der Augennerven. *Handbuch der gesamte Augenheilkunde* VI, Part 2. Berlin: Springer, 1899.

Bisiach, E. Commentary in *Behavioral and Brain Sciences*, 1980, *3*, 499–500.

Bisiach, E., Capitani, E., Luzzatti, C., & Perani, D. Brain and conscious representation of outside reality. *Neuropsychologia*, 1981, *19*, 543–551.

Brown, J. W. Language representation in the brain. In H. Steklis & M. Raleigh (Eds.), *Neurobiology of social communication in primates*. New York: Academic Press, 1979.

Brown, J. W. Review of deep dyslexia. *Brain and Language*, 1981, *14*, 386–392.

Brown, J. W. Hierarchy and evolution in neurolinguistics. In M. Arbib, D. Caplan, & J. Marshall (Eds.), *Neural models of language process*. New York: Academic Press, 1982.

Brown, J. W. Emergence and time in microgenetic theory. *Journal of the American Academy of Psychoanalysis*, 1983, *11*, 35–54. (a)

Brown, J. W. The microstructure of perception: Physiology and patterns of breakdown. *Cognition and Brain Theory*, 1983, *6*, in press. (b)

Brown, J. W., Leader, B., & Blum, C. Hemiplegic writing in severe aphasia. *Brain and Language*, 1983, in press.

Brown, J. W. *Mind, brain and consciousness*. New York: Academic Press, 1977.

Chedru, F. Space representation in unilateral spatial neglect. *Journal of Neurology, Neurosurgery and Psychiatry*, 1976, *39*, 1057–1061.

Denny-Brown, D., & Fischer, E. Physiological aspects of visual perception. *Archives of Neurology*, 1976, *33*, 228–242.

Dide, M. Les désorientations temporo-spatiales et la prépondérance de l'hémisphere droit dans les agnoso-akinésies proprioceptives. *Encephale*, 1938, *33*, 277–294.

Duensing, F. Raumagnostische und ideatorisch-apraktische Störung des gestaltenden Handelns. *Deutsch Zeitschrift Nervenheilkunde*, 1953, *170*, 72–94.

Gazzaniga, M. Paper presented at the Conference on Language and Cognitive Processing in the Right Hemisphere, Institute for Research in Behavioral Neuroscience, New York, 1980.

Gloning, I., Gloning, K., & Hoff, H. *Neuropsychological symptoms and syndromes in lesions of the occipital lobe and adjacent areas.* Paris: Gauthier-Villars, 1968.

Holtzman, J., Sidtis, J., Volpe, B., & Gazzaniga, M. Attentional unity following brain bisection in man. *Neuroscience Abstracts,* 1980, *6,* 195.

Kinsbourne, M., & Warrington, E. A disorder of simultaneous form perception. *Brain,* 1962, *85,* 461–486.

Kleist, K. *Gehirnpathologie.* Leipzig: Barth, 1934.

Lange, J. Agnosien und Apraxien. In Bumke & Foerster (Eds.), *Handbuch der Neurologie.* 1936, *6,* 807–960.

Mendilaharsu, C., Miglionico, A., Mendilaharsu, S., Budelli, R., & DeSouto, H. A propos d'une epreuve d'etude de l'apraxie constructive pour differentier les lesions de l'hemisphere droit et du gauche. *Acta Neurologica Latinoamericana,* 1968, *14,* 138–154.

Mayer-Gross, W. The question of visual impairment in constructional apraxia. *Proceedings of the Royal Society of Medicine,* 1936, *29,* 1396–1400.

Nebes, R. Direct examination of cognitive function in the right and left hemispheres. In M. Kinsbourne (Ed.), *Asymmetrical function of the brain.* Cambridge: Cambridge University Press, 1978.

Nielsen, H. Is constructional apraxia primarily an interhemispheric disconnection syndrome? *Scandinavian Journal of Psychology,* 1975, *16,* 113–124.

Piercy, M., Hécaen, H., & Ajuriaguerra, J. de. Constructional apraxia associated with unilateral cerebral lesions—left and right sided cases compared. *Brain,* 1960, *83,* 225–242.

Trevarthen, C. Experimental evidence for a brain stem contribution to visual perception in man. *Brain, Behavior and Evolution,* 1970, *3,* 338–352.

Zaidel, E. Personal communication, 1980.

Zihl, J., & von Cramon, D. The contribution of the 'second' visual system to directed visual attention in man. *Brain,* 1979, *102,* 835–856.

STUDIES OF
NORMAL SUBJECTS

The Linguistic and Emotional Functions of the Normal Right Hemisphere

M. MOSCOVITCH

This first part of this chapter deals with the problem of right hemisphere contribution to language comprehension and production in normal people. Examination of this issue within an information-processing framework suggests that, although the right hemisphere has some linguistic capacities that are not negligible, its contribution to normal language is minimal in those areas that are traditionally considered linguistic, such as syntax, phonology, and semantics. Much more noticeable is the influence of the right hemisphere on verbal memory and on the pragmatic, communicative use of language (i.e., its discourse function). The latter effect may to some extent depend on the right hemisphere's superiority in mediating emotions. The second part of this chapter, therefore, deals with recent developments in research on the lateralization of emotion.

LANGUAGE[1]

Research on different populations of brain-damaged patients suggests that the right hemisphere is capable of supporting language to some degree. We

[1]Many of the points mentioned in this section are reviewed at greater length in Moscovitch (1981, in press a).

COGNITIVE PROCESSING IN
THE RIGHT HEMISPHERE

know, for example, that aphasic patients with left hemisphere lesions may sometimes retain certain functions, particularly semantic ones. Broca's aphasics may be relatively more impaired syntactically than semantically. Individuals with phonemic or deep dyslexia as a result of left hemisphere lesions have difficulty reading phonetically but are less impaired in extracting meaning from script via another route. In both of these syndromes, investigators suspect that the right hemisphere may be performing the linguistic functions observed, although at the moment there is little evidence to back this up. In a number of patients with a variety of asphasic syndromes, however, Kinsbourne (1971) and Czopf (1972) have shown that aphasic speech was arrested by anesthetization of the right, but not the left, hemisphere with sodium amytal. The linguistic activities of the right hemisphere have also been investigated in patients who have undergone hemispherectomy and commissurotomy. As expected from the aphasia literature, some of these patients, but by no means the majority, show preserved syntax for simple but not complex sentences. Their lexicon, though impoverished, seems nonetheless substantial, reaching the level of about 14-years-old in one patient. If it is the case, as these studies suggest, that the right hemisphere has a substantial lexicon, then do normal people draw on the linguistic capacity or competence of the right hemisphere? It is this sort of question we wish to address.

The crucial evidence for answering questions about right hemisphere contribution to normal linguistic performance comes from two different populations—normal people and people with right hemisphere lesions. Turning first to the evidence from normal people we can see that, despite severe limitations in the techniques available to study hemispheric differences, definite progress has been made.

Research in both audition and vision has generally supported findings from the clinical literature that hemispheric asymmetries are found primarily at later, higher order stages of information processing (see Berlin & McNeil, 1976; Moscovitch, 1979; Madden & Nebes, 1980; Bradshaw & Nettleton, 1981, for reviews; and Kimura & Durnford, 1974, for a dissenting view). Recent studies from our own and others' laboratories, using visual masking techniques, have added further support to this position.

In our studies, three-letter words arranged vertically were presented tachistoscopically for durations ranging from 2 to 16 msec to either the right or left visual field followed by either a flash or pattern mask after a 2–24-msec interstimulus interval (ISI). The subject's task was to identify the word. As the ISI between the target and mask was increased, identification was improved until it reached a criterion of four consecutive correct responses which was taken as the critical ISI. Because the flash mask is effective only when it is presented to the same eye as the target, it is considered to act peripherally (Turvey, 1973). The pattern mask is effective even when it is presented to the eye opposite the target and is consequently assumed to act centrally at, or beyond, the point at which input from the two eyes converges (Turvey, 1973). If hemispheric differences are absent at the early processing stages but are found at later ones, then one might expect that perceptual asymmetries for word identification would occur only in the patterned, central masking condition. As predicted, the critical ISI at which the target escaped the mask was shorter in the right field–left hemisphere only in the pattern mask condition. In the flash mask condition, no hemifield differences were noted (see Figure 4.1).

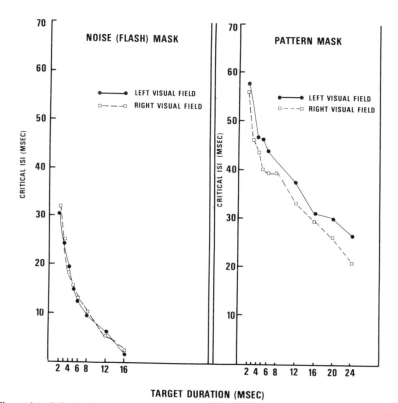

Figure 4.1. Relation between target duration and mean critical ISI for masking by noise and pattern (50 msec duration) when the target and mask appear in the same visual field. The target is a three-letter word presented vertically. (From Moscovitch, 1979).

A subsequent study conducted in collaboration with Mark Byrd confirmed and extended this finding. Because critical ISI is a measure of performance only at one point in the identification function, we decided to look at accuracy of target identification at different stimulus onset asynchronies (SOA) between the target and the mask. It may be the case, for example, that at low SOAs identification, though poor, may favor one visual field whereas at higher SOAs, as identification improves, performance may favor the opposite field. The reason for this is that when identification is poor the subject relies primarily on the visual feature extraction capabilities of the right hemisphere whereas when stimulus clarity improves the critical factor is linguistic or verbal analysis. As before, subjects were presented with vertical three-letter targets, followed by a flash or pattern mask at different SOAs. As Figure 4.2 shows, a large and consistent advantage in favor of the right field–left hemisphere was evident only in the pattern mask condition. Significantly, this advantage appeared as soon as any identification was possible and was maintained virtually unchanged at all subsequent SOAs.

What might be the structural locus at which these asymmetries first ap-

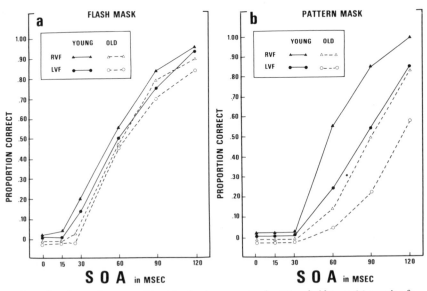

Figure 4.2. Proportion correct identification by young (under 30) and old (over 65) people of a three-letter target presented in the right or left visual field for a duration of 2 msec. The mask was either a flash or a pattern that was presented for a duration of 50 msec in both fields at varying SOAs from the target. (From Moscovitch, 1982.)

pear? A clue comes from masking studies that Schlotterer, Crapper, and I conducted on patients suffering from senile dementia of the Alzheimer type. We found that compared to age-matched controls and young normal subjects, Alzheimer patients showed a marked decrement in identification of a foveally presented letter in the pattern mask condition relative to that of the flash mask. The SOA at which identification was perfect in the pattern mask condition was over 45 msec longer in Alzheimer patients than in controls (Figure 4.3). Because the degenerative changes characteristic of Alzheimer's disease, such as the presence of neurofibrillary tangles and senile

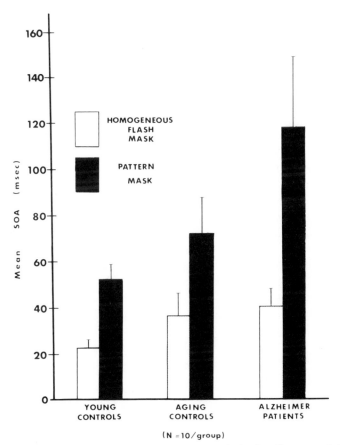

Figure 4.3. Mean critical SOA between target and mask at which a foveally presented single letter target is identified correctly on four successive trials. The mask was either a flash or a pattern of 50 msec duration that was superimposed on the target. (From Schlotterer, 1977.)

placques, are relatively rare prior to striate cortex but proliferate in areas subsequent to it such as the prestriate and temporal lobes, our results suggest that the pattern mask acts subsequent to striate cortex.

Beyond the early stages, from both a functional and structural point of view, information is processed differently by each hemisphere. This applies to all kinds of information or types of stimulus input whether linguistic or nonlinguistic. Where differences in performance mediated by the right and left hemisphere are large, as in processing the syntactic or the phonological properties of language, one can assume that the inferior hemisphere's capacities are simply inadequate or inappropriate for the task. In many instances, however, as in processing the semantic properties of language, or in classifying objects and interpreting events, hemispheric differences, as measured in absolute performance levels, are likely to be smaller because each hemisphere contributes in its own way to the task at hand.

These observations apply primarily to clinical populations such as split-brain patients or patients with unilateral brain damage. In testing for hemispheric specialization in normal people, one is limited to studying perceptual or motor asymmetries that are small even when they are presumed to reflect large differences between the cerebral hemispheres. This is understandable if one considers that the hemispheres are free to communicate with each other. Thus, it is assumed that a consistent advantage of 30 msec in latency or 10% in accuracy for one visual field or ear over the other in recognition indicates that the hemisphere contralateral to the favored field is dominant for the task at hand. To make matters worse, these differences are often fragile in that a variety of attentional factors can bias performance toward or away from a given sensory field.

Nonetheless, some reaction time techniques have been devised that are resistant to these performance variables (Geffen, 1978) or that make it possible to factor out these variables and determine the relative contributions of each hemisphere to a given task (Moscovitch, 1973; Berlucchi, 1974; Zaidel, personal communication). One such technique involves examining how RT differences between the left and right sensory field vary with responding hand in a task that requires a yes–no decision that can be signaled by a button press. A consistent sensory field advantage that is maintained regardless of response hand indicates that the task is functionally localized to a single hemisphere whereas an interaction of responding hand with the sensory field indicates that both hemispheres contribute to performance. Using this type of analysis, experiments have shown that tasks requiring phonological decisions are functionally localized to the left hemisphere, a finding consistent with the clinical literature (Moscovitch, 1973, 1976, 1979).

Similarly *some* pattern recognition tasks (e.g., face recognition) are functionally localized to the right hemisphere. Although the neurological literature indicates that damage to either hemisphere may impair face recognition and that damage to both is usually necessary to produce prosopagnosia, (Meadows, 1974; Benton, 1980), the results of studies on normal people suggest that for some face recognition tasks the left hemisphere's contribution is negligible, whatever its underlying capacity might be (see Moscovitch, 1979, for review).

When applied to other questions, such as the right hemisphere's contribution to processing verbal information semantically, the techniques produce mixed results. For example, the clinical literature suggests that the right hemisphere has a lexicon consisting primarily of concrete words that are represented semantically but cannot be easily manipulated phonologically, if at all. One would therefore expect abstract and function words to produce a consistent right field–left hemisphere advantage whereas concrete words would show no advantage or would produce sensory field RT differences that would vary with responding hand. Whereas some studies report stronger left hemisphere advantage for abstract than for concrete words, an equal number of studies failed to find any difference (see Moscovitch, 1981, for review). Our own studies fall into the latter caegory. For example, Janet Olds and I attempted to replicate Day's (1977, 1979) finding that in a lexical decision task, a consistent left field advantage is found only for abstract words. As Table 4.1 shows, we found a right field–left hemisphere advantage for concrete words as well as abstract ones. Although statistically only the overall right-field advantage was significant, the data are not as conclusive as one would like since there is a hint that concrete words produce smaller perceptual asymmetries than abstract ones.

Table 4.1
GO–NO–GO REACTION TIME (MSEC) TO CONCRETE AND ABSTRACT WORDS
PRESENTED EITHER IN THE LEFT OR RIGHT VISUAL FIELD [a]

	Left hand		Right hand	
	Left visual field	Right visual field	Left visual field	Right visual field
Concrete	673	643	674	666
Abstract	671	622	709	643

[a]Subjects distinguished between words and nonwords by responding with either the left or right hand only if a word appeared.

What these studies suggest is that, regardless of the right hemisphere's proven capacity to process verbal information semantically, normal people tend to rely primarily on the left hemisphere's superior abilities in this domain. This type of functional localization may occur either because the left hemisphere inhibits the right with regard to linguistic functions, the left hemisphere completes the task before the right, or the subject chooses a strategy that is more compatible with left than with right hemisphere processes. Whatever the reason, the right hemisphere's inherent abilities are not reflected in normal performance, and functions therefore appear to be localized to the left.

The literature on patients with right hemisphere damage supports this hypothesis. At the moment there are only two papers, by Lesser (1974) and by Gainotti, Caltagirone, Miceli, and Masullo (1981, and Chapter 8, this volume) that show even a mild semantic impairment following right hemisphere lesions. In their studies, lexical-semantic comprehension of spoken or written words and sentences was impaired in patients with right hemisphere lesions although syntax and phonology were normal. It remains to be determined, however, whether these semantic deficits are specifically linguistic or whether they arise from some more general cognitive impairment which affects the semantic system more than the phonological or syntactic one.

Under some circumstances, however, the right hemisphere's linguistic abilities, particularly its semantic ones, may emerge and influence normal performance, which would account for the occasional observation of right hemisphere processing of concrete words. Althouth the conditions necessary for this to occur have yet to be elucidated, there are some promising candidates. One involves overloading the left hemisphere and thereby enabling the right hemisphere's capacities to emerge. This would be consistent with the model illustrated in Figure 4.4 in which the two hemispheres are conceived as separate, but interdependent, information-processing systems. When one system is overloaded, the other's contribution to a particular task may become more evident (see Hellige & Cox, 1976; Hellige, Cox, & Litvac, 1979; Friedman & Polson, 1982).

A second possibility involves the presentation of stimuli or of tasks that naturally engage the superior visuospatial processing mechanisms of the right hemisphere. Wilkins and Moscovitch (1978) found that patients with left temporal lobectomy but not those with right, had difficulty in rapidly naming line drawings or classifying line drawings and words as representing something living versus man-made. They were, however, perfectly normal at classifying the same material by size, even though control subjects and

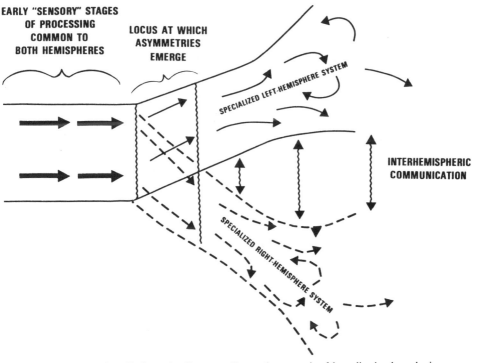

Figure 4.4. Model of information flow according to the transmitted lateralization hypothesis. (From Moscovitch, 1979.)

patients with right temporal lobectomy found this task somewhat more difficult (see Tables 4.2 and 4.3). Presumably, size classification may require analogical visuospatial processes that are more likely to be mediated by the right hemisphere than the left. Similar processes are involved in imagery-mediated verbal recall. Although right temporal lobectomy is not as dev-

Table 4.2
MEAN CLASSIFICATION SCORES[a]

	"Living–made"		"Larger–smaller"	
	Drawings	Words	Drawings	Words
Left temporal	12.1	12.3	13.1	13.3
Right temporal	14.4	13.6	13.1	11.4
Normal control	14.5	14.4	12.9	12.5

[a]Maximum score—16, average chance score—8.

Table 4.3
MEAN NAMING SCORES[a]

Group	Without cue	With cue
Left temporal	11.4	11.6
Right temporal	13.3	12.6
Normal control	14.7	13.9

[a]Maximum score—16; average chance score—8.

astating on verbal recall as left temporal lobectomy, it does lead to a noticeable impairment on tasks that have a strong imagery component. Jones (1976), confirming Patten (1972), reported that control subjects and patients with left temporal lobectomy improve their performance in a verbal paired associate task by using imagery mnemonics but patients with right temporal lobectomy do not. In a subsequent study, it was established (Jones-Gotman & Milner, 1978; Jones-Gotman, 1979) that an intact right temporal lobe is critical for normal performance on verbal tasks that have an imagery components, such as recalling concrete words.

The different contributions of both hemispheres to verbal recall was even more noticeable when pictorial stimuli are used. Jaccarino (1975; cf. Milner, 1978) found that damage to either the right or left temporal lobe resulted in impaired recall of the names of line drawings that were presented a day earlier. That right temporal damage can influence even *immediate* verbal recall was demonstrated by Moscovitch (1976). He presented patients with 16 randomly ordered drawings of common objects, each of which belonged to one of four taxonomic or shape categories (see Figure 4.5). In recalling the names of these drawings, normal subjects usually cluster their responses according to both lexical and shape categories (Frost, 1972). Patients with right temporal lobectomy, however, clustered only by taxonomic category whereas patients with left temporal lobectomy clustered primarily by shape but inconsistently by taxonomic category (Table 4.4).

Similar biases in clustering could be produced in normal people by presenting drawings bilaterally (see Figure 4.6) with a concurrent task that affects the processing capacities of one hemisphere more than the other. In the concurrent nonverbal task, which is presumed to affect right hemisphere processing, the subject identifies central nonsense figures while encoding a bilaterally presented drawing (see Figure 4.6), whereas in the concurrent verbal task, the subject names a central, vertically presented word. In the control condition, the center is left blank. As Table 4.5 shows, taxonomic

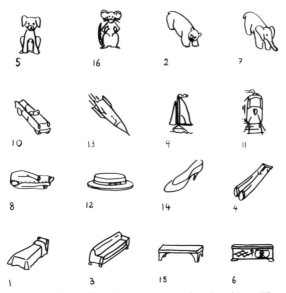

Figure 4.5. An example of a set of line drawings presented to the subjects. The number next to each drawing indicated the order of presentation. I thank Nancy Frost for making these drawings available to me. (Reprinted from Right Hemisphere Language by M. Moscovitch by permission of Aspen Systems Corporation, © 1981.)

clustering is predominant in the nonverbal concurrent condition, and spatial clustering in the verbal concurrent condition.

These results are consistent with out hypothesis that beyond the early stage of processing each hemisphere encodes the identical information in a manner commensurate with its abilities (for similar research on faces, see Sergent, 1982; Proudfoot, 1982). On verbal tasks, however, special techniques are required to free the right hemisphere from the dominance of the left and to reveal its contribution to normal performance.

Table 4.4
MEAN ITEMS RECALLED AND MEAN CLUSTERING[a]

Group	Mean items recalled	Spatial ARC	Verbal ARC
Normal control	11.0	.14[b]	.36[b]
Right temporal	10.7	− .07	.31[b]
Left temporal	8.5	-.27[b]	.34

[a]Note ARC = adjusted ration for clustering (Roenker, Thompson, & Brown, 1971).
[b]$t < .05$.

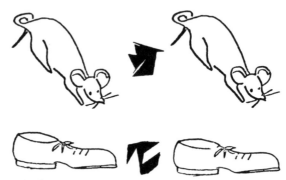

Figure 4.6. Example of two line drawings and the accompanying nonverbal interfering stimuli which were presented tachistoscopically. (Reprinted from Right Hemisphere Language by M. Moscovitch by permission of Aspen Systems Corporation, © 1981.)

Apart from memory, the domain in which the right hemisphere's contributions to verbal performance are most evident is not that of traditional linguistics, such as phonology, syntax, and semantics, but rather that of the paralinguistic aspects of language, such as intonation, emotional tone, context, inference, and connotation—in short, the domain of pragmatics or the discourse function of language (Bates, 1976). It was Hughlings Jackson who first called attention to the right hemisphere's contribution to linguistic performance. In particular, he thought that the less propositional, more automatic aspects of language, such as emotional utterances, might be mediated by the right hemisphere. Recent studies have supported his intuitions. Patients with right hemisphere lesions are impaired in producing and perceiving the correct emotional tone of linguistic utterances (Heilman, Scholes, & Watson, 1975; Ross & Mesulam, 1979), react inappropriately to humorous material (Gardner, Ling, Falmm, & Silverman, 1975; Wapner,

Table 4.5

MEAN ITEMS RECALLED AND MEAN CLUSTERING

Group	Mean items recalled	Spatial ARC	Verbal ARC
Control	8.5	.12	.20[a]
Nonverbal concurrent	7.2	− .19	.39[a]
Verbal concurrent	4.2	.37[a]	.04

[a] $t < .05$.

Hambly, & Gardner, 1981) interpret metaphors incorrectly (Winner & Gardner, 1977), have difficulty solving subtle sentence anagrams (Cavalli, DeRenz, Faglioni, & Vitale, 1981), and have a poor appreciation of antonymic contrasts (Gardner, Silverman, Wapner, & Zurif, 1978), actor–object relations (Heeschen, 1980), and connotative aspects of pictures (Gardner & Denes, 1973). These observations are consistent with results of laterality studies in normal people (e.g., Blumstein & Cooper, 1974; Haggard & Parkinson, 1971; Safer & Leventhal, 1977; Zurif, 1974). Patients with right hemisphere damage seem to have no difficulty comprehending individual sentences, but they do have difficulty relating a sentence to a larger context, understanding its emotional connotation, and drawing the proper inferences from it (Wapner *et al.*, 1982). Without the right hemisphere, communication, in its broadest sense, may not proceed normally.

EMOTION

Apart from studying the emotional uses of language, investigators have also begun to examine the broader issue of the lateralization of emotional functions in general (see Campbell, in press, and Tucker, 1981, for reviews). Two hypotheses are currently receiving consideration. One is that negative emotions are mediated primarily by the right hemisphere and positive ones by the left; the other is that all emotions are mediated primarily by the right hemisphere.

The former hypothesis has its origin in Goldstein's (1948) observations that catastrophic reactions are more likely to accompany damage to the left hemisphere than to the right, whereas the opposite is true for indifference reactions. The idea that negative and positive affect are mediated by different hemispheres was reinforced by Rossi and Rosadini's (1967) report that patients tend to euphoria after recovering from right hemisphere anesthetization with sodium amytal and to depression after left hemisphere anesthetization. Gainotti's (1972) studies of mood changes following left or right hemisphere lesions supported this hypothesis.

Despite the difficulty of replicating Rossi and Rosadini's findings (Milner, 1967; Kolb & Milner, 1981), and the possibility that the mood changes observed by Gainotti were confounded with aphasia and neglect, their studies inspired a great deal of research on normal people, some of which is consistent with the hypothesis that negative and positive affect are mediated by different hemispheres. Motion picture sequences viewed with the left visual field are judged more negative than those viewed with the right field

(Dimond & Farrington, 1977), and questions concerned with negative, rather than positive, affect produce greater leftward eye movements (Schwartz, Davidson, & Maer, 1975) and right hemisphere EEG desynchronization (Davidson & Schwartz, 1976). Facial motor asymmetries ("facedness") are more likely to be biased to the left side for negative facial expressions, such as anger, sorrow, or disgust, than for positive ones (Sackeim, Gur, & Saucy, 1978). Similarly, tachistoscopic identification produces a larger left visual field advantage in identifying emotionally negative than positive facial expressions (Ley & Bryden, 1979; Reuter-Lorenz & Davidson, 1981).

Unfortunately, many of these findings are contradicted by other evidence. A number of studies in the production and perception of facial expressions report no significant differences between positive and negative expressions. Both produce a left sided–right hemisphere advantage in normal right-handers (Ladavas, Umilta, & Ricci-Bitti, 1980; Strauss & Moscovitch, 1981; Suberi & McKeever, 1977; Buchtel, Campari, DeRisio, & Rota, 1978; Borod & Caron, 1980; Campbell, 1978, 1979, in press; Landis, Assal, & Perret, 1979). Identification of positive and negative tones of voice produce comparable left ear advantages on dichotic listening studies (Safer & Leventhal, 1977). Lastly, Heilman, Scholes, and Watson (1975) have found that damage to the right parietal region impairs the identification and production of both positive and negative emotions, even if they are conveyed verbally. Together, these clinical and laboratory studies support the second hypothesis that the right hemisphere is superior to the left in mediating all emotional functions.[2]

It is difficult to know how to resolve all these discrepancies. Because we have found evidence in favor of both hypotheses even in our own laboratory, examination of our studies might shed some light on the controversy. We have looked primarily at asymmetries in the production and perception of facial expression. Studies on facial motor asymmetries, except for our own and Ekman, Hager, and Friesen's (1981), have looked only at posed emotional expressions. Differences between the left and right half of the face were found either by observing a videotape of the expression or by comparing photographic composites of it. The composites were formed by cutting a full-face photograph in half and putting together two left halves or two right halves. Of studies using this technique, only those by Sackeim *et*

---

[2]A third alternative is that the mode in which the emotion is expressed determines the hemisphere to which it is lateralized. The verbal mode leads to left hemisphere lateralization and the nonverbal mode to right (Kolb & Taylor, 1981).

al. (1978) suggest that negative expressions are mediated solely by the right hemisphere. Sackeim *et al.* found no consistent asymmetries for positive facial expressions. The photographs they used were of posed facial expressions that were made available by Ekman. According to Ekman (1980), the reason positive expressions were not more intense on the left side is that these were the only expressions that were emitted spontaneously. Ekman argues that voluntary control over the facial musculature, such as occurs in posed expressions, is lateralized to the right hemisphere, but that control over spontaneous, emotional facial expressions is bilateral. In a study in which spontaneous emotional expressions were photographed and carefully analyzed according to the Facial Affect Coding System (FACS), Ekman *et al.* (1981) found no evidence for consistent asymmetries whereas they did find a consistent left-sided bias for posed expressions.

Their failure to find consistent asymmetries for spontaneous, emotional facial expressions is contrary to our own findings (Moscovitch & Olds, 1982). We videotaped individuals as they related emotional experiences to an interviewer (Figure 4.7). Although our video images could not be submitted to the fine, detailed analysis of FACS, they were sufficiently good to pick up the grosser facial movements that constitute an expression. Whereas most expressions appeared to be symmetrical, of those that were asymmetrical, the majority occurred on the bottom of the left side of the face in both male and female right-handers. Moreover, the occurrence of a facial expression reduced the right hand's tendency to gesture more frequently than the left during speech. Neither of these effects were found consistently in left-handers (Figures 4.8 and 4.9). Subsequent developmental studies showed that these facial asymmetries, as well as their effect on hand gestures, emerge by the age of 6–7 (Strauss, Moscovitch, & Olds, 1981).

Admittedly, the facial expressions that we monitored may not have been truly emotional. Rather they may have acted as the facial equivalents of hand signals or gestures. As such they may be more voluntary than truly emotional expressions. Nonetheless, they were spontaneous and it is clear from our studies that such facial expressions are lateralized to the left. Whether truly emotional expressions are similarly lateralized is still in doubt. In analyzing emotional expressions, Ekman *et al.* (1981) looked only at the apex of the expression. It remains to be seen whether similar results would be obtained were the expression analyzed through its development and decline. Schiff and MacDonald (in preparation) have shown that solving a difficult cognitive task affects the musculature on the left side of the face more than that on the right even when the subject is not aware of being

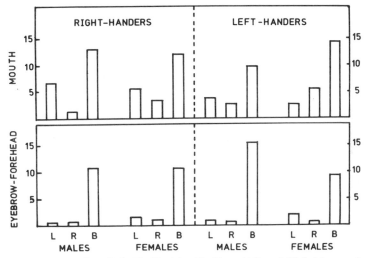

Figure 4.8. Mean number of left side (L), right side (R), and bilateral (B) facial expressions (in the mouth and forehead region) for right-handed and left-handed males and females.

observed. This suggests that it is not only voluntary control of the facial musculature that is mediated by the right hemisphere.

In summary, some of the discrepancies regarding asymmetries of facial expression result from using posed versus unposed expressions, and from using videotapes versus photographic composites. When these factors are taken into account, as well as other factors such as scanning biases in viewing videotapes and photographs (Campbell, in press; Heller & Levy, 1981), many of the discrepancies become resolved. It remains to be seen, however, whether the production of truly emotional facial expressions is lateralized.

On the perception end, similar careful analyses of procedures and stimulus materials may be informative. In a series of experiments (Strauss & Moscovitch, 1981), a pair of Ekman faces appeared simultaneously in either the right or left field. Subjects judged whether the expressions on the two faces were the same or different. A consistent left visual field–right hemisphere advantage was found only when the same emotion was expressed by different people. Similar left field advantages were obtained when the sub-

---

Figure 4.7. (*Opposite page*) Photographs of well-known personalities and the author showing asymmetrical facial expressions. Notice that the expression is more pronounced on the left side of the face in about 80% of the right-handed individuals. (p) and (w) are left handed. (From Moscovitch & Olds, 1982.)

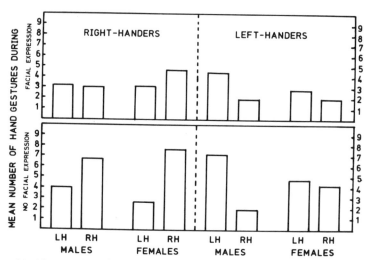

Figure 4.9. Mean number of right hand (RH) and left hand (LH) gestures that occur in the presence or absence of a facial expression in right-handed and left-handed males and females.

ject judged whether the expression was the same or different from a target expression that he held in memory. In these experiments there was no indication that the identification of positive and negative expression was lateralized to different hemispheres. These results are consistent with reports by Safer (1981) and Suberi and McKeever (1977), but not with those of Ley and Bryden (1979) and Reuter-Lorenz and Davidson (1981). Ley and Bryden found a slightly greater left field advantage for negative expressions. Because they used caricatures rather than real faces and because the positive and negative expressions varied in intensity, their results, though interesting, are not conclusive. Reuter-Lorenz and Davidson, however, also used Ekman faces, yet their results were different from ours. They found that happy faces were detected more quickly in the right visual field and sad ones in the left. Their results and procedures, however, did differ from ours in important respects. Rather than have subjects identify the emotional expression or compare two expressions, they presented a neutral face to one field and an emotional face to the other and had subjects simply detect which field contained the emotionally expressive face by responding with the corresponding hand. Moreover, only happy and sad expressions were used and these were not always of equal intensity. Lastly, the error rate was over 30% and did not always conform to the pattern produced by the latency data, making the latter difficult to interpret.

In a replication of this study, Reuter-Lorenz, Givis, and I (Reuter-Lorenz, Givis, & Moscovitch, in press) used the same detection procedure as had Reuter-Lorenz and Davidson, but modified their stimulus presentation somewhat. We used two happy expressions—an intense one with an open-mouthed, toothy smile, and a less intense one in which the mouth was closed. The open-mouthed smile was judged by independent raters to be as intense emotionally as the sad expression. We used right-handers as well as two groups of left-handers, those who wrote with an inverted hand posture and those who did not. The left-handers were included to test Levy and Reid's (1978) hypothesis that inverted left-handers have the same hemispheric organization as right-handers whereas noninverted left-handers have the opposite organization. The results of our study, which are shown in Figure 4.10, confirmed Reuter-Lorenz and Davidson's finding that happy and sad facial expressions are perceived best by the left and right hemisphere, respectively. Significantly, stimulus intensity did not seem to offset the pattern of perceptual asymmetries. The open mouth happy expression produced faster responses than the closed mouth smile, but not a greater right field advantage. Although error rate was still high at the exposure duration of 250 msec that we used, the error pattern was the same as the latency one. The results were also consistent with Levy and Reid's hypothesis. Inverted left-handers had the same pattern of perceptual asymmetries as right-handers whereas noninverted left-handers had the opposite patterns.

Thus, even when speed–accuracy.trade-offs are not a factor, happy faces, whatever their intensity, are detected more quickly in one visual field and sad faces in the other. These findings are not easily reconciled with other studies that employ similar stimuli yet report no interaction of visual field and emotion. As we noted earlier, the critical difference may be that in both her studies Reuter-Lorenz and her colleagues asked subjects merely to detect an emotional expression or differentiate it from a neutral one, whereas the other investigators always asked their subjects to identify the emotional expression or compare it to another one. Yet it is difficult to see how this fact by itself can explain the differences among the studies. One might argue that cognitive awareness of all emotional expressions is mediated by the right hemisphere, whereas simple detection can proceed more quickly on the left if the face is a happy one, on the right, if it is a sad one. The question, however, remains—what is it about happy faces that makes them easily detected by the left hemisphere? One possibility that Reuter-Lorenz, Elizabeth Ladavas, and I are testing is that the stimulus configuration of a

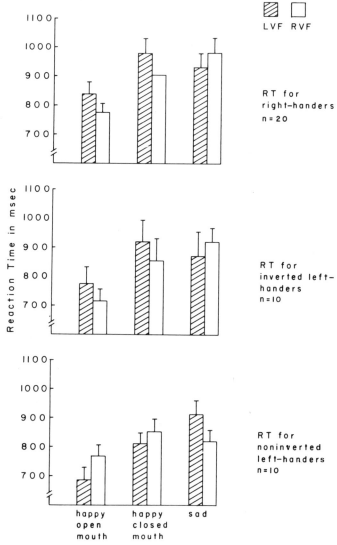

Figure 4.10. Left and right visual field reaction times to open mouthed happy, closed mouthed happy, and sad facial expressions by right-handers, and inverted and noninverted left-handers.

happy face is different from that of a sad face and, indeed, from that of all other expressions. Information about happy expressions is conveyed primarily, if not exclusively, by the lower part of the face, whereas both the lower and upper part of the face carry information about sad expressions. To detect whether a happy face is emotional, one need only concentrate on the lower part of the face, particularly around the mouth. It is for this focal, analytic work that the left hemisphere is presumed to be specialized (Levy, 1974; Bradshaw & Nettleton, 1981). In any event, this task is well within the higher order perceptual capabilities of the left hemisphere. Detecting sad expressions, on the other hand, or any other expression for that matter, may require that information from various parts of the face be related to each other, a process that seems best suited to the specialized functions of the right hemisphere. This line of reasoning suggests that there is nothing special about the processes involved in perceiving emotional facial expressions. Although a number of investigators have tried to show that processing emotional expression requires different mechanisms from those used to process other nonverbal stimuli, the evidence they adduce is not that strong (Ley & Bryden, 1979; Suberi & McKeever, 1977; Strauss & Moscovitch, 1981).

It should be remembered that we have yet to prove whether any of these hypotheses is correct. It may well be that our experiments will not refute the idea that one hemisphere is specialized to process positive emotions and the other, negative ones; or it may be that emotional expressions are indeed processed differently from faces and other complex, nonverbal stimuli. Our approach, however, is to examine carefully the stimulus properties of the materials we use and the cognitive operations they might induce before we reach this much broader conclusion about the general properties of the two hemispheres (Moscovitch, in press b). Similar careful analyses of stimuli and responses would be fruitful in studies using other techniques, such as electrophysiological ones, to assess hemispheric asymmetries for emotion. Without such analyses the discrepancies in the literature are not likely to be resolved (Sergent, 1982a, 1982b; Sergent & Bindra, 1981).

If it is indeed shown that the cerebral hemispheres are specialized in processing emotions, how might that specialization have arisen? Because there is little experimental evidence that bears on this question, I shall indulge in speculation. My own bias is that all emotions are mediated by the right hemisphere. Stimuli producing strong emotional reactions are likely to be those that demand an immediate response. It makes sense to have the mechanisms that mediate emotions in close association with mechanisms that are best at processing complex, holistic information quickly. Whether the right hemisphere was first specialized for processing significant, emotional stimuli and its other processing skills were an outgrowth of that specialization or vice versa is a question that may well intrigue psychologists in the future.

REFERENCES

Bates, E. *Language and context*. New York: Academic Press, 1976.

Benton, A. L. The neuropsychology of facial recognition. *American Psychologist*, 1980, *35*, 176–186.

Berlin, C. I., & McNeil, M. R. Dichotic listening. In N. J. Lass (Ed.), *Contemporary issues in experimental phonetics*. New York: Academic Press, 1976.

Berlucchi, G. Cerebral dominance and interhemispheric communication in normal man. In F. O. Schmitt & F. G. Worden (Eds.), *The neurosciences: Third study program*. Cambridge, Mass.: MIT Press, 1974.

Blumstein, S., & Cooper, W. E. Hemispheric processing of intonation contours. *Cortex*, 1974, *10*, 146–158.

Borod, J. C., & Caron, H. S. Facedness and emotion related to lateral dominance, sex, and expression type. *Neuropsychologia*, 1980, *18*, 237–241.

Bradshaw, J. L., & Nettleton, N. C. The nature of hemispheric specialization in man. *The Behavioral and Brain Sciences*, 1981, *4*, 51–91.

Buchtel, H. A., Campari, F., DeRisio, C., & Rota, R. Hemispheric differences in discriminative reaction time to facial expression. *Italian Journal of Psychology*, 1978, *5*, 159–169.

Campbell, R. Asymmetries in interpreting and expressing a posed facial expression. *Cortex*, 1978, *14*, 327–343.

Campbell, R. Left handers' smiles. *Cortex*, 1979, *15*, 571–380.

Campbell, R. The lateralization of emotion: A critical review. *International Journal of Psychology*, in press.

Caramazza, A., & Berndt, R. S. Semantic and syntactic processes in aphasia: A review of the literature. *Psychological Bulletin*, 1978, *85*, 898–918.

Caramazza, A., Gordon, J., Zurif, E. B., & DeLuca, D. Right-hemispheric damage and verbal problem solving behavior. *Brain and Language*, 1976, *3*, 41–46.

Cavalli, M., DeRenzi, E., Faglioni, P., & Vitale, A. Impairment of right brain-damaged patients on a linguistic cognitive task. *Cortex*, 1981, *17*, 545–556.

Coltheart, M. Deep dyslexia: A right hemisphere hypothesis. In M. Coltheart, K. Patterson, & J. C. Marshall (Eds.), *Deep dyslexia*. London: Routledge & Kegan Paul, 1980.

Critchley, M. Speech and speech loss in relation to duality of the brain. In V. B. Mountcastle (Ed.), *Interhemispheric relations and cerebral dominance*. Baltimore, Md.: Johns Hopkins University Press, 1962.

Czopf, J. Über die Rolle der nicht dominant Hemisphäre in der Restitution der Sprache der Aphäsischen. *Archiv für Psychiatrie und Nerven krankheiten*, 1972, *216*, 162–171.

Davidson, R., & Schwartz, G. Patterns of cerebral lateralization during cardiac biofeedback versus the self-regulation of emotion: Sex differences. *Psychophysiology*, 1976, *13*, 62–74.

Day, J. Right-hemispheric language processing in normal right-handers. *Journal of Experimental Psychology: Human Perception and Performance,* 1977, *3,* 518–528.

Day, J. Visual half-field word recognition as a function of syntactic class and imageability. *Neuropsychologia,* 1979, *17,* 515–519.

Dennis, M. Capacity and strategy for syntactic comprehension after left or right hemidecortication. *Brain and Language,* 1980, *10,* 287–317.

Dimond, S. J., & Farrington, L. Emotional responses to films shown to the right or left hemisphere of the brain measured by heartrate. *Acta Psychologica,* 1977, *41,* 255–260.

Ekman, P. Asymmetry in facial expression. *Science,* 1980, *209,* 833–834.

Ekman, P., Friesen, W. V., & Ellsworth, P. *Emotion in the human face: Guidelines for research and an integration of findings.* New York: Pergammon Press, 1972.

Ekman, P., Hager, J. C., & Friesen, W. V. The symmetry of emotional and facial actions. *Psychophysiology,* 1981, *18,* 101–106.

Friedman, A., & Polson, M. C. The hemispheres as independent resource-systems: Limited-capacity processing and cerebral specialization. *Journal of Experimental Psychology: Human Perception and Performance,* 1982, *8,* 146–157.

Frost, N. Encoding and retrieval in visual memory tasks. *Journal of Experimental Psychology,* 1972, *95,* 317–326.

Gainotti, G. Emotional behavior and hemispheric side of lesion. *Cortex,* 1972, *8,* 41–55.

Gainotti, G., Caltagirone, C., Miceli, G., & Masullo, C. Selective semantic-lexical impairment of language comprehension in right-brain-damaged patients. *Brain and Language,* 1981, *13,* 201–211.

Gardner, H., & Denes, G. Connotative judgements by aphasic patients on a pictorial adoptation of the semantic differential. *Cortex,* 1973, *9,*183–196.

Gardner, H., Ling, P. K., Flamm, L., & Silverman, J. Comprehension and appreciation of humorous material following brain damage. *Brain,* 1975. *98,* 399–412.

Gardner, H., Silverman, J., Wapner, W., & Zurif, E. The appreciation of antonymic contrast in aphasia. *Brain and Language,* 1978, *6,* 301–317.

Gazzaniga, M. S. *The bisected brain.* New York: Appleton-Century-Crofts, 1970.

Gazzaniga, M. S., & LeDoux, J. *The integrated mind.* New York: Plenum Press, 1978.

Geffen, G. The development of the right ear advantage in dichotic listening with focused attention. *Cortex,* 1978, *14,* 11–17.

Goldstein, K. *The organism.* New York: American Book, 1948.

Goodglass, H. Studies in the grammar of aphasics. In S. Rosenburg & J. Koplin (Eds.), *Developments in applied psycholinguistic research.* New York: Macmillan, 1968.

Gowers, W. R. *Lectures on the diagnosis of diseases of the brain.* London: Churchill, 1887.

Haggard, M. P., & Parkinson, A. M. Stimulus to sk factors as determinants of ear advantages. *Journal of Experimental Psychology,* 1971, *23,* 168–177.

Hécaen, H., & Albert, M. L. *Human neuropsychology.* New York: Wiley-Interscience, 1978.

Heeschen, C. Strategy of decoding actor–object relations by aphasic patients. *Cortex,* 1980, *16,* 5–19.

Heilman, K. M., Scholes, R., & Watson, R. Auditory affective agnosia. *Journal of Neurology, Neurosurgery, and Psychiatry,* 1975, *38,* 69–72.

Heller, W., & Levy, J. Perception and expression of emotion in right-handers and left-handers. *Neuropsychologia,* 1981, *19,* 263–272.

Hellige, J. B., & Cox, P. J. Effects of concurrent verbal memory on recognition of stimuli from the left and right visual fields. *Journal of Experimental Psychology: Human Perception and Performance,* 1976, *2,* 210–221.

Hellige, J. B., Cox, P. J., & Litvak, L. Information processing in the cerebral hemispheres: Selective hemispheric activation and capactiy. *Journal of Experimental Psychology: General,* 1979, *108,* 251–279.

Jaccarino, G. *Dual encoding in memory: Evidence from temporal-lobe lesions in man.* M. A. thesis, McGill University, 1975.

Jones, M. K. Imagery as a mnemonic aid after left temporal lobectomy; contrast between specific and generalized memory disorders. *Neuropsychologia,* 1976,*12,* 21–30.

Jones-Gotman, M. Incidental learning of image mediated or pronounced words after right temporal lobectomy. *Cortex,* 1979, *15,* 187–198.

Jones-Gotman, M., & Milner, B. Right temporal-lobe contribution to language-mediated verbal learning. *Neuropsychologia,* 1978, *16,* 61–71.

Kimura, D., & Durnford, M. Normal studies on the function of the right hemisphere in vision. In S. J. Dimond & J. G. Beaumont (Eds.), *Hemisphere function in the human brain.* London: Elek Scientific Books, 1974.

Kinsbourne, M. The minor cerebral hemisphere as a source of aphasic speech. *Archives of Neurology,* 1971, *25,* 302–306.

Kolb, B., & Milner, B. Observations on spontaneous facial expression after intracarotid injection of sodium amytal. *Neuropsychologia,* 1981,*19,* 505–514.

Kolb, B., & Taylor, L. Affective behavior in patients with localized cortical excisions: Role of lesion site and side. *Science,* 1981, *214,* 89–91.

Ladavas, E., Umilta, C., & Ricci-Bitti, P. Evidence for sex difference in right hemisphere dominance for emotions. *Neuropsychologia,* 1980, *18,* 361–366.

Landis, T., Assal, G., & Perret, E. Opposite cerebral hemispheric asymmetries for visual associative processing of emotional tonal expressions and objects. *Nature,*1979, *278,* 709–740.

Lesser, R. Verbal comprehension in aphasia: An English version of three Italian tests. *Cortex,* 1974, *10,* 247–263.

Levy, J. Psychobiological implications of bilateral asymmetry. In S. J. Dimond and G. Beaumont (Eds.), *Hemisphere function in the human brain.* London: Elek Books, 1974.

Levy, J., & Reid, M. L. Variations of cerebral organization as a function of handedness, hand posture in writing, and sex. *Journal of Experimental Psychology: General,* 1978, *107,*119–144.

Levy, J., & Trevarthen, C. Perceptual, semantic, and phonetic aspects of elementary language processes in split brain patients. *Brain,* 1977, *100,*105–118.

Ley, R. G., & Bryden, M. P. Hemispheric differences in recognizing faces and emotion. *Brain and Language,* 1979, *7,* 120–138.

Madden, D. J., & Nebes, R. D. Visual perception and memory. In M. C. Wittrock (Ed.), *The brain and psychology.* New York: Academic Press, 1980.

Madden, D. J., Nebes, R. D., & Berg, W. D. Signal detection analysis of hemispheric differences in visual recognition memory. *Cortex,* 1981, *17,* 491–502.

Marshall, J. C., & Newcombe, F. Patterns of paralexia: A psycholinguistic approach. *Journal of Psycholinguistics,* 1973, *2,* 175–199.

McKeever, W. F., & Suberi, M. Parallel but temporally displaced visual half field metacontrast functions. *Quarterly Journal of Experimental Psychology,* 1974, *26,* 258–265.

Meadows, J. C. The anatomical basis of prosopagnosia. *Journal of Neurology, Neurosurgery, and Psychiatry,* 1974, *37,* 489–501.

Milner, B. Discussion on cerebral dominance in man. In C. H. Millikan & F. L. Darley (Eds.), *Brain mechanisms underlying speech and language.* New York: Grune and Stratton, 1967.

Milner, B. Clues to cerebral organization. In P. A. Buser & T. Rougel-Buser (Eds.), *Cerebral correlates of conscious experience* (INSERM symposium No. 6). Amsterdam: Elsevier/North-Holland Biomedical Press, 1978.

Moscovitch, M. Language and the cerebral hemispheres: Reaction-time studies and their implications for models of cerebral dominance. In P. Pliner, T. Alloway, & L. Krames (Eds.), *Communication and affect: Language and thought.* New York: Academic Press, 1973.

Moscovitch, M. On the representation of language in the right hemisphere of right-handed people. *Brain and Language,* 1976, *3,* 47–71.

Moscovitch, M. Information processing and the cerebral hemispheres. In M. S. Gazzaniga (Ed.), *Handbook of behavioral neurobiology* (Vol. 2). New York: Plenum Press, 1979.

Moscovitch, M. Right hemisphere language. *Topics in Language Disorders,* 1981, *1,* 41–61.

Moscovitch, M. Stages of processing and hemispheric differences in language in the normal subject. In M. G. Studdert-Kennedy (Ed.), *Neurobiology of language processes.* Cambridge, Mass.: M.I.T. Press, in press. (a)

Moscovitch, M. Global and local analysis of perceptual asymmetries. *The Behavioral and Brain Sciences,* in press. (b)

Moscovitch, M., & Olds, J. Asymmetries in spontaneous facial expressions and their possible relation to hemispheric specialization. *Neuropsychologia,* 1982, *20,* 71–81.

Moscovitch, M., Scullion, D., & Christie, D. Early vs. late stages of processing and their relation to functional hemispheric asymmetries in face recognition. *Journal of Experimental Psychology: Human Perception and Performance,* 1976, *2,* 401–416.

Neilson, J. M. *Agnosia, apraxia, aphasia: Their value in cerebral localization.* New York: Hoeber, 1946.

Patten, B. W. The ancient art of memory. *Archives of Neurology,* 1972, *26,* 25–31.

Proudfoot, R. E. Hemispheric asymmetry for face recognition: Some effects of visual masking, hemiretinal stimulation and learning task. *Neuropsychologia,* 1982, *20,* 129–144.

Reuter-Lorenz, P., & Davidson, R. J. Differential contributions of the two cerebral hemispheres to the perception of happy and sad faces. *Neuropsychologia,* 1981, *19,* 609–613.

Reuter-Lorenz, P. Givis, R., & Moscovitch, M. Hemispheric specialization and the perception of emotion: Evidence from right-handers are from inverted and noninverted left-handers. *Neuropsychologia,* in press.

Roenker, A. L., Thompson, C. P., & Brown, S. C. Comparisons of measures for the estimation of clustering in free recall. *Psychological Bulletin,* 1971, *76,* 45–48.

Ross, E. D., & Mesulam, M. M. Dominant language functions of the right hemisphere: Prosody and emotional gesturing. *Archives of Neurology,* 1979, *36,* 144–148.

Rossi, G. F., & Rosadini, G. Experimental analysis of cerebral dominance in man. In C. H. Millikan & F. L. Darley (Eds.), *Brain mechanisms underlying speech and language.* New York: Grune and Stratton, 1967.

Russel, W. R., & Espir, M. L. R. *Traumatic aphasia: Its syndromes, psychopathology, and treatment.* London: Oxford University Press, 1961.

Sackeim, H., Gur, R., & Saucy, M. Emotions are expressed more intensely on the left side of the face. *Science,* 1978, *202,* 434–436.

Safer, M., & Leventhal, H. Ear differences in evaluating emotional tones of voice and verbal content. *Journal of Experimental Psychology: Human Perception and Performance,* 1977, *3,* 75–82.

Schlotterer, G. *Changes in visual information processing with normal aging and progressive dementia of the Alzheimer type.* Unpublished Ph.D. thesis, University of Toronto, 1977.

Schiff, B., & MacDonald, H. Unpublished Honours Thesis, University of Toronto, 1981.

Schwartz, M.F., Davidson, R. J., & Maer, F. Right hemisphere lateralization for emotion in the human brain: Interaction with cognition. *Science,* 1975, *197,* 286–288.

Schwartz, M. F., Saffran, E. M., & Marin, O. S. M. The word order problem in agrammatism, I: Comprehension. *Brain and Language,* 1980, *10,* 249–262.

Searlman, A. A review of right hemisphere linguistic abilities. *Psychological Bulletin,* 1977, *84,* 503–528.

Sergent, J. The cerebral balance of power: Confrontation or cooperation? *Journal of Experimental Psychology: Human Perception and Performance,* 1982, *8,* 253–272.

Sergent, J., & Bindra, D. Differential hemispheric processing of faces: Methodological considerations and reinterpretation. *Psychological Bulletins,* 1981, *84,* 531–554.

Strauss, E., Moscovitch, M., & Olds, J. *Children's production of facial expressions.* Paper presented at the International Neuropsychological Society Meeting, Italy, June 1981.

Suberi, M., & McKeever, W. Differential right hemispheric memory storage of emotional and non-emotional faces. *Neuropsychologia,* 1977, *15,* 757–769.

Tomlinson, B. E., Blessed, G., & Roth, M. Observation on the brains of demented old people. *Journal of Neurological Sciences,* 1970, *4,* 205–242.

Tucker, D. M. Lateral brain function, emotion, and conceptualization. *Psychological Bulletin,* 1981, *89,* 19–46.

Turvey, M. On peripheral and central processes in vision: Inferences from an information-processing analysis of masking with patterned stimuli. *Psychological Review,* 1973, *80,* 1–52.

Wapner, W., Hamby, S., & Gardner, H. The role of the right hemisphere in the apprehension of complex linguistic materials. *Brain and Language,* 1981, *14,* 15–33.

Wilkins, A., & Moscovitch, M. Selective impairment of semantic memory after temporal lobectomy. *Neuropsychologia,* 1978, *16,* 73–79.

Winner, E., & Gardner, H. The comprehension of metaphor in brain-damaged patients. *Brain,* 1977, *100,* 717–729.

Zaidel, E. Lexical organization in the right hemisphere. In P. A. Buser & A. Rougel-Buser (Eds.), *Cerebral correlates of conscious experience.* Amsterdam: Elsevier/North-Holland, 1978. (a)

Zaidel, E. Concepts of cerebral dominance in the split-brain. In P. A. Buser & A. Rougel-Buser (Eds.), *Cerebral correlates of conscious experience.* Amsterdam: Elsevier/North-Holland, 1978. (b)

Zangwill, O. L. Speech. In J. Field, H. W. Magocen, & K. E. Hill, (Eds.), *Handbook of physiology* (Vol. 3). Washington, D.C.: American Psychological Society, 1960.

Zurif, E. B. Auditory lateralization: Prosodic and syntactic features. *Brain and Language,* 1974, *1,* 391–404.

Zurif, E. B., & Caramazza, A. Psycholinguistic structures in aphasia. In H. Whitaker & H. A. Whitaker (Eds.), *Studies in neurolinguistics* (Vol. 1). New York: Academic Press, 1976.

Zurif, E., Caramazza, A., & Myerson, R. Grammatical judgements of agrammatic aphasics. *Neuropsychologia,* 1972, *10,* 405–417.

5

Right Hemispheric Specialization for the Expression and Appreciation of Emotion: A Focus on the Face[1]

JOAN C. BOROD
ELISSA KOFF
HERBERT S. CARON

A decade of research has implicated the right cerebral hemisphere as dominant for both the expression of emotion and the appreciation of emotional situations. Although these aspects of emotional processing may be quite separate, their interrelatedness is obvious, for in order to express emotion a person must be able to perceive and process stimuli. It may be that the right hemisphere is specialized for emotion in the same way that the left hemisphere is specialized for language, with expression or production related to more anterior brain structures, and with appreciation or comprehension related to more posterior structures. Although there is currently no strong evidence for this functional-neuroanatomic analogy, the expression–appreciation distinction is a useful model and will serve as the basis of the

[1]This work was supported by USPHS Grants NS06209 and NS07615 to the Aphasia Research Center and by Bio-Medical Research Support Grant 1–S07RR07186–02 to Wellesley College. Portions of this chapter were presented at the annual meetings of the International Neuropsychology Society in New York, 1979, and in San Francisco, 1980, and at the Society for Research in Child Development Symposium, "The Development of Affect and Its Relation to Cerebral Asymmetry," in Tarrytown, New York, October 1980.

following literature review on hemispheric specialization for emotion. The review will present findings from experimental studies with normal and neurologically impaired populations, and from clinical observation of neurological and psychiatric populations. These studies will be presented with respect to three sources of emotional information: facial, intonational, and situational–behavioral. Primary focus will be on studies involving the face, as the face appears to be so central in the communication of emotion. Following the literature review, we will summarize our studies of emotional expression using facial asymmetry as a behavioral index.

Our research began with the observation that the two sides of the face demonstrated striking asymmetries for extent of movement, intensity of expression, and quality of emotion. We wondered whether these asymmetries were systematic and, if so, what their relationship to other lateralized functions might be. Further, we were curious about the implications of such asymmetries for the study of neuropsychology and behavioral neurology, particularly in light of the observation that the lower portion of the face is predominantly innervated by the contralateral cerebral hemisphere (Brodal, 1957; Kuypers, 1958). As volitional facial expression and movement presumably involve cortical control, we thought that facial asymmetries might constitute another index of lateral dominance and provide a window onto brain–behavior relationships. Also, since most studies of the expression of emotion used nonnormal populations, if facial asymmetry proved to be a reliable phenomenon, it would provide a method for the study of emotional expression in the normal subject. Accordingly, we examined facial asymmetry during posed emotional expression in normals, taking into account expression type (positive versus negative), sex of subject, and traditional measures of lateral dominance.

GENERAL CONSIDERATIONS

A variety of studies, employing diverse methodologies and stimuli, have supported a right hemisphere advantage for the processing of emotional information. Among the most frequently used measures are ear differences in response to dichotic presentation of affectively toned verbal and nonverbal material, and visual field differences in response to tachistoscopic presentation of faces and facial expressions. Lateral eye movements (LEMs) and a variety of physiological parameters, such as EEG, also have been studied for evidence of differential hemispheric activity. Both normal and unilaterally brain-damaged individuals have served as subjects. Given the typical contralateral innervation of the central nervous system (E. Gardner, 1975), superiority of the left side (e.g., left visual field) implies greater relative activation or involvement of the right hemisphere.

In the visual modality, typical paradigms include perceptual discrimination tasks (requiring same–different judgments) and recognition tasks (requiring subjects to match a face with a previously presented one, or to choose a previously presented face from among distractors). Typical dependent variables are speed and accuracy. In the auditory domain, subjects commonly are asked to discriminate whether two emotionally toned sentences or vocalizations are the same or different, and to identify the affect being expressed in the stimulus. Although some production studies have been reported, the bulk of the literature concentrates upon comprehension of emotional information conveyed via the face or the vocal apparatus.

The literature often is difficult to interpret, as well as contradictory, owing to methodological vicissitudes and a variety of potentially confounding variables, including sex, handedness, and age. Sometimes the values of these variables are unspecified, while at other times only one subject group is studied. Another source of confusion derives from the lack of an adequate operational definition of emotion; this is particularly evident in studies concerned with emotional valence (e.g., positive versus negative), where emotions often seem to arbitrarily be forced into bipolar categories.

Interpretation of results also is problematic because of the lack of consensus about the meaning of some of the typical findings in laterality research. For example, does the absence of a visual field (or ear) advantage imply bilateral activity, or the superimposition of the activity of the nondominant hemisphere? This issue of interpretation confounds the literature on brain-damaged populations as well; here a major functional question is whether the behavior observed after brain damage is being mediated by the damaged area, or is reflecting some sort of disinhibitory process. The anatomic version of this question concerns the locus of control of this behavior; that is, is it the damaged area, a homologous area in the opposite hemisphere, or some subcortical site? Finally, comparisons of patient groups (e.g., right versus left hemisphere damaged) frequently are difficult to interpret because of group differences in etiology, location, size, and duration of lesion.

APPRECIATION STUDIES

Faces

Numerous studies have supported left visual field–right hemisphere superiority for the recognition of static faces, ranging from cartoons and line drawings bearing little resemblance to real faces, to more or less realistic photographs (Geffen, Bradshaw, & Wallace, 1971; Gilbert, 1973; Hilliard, 1973; Ley & Bryden, 1979; Rizzolatti, Umilta, & Berlucchi, 1971). Such data are consistent with results from studies of unilaterally brain-damaged patients (e.g., Hécaen & Angelergues, 1962; DeRenzi, Faglione, & Spinnler, 1968; DeRenzi & Spinnler, 1966) indicating defects in face recognition associated with right but not left brain damage.

Early explanations for these data suggested that the right hemisphere advantage was an extension or derivation of that hemisphere's established specialization for visuospatial material; a contrasting suggestion was that face recognition was a special and unique function of the right hemisphere, independent of the specificity for visuospatial material, and perhaps neuroanatomically distinct. A third possibility was that it was the expression on the face, rather than the face per se, that attracted the attention of the right hemisphere, and that this might derive from the dominance of the right hemisphere for the processing of emotional material in general, of which facial expression is an exemplar.

A number of recent studies concerned with the more cognitive or interpretive aspects of the processing of emotional stimuli have supported this last notion, in both the visual and auditory modalities. Further, several studies have suggested that processing of emotional information may be differentially lateralized, with right hemisphere specialization for negative emotions and left hemisphere specialization for positive emotions.

Although in general the literature supports a right hemisphere advantage for the recognition of faces, there is some suggestion that the left hemisphere could be involved as well. Which hemisphere is activated appears to depend upon the functional demands of the task (see Sergent & Bindra, 1981, for review). In general, left visual field advantages are obtained when a task requires holistic judgments, but right visual field superiority is sometimes seen when more analytic judgments are demanded (e.g., Berent, 1977). However, when a task requires recognition of emotional expressions, a left visual field advantage has been demonstrated with photographs of faces (Buchtel, Campari, DeRisio, & Rota, 1978; Suberi & McKeever, 1977), as well as with cartoon faces (Ley & Bryden, 1979). The Ley and Bryden (1979) and Suberi and McKeever (1977) studies attempted to dissociate recognition of faces per se from recognition of emotion; in both cases, a right hemisphere superiority for recognition of emotional faces appeared to be independent of a right hemisphere superiority for face recognition. Further, McKeever and Dixon (1981) have reported that the right hemisphere superiority for processing emotional expression is unrelated to visuospatial perception.

The preceding research has been extended to brain-damaged patients by Dekosky, Heilman, Bowers, and Valenstein (1980), who demonstrated that, relative to patients with left hemisphere impairment, patients with right hemisphere impairment had deficits in naming facial emotions and in discriminating neutral as well as emotional expressions in photographs of the face. They also had problems naming emotions represented in line drawings of scenes with emotional content. When inability to recognize faces (prosopagnosia) was controlled, however, all differences between right- and left-damaged groups disappeared, although both remained significantly impaired relative to controls. In contradistinction, Cicone, Wapner, and Gardner (1980) did not find a relationship between performance on an emotional perception task and a facial recognition task, suggesting that deficits associated with right hemisphere damage cannot be accounted for by prosopagnosia alone.

Intonation

It is generally accepted that the right hemisphere of normal right-handed subjects is dominant for processing intonation contours of short sentences (Blumstein & Cooper, 1974) and melody (Borod & Goodglass, 1980; Kimura, 1964). In addition, studies show a right hemisphere effect for nonverbal emotional vocalizations (e.g., crying, laughing) as well as for emotional tone of speech (e.g., anger, happiness). Using the dichotic listening procedure, a left ear advantage has been reported for emotional tone of natural speech (Haggard & Parkinson, 1971), and for nonverbal emotional vocalizations (Carmon & Nachson, 1973; King & Kimura, 1972). Similar results favoring the left ear have been found with monaural presentation of emotionally toned human speech (Safer & Leventhal, 1977). In addition, in the domain of music, a left ear superiority has been reported for the identification of the emotional tone of short musical passages presented dichotically (Bryden, Ley, & Sugarman, 1982).

With respect to brain-damaged patients, Heilman, Scholes, and Watson (1975) showed that patients with right temporoparietal lesions were significantly less able to judge the emotional tone of spoken sentences than were patients with similar lesions on the left side. Neither group was impaired in judging the content of the same sentences. A later study by Tucker, Watson, and Heilman (1977) confirmed this finding; patients with right parietal damage were shown to have difficulties compared to left-damaged patients in comprehending and discriminating emotional tone of speech. In contrast, Schlanger, Schlanger, and Gerstman (1976) found no differences in comprehension of emotionally toned sentences as a function of hemisphere. These discrepant results may be a function of lesion site, since the lesions in the Schlanger *et al.* study were distributed much more widely than in the Heilman *et al.* study.

Wechsler (1973) extended the investigation of laterality for emotion to memory for emotionally toned material, by looking at recall for affectively charged versus neutral material. Greater impairment of recall for emotionally charged material was observed in right-brain-damaged patients compared to left, whereas no difference between the groups was seen in recall of neutral material.

Emotional Situations

Another group of studies employs cognitive strategies to create emotional situations. In studies of normal subjects, typical measures of relative hemispheric involvement include lateral eye movements (LEM) and physiological indices such as EEG, electromyography (EMG), and heart rate response.

Lateral eye movements, in response to questions requiring reflective thinking, have been hypothesized to indicate activation of the hemisphere contralateral to the direction of eye movement (see Erlichman & Weinberger, 1978, for review and caveats about interpretation of data). Schwartz, Davidson, and Maer (1975) observed LEM in response to emotional and nonemotional questions, and found that normal right-handed subjects tended to shift their gaze to the left (suggesting greater right hemisphere activation) when responding to emotional questions.

Tucker, Roth, Arneson, and Buckingham (1977) examined the relationship of stress, itself presumed to be a type of emotional situation, to LEM. Stress was induced by telling subjects that their answers to emotional and nonemotional questions would reflect intellectual and personality characteristics. They found significantly more left eye movement to emotional than nonemotional questions and a right hemisphere effect for stress which appeared to be independent of question content. Increases in left eye movement were significant only for stress in males, and only for emotional questions in females, suggesting that the sexes may respond differently to emotional situations. Similarly, an interview situation that included embarrassing questions elicited left LEM with high frequency (Libby & Yaklevich, 1973). Hiscock (1977), on the other hand, found no consistency in eye movements among subjects in whom anxiety had been induced. As all his subjects were male, these data contrast markedly with those of Tucker *et al.* (1977).

Asymmetries in bilateral EEG in response to emotional situations also appear to support a right hemisphere effect. Asking subjects to recreate feelings associated with affective and nonaffective experiences in their pasts, Davidson, Schwartz, Pugash, and Bromfield (1976) found relatively greater right hemisphere activation when affective states were generated, as measured by EEG from the parietal areas; however, this effect was significant only for the females. Films containing emotional materials also appear to elicit relatively greater right parietal activation (Davidson, Schwartz, Saron, Bennett, & Goleman, 1978), particularly when negative affect is being processed.

The notion that the right hemisphere may be more engaged by negative emotions, and the left hemisphere by positive emotions, has been supported in several recent studies. Observing LEM in response to questions involving the positive emotions of happiness and excitement, and the negative emotions of fear and sadness, Ahern and Schwartz (1979) found that the excitement elicited more right and fewer left looks than fear for both verbal and spatial types of questions. Corroboration comes from facial electromyography (EMG) data (Scwartz, Ahern, & Brown, 1979), recorded bilaterally from two sets of muscles (zygomatic and corrugator) in response to the same questions. Positive emotion questions elicited relatively greater activity in the right zygomatic muscle (implying left hemisphere activation) than in the left, whereas negative emotion questions elicited relatively greater activity in the left zygomatic muscle, during responses to the reflective questions. In another paradigm, films depicting emotional situations were selectively projected to the left or right hemisphere through a specially designed contact lens system (Dimond & Farringtion, 1977; Dimond, Farrington, & Johnson, 1976). A greater heart rate response was generated when a cartoon was projected to the left than to the right hemisphere, whereas the opposite effect was noted during a film of a surgical operation. In contrast, using EEG power measures, Harman and Ray (1977) found no significant difference between responses to positive and negative emotions in the right hemisphere, and a sharp increase in left hemisphere activity during recall of negative experiences and a sharp decrease during recall of positive experiences.

Studies of comprehension of emotional situations by brain-damaged patients are few in number. Two that have reported indicate that patients with right hemisphere lesions are unable to appreciate the humor depicted in cartoons (Gardner, Ling, Flamm, & Silverman, 1975), or in familiar emotional situations represented in simple line drawings (Cicone, Wapner, & Gardner, 1980).

EXPRESSION STUDIES

Expression or production of emotion has not been studied to the same extent as appreciation or comprehension. When expression has been studied, subjects typically are requested to produce posed expressions upon command, as it is considerably more difficult to devise elicitation conditions for spontaneous than deliberate emotional expressions. Deliberate, or volitional, movements are those that are clearly intended by the individual or requested of him or her; spontaneous movements are those unintended movements that arise as part of an instinctual reaction to an appropriately evocative emotional situation (Myers, 1976). Although this distinction may be theoretically and clinically useful, pragmatically it is difficult to control for unintended movements during deliberate expression of emotion. Indeed, this distinction has evolved out of consideration of clinical neurological observations rather than of experimental findings. Different mechanisms of control have been suggested for these phenomena: Cortical or pyramidal control has been implicated in deliberate emotional expression, and another system—possibly subcortical, limbic, or extrapyramidal—in spontaneous emotional expression (Kahn, 1964; Tschiassny, 1953).

Although the conclusions concerning production of emotion generally agree with those concerning appreciation or comprehension, as we have noted, most studies examine deliberate or intentional production of emotion, and in fact, very little is known about spontaneous emotional expression. Also, in contrast to the appreciation studies, the majority of production studies concern brain-damaged patients, in whom deficits in expression have been well documented.

Faces

In normal right-handers, a greater intensity of emotional expression or greater extent of muscle movement on the left side of the face has been found for posing emotional expressions (Borod, Koff, & White, in press; Campbell, 1978), for posing expressions while imagining emotional situations (Borod & Caron, 1980), for relating emotional experiences (Moscovitch & Olds, 1979), and for deliberately arranging the muscles of the face into a particular emotional pattern (Sackeim & Gur, 1978). (For review of the facial asymmetry literature, see Borod & Koff, in press a.) Left dominance also has been found for nonemotional movement of the facial musculature (Borod & Koff, in press b; Chaurasia & Goswami, 1975; Koff, Borod, & White, 1981). Some studies, however, have failed to demonstrate systematic left-sided facial asymmetry for posed expression (Knox, 1972; Strauss & Kaplan, 1980; van Gelder, 1981). These latter studies, as well as those by Campbell (1978) and Sackeim and Gur (1978), used as stimuli composite faces, which are created by vertically bisecting a still photograph and reassembling the halves into left–left and right–right composites.

Inconsistencies among the studies using composites may be related to methodological difficulties and artifacts introduced by still photography and composites (Bruner & Taguiri, 1954; Ekman, Friesen, & Ellsworth, 1972; Izard, 1971). The use of still photography is limiting in that it rules out the opportunity to inspect the expression as it unfolds or to choose the peak, and may be less ecologically valid than observing the full face in natural motion. One problem with composites is that they cannot account for asymmetries intrinsic to some expressions (e.g., the derisive smile or the snarl), as the composite method makes all expressions perfectly symmetrical. Another problem is that the left and right composites are often of different widths, which may affect apparent intensity.

In regard to brain-damaged patients, Buck and Duffy(1980) found right-hemisphere-damaged patients less able than left-hemisphere-damaged patients to communicate affect spontaneously via facial expression in response to emotionally laden slides. Ross and Mesulam (1979) noted, following right hemisphere damage, a lack of variety in facial expressions in one patient, and in another a paucity of the facial movements that typically accompany both speech and fluctuations in mood.

In contrast, Kolb, Milner, and Taylor (1979) failed to observe differences as a function of side of lesion in the production of spontaneous facial expression during 15 minutes of standard neuropsychological testing. Patients with frontal lobe lesions in either hemisphere produced fewer facial expressions than patients with lesions in the temporal or parieto-occipital regions on either side. Heilman and Valenstein (1979), looking at posed emotional expression, also failed to find differences in performance between right- and left-brain-damaged patients. These data are consistent with the literature on patients with central and emotional facial paralysis (e.g., Feiling, 1927; Monrad-Krohn, 1924; Spiller, 1912), which reveals a random distribution for the side of lesion associated with facial asymmetry, whether facial expressions are made spontaneously or to command.

Intonation

With respect to intonation, information is limited and comes principally from studies of brain-damaged patients. Ross and Mesulam (1979) described two patients who lost the ability to spontaneously express emotion through speech after right hemisphere damage. Voices became monotonous, colorless, and lacked emotional inflection; one of the patients reported a loss of the ability to laugh and cry normally. Both patients were aware of their disabilities, and stated that they were experiencing emotions appropriately while unable to express them outwardly, and neither reported difficulty comprehending the emotional intentions of other people. This inability to inflect speech emotionally following right hemisphere damage also was observed in a group of patients studied by Tucker, Watson, and Heilman (1977). The ability of these patients to produce emotionally toned sentences upon command was markedly inferior to that of a group of non-brain-damaged controls. A special role for the right hemisphere in the mediation of affective speech was suggested as early as 1879, with Hughlings-Jackson's observation that affective speech frequently was spared in aphasic patients with left hemisphere damage who had lost the ability to use propositional speech. Tucker *et al.* (1977) reported the converse for patients with right hemisphere damage; while they were unable to utilize affective speech, they often used propositional speech to express emotions.

Emotional Situations

With respect to production, behavioral evidence comes from subjects with neurological impairment, temporal lobe epilepsy, and psychiatric and psychosomatic disorders. The literature on unilateral brain damage describes differential effects upon emotional behavior as a consequence of side of lesion (Gainotti, 1972; Hécaen, 1962): The affect of patients with right hemisphere damage typically is described as indifferent (involving euphoria, inappropriate joking, and minimization of deficits), that of patients with left hemisphere damage is described as catastrophic (also depressed). In patients who received unilateral carotid artery injections of sodium amytal, reports of striking changes in affect are consistent with these clinical observations. The injections, administered prior to surgery to determine the language-dominant hemisphere, result in the temporary inactivation of the hemisphere ipsilateral to the injection site. Perria, Rosadini, and Rossi (1961) and Terzian (1964) both noted a catastrophic response upon injection of the left carotid and an indifference response following injection of the right carotid. Although these data appear supportive of differential responsivity of the hemispheres, a later attempt to replicate these findings was unsuccessful (Milner, 1967).

While one interpretation of these data supports the notion that the right hemisphere is uniquely specialized for emotion, another view is that these data are compatible with right hemisphere specialization for negative emotions and left hemisphere specialization for positive emotions. In the former view, the indifference reaction is taken as a lack of emotional responsivity; in the latter view, the euphoria that sometimes accompanies right hemisphere damage is attributed to the intact left hemisphere.

The literature on temporal lobe epilepsy (TLE) has provided additional support for the notion of right hemisphere specialization for emotion. Patients with right TLE have been charaterized as extremely emotive, manifesting such symptoms in the interictal phases as anger, sadness, elation, agitation, aggression, and denial or minimization of negative feelings; left TLE patients show ruminative intellectual tendencies, tend to be socially isolated, obsessive, and humorless, and have a predilection for overly harsh self-descriptions (Bear & Fedio, 1977; Seidman & Mirsky, 1980). Such descriptions are not inconsistent with Flor-Henry's (1969) report of a relationship between right TLE and affective disorders (i.e., manic-depressive reactions), and between left TLE and thought disorders (i.e., schizophreniclike reactions).

Finally, the psychiatric literature suggests that particular emotional disorders may be associated primarily with one hemisphere or the other. For example, there is a preponderance of left-sided complaints, which, given the contralateral connectivity of sensorimotor pathways, implicates the right hemisphere, in hysterical conversion symptoms (Galin, Diamond, & Braff, 1977; Ley, 1978; Stern, 1977) and in hypochondriasis (Kenyon, 1964). Left-sided symptoms also have been noted in patients with phobias (Mackie, 1967), psychotic identity problems (Hirsch, 1966), rheumatism (Edmonds, 1947; Halliday, 1937), and unilateral pain (Agnew & Merskey, 1976). There also is a growing body of data implicating the right hemisphere in affective disorders and the left hemisphere in schizophrenia (see Tucker, 1981, for review).

DESCRIPTION OF EXPERIMENTS

Everyday experience and scientific study suggest that the face is the central organ for communication and emotional expression. It is well known that of all animals, the human being has the most extensively developed facial musculature, and depends most heavily on facial function as a facilitator of social interaction (Roberts, 1966). Historically, the psychologist was preceded in the study of facial expression by the anatomist, the painter, and the actor. Sir Charles Bell, a nineteenth-century anatomist, was one of the first to underline the significance of anatomy for the painter and the importance of facial musculature for theatrical expression (Woodworth & Schlosberg, 1954). By the end of that century, Darwin (1890) had defined the primary emotions as fear, rage, laughter, crying, disgust, and surprise, and envisioned them as functional products of evolution. Although Darwin assumed that emotional expressions were direct reflections of bodily conditions, others (Landis, 1924) suggested that some emotional expressions (e.g., devotion, scorn) were more appropriately viewed as products of the social environment (i.e., learned). Research with human infants (Poeck, 1969), blind children (Fulcher, 1942), and animals (Lang & Schenkel, 1969; Tembrock, 1949) characterizes the development of facial expressions as initially occurring reflexively, then imitatively, and then, through social contact, becoming more specific and refined.

Darwin (1890) seems to have been the first to notice the phenomenon of asymmetry during social communication. His discussion, entitled "Sneering and Defiance," contains the first documented assessment of facial asymmetry. Following reports that Australian natives, when angry, drew the upper lip to one or the other side, Darwin instructed four subjects to uncover the canine tooth on one side of the face in sneering. Two could expose the canine only on the left side, one only on the right side, and the fourth on neither side. This distribution, albeit based on a sample of four, foreshadows the findings from our own studies.

Fifty years later, Lynn and Lynn (1938, 1943) reported the first extensive study of facial asymmetry and introduced the term "facedness" to denote the relative extent of muscular movement on the left and right sides of the face. They measured facedness during spontaneous smiling and laughter, and found the majority of subjects to demonstrate no asymmetry. Smaller but equal numbers of subjects were found to be right- and left-faced. Although no relationship obtained between facedness and handedness or footedness, facedness and ocular dominance were correlated (1943).

More or less simultaneously, Wolff (1933, 1943) pioneered the study of facial asymmetry for emotional quality. Wolff's research using composite photographs suggested that the right side of the face projects the "social facade," whereas the left reveals the "unconscious self." Although subsequent studies (Karch & Grant, 1978; Lindzey, Prince, & Wright, 1952; Seinen & Van Der Werff, 1969; Stringer & May, 1980) have confirmed that the two sides of the face reflect different emotional qualities, no consensus has emerged on the specific emotions or emotional valences associated with each hemiface.

Since the early 1940s, there have been no reported studies assessing the quantitative component of facial asymmetry, that is, the relative extent or intensity of facial expression on the left and right sides of the face. The only other source of discussion of facial asymmetry is the clinical neurological literature. DeJong (1979), in discussing the diagnosis of facial nerve disorders, cautioned that minimal facial paralysis must be differentiated from any morphological facial asymmetry. The meaning of such asymmetries and their implications for brain–behavior relationships have only been seriously studied in the past 5 years.

General Hypotheses

Our work, begun in the mid-1970s, was based on observations of facial asymmetry during emotional expression. We were particularly interested in volitional (posed) emotional expression, as such expression presumably involves cortical control and might ultimately provide an indication of underlying neuroanatomical processes. Although the upper portion of the face is innervated by substantial bilateral projections from the frontal motor cortex, the lower part of the face is innervated predominantly by the contralateral cerebral hemisphere (Brodal, 1957; Kuypers, 1958). The facial nucleus is subdivided: The ventral part of the nucleus, which supplies the muscles around the eyes, receives fibers from both motor areas, whereas the dorsal part of the nucleus, which supplies the muscles of the lips, nose, and cheek, receives fibers predominantly from the contralateral motor cortex (Clark, 1975; E. Gardner, 1975).

We were interested in determining which side of the face was more involved during posed emotional expression. There were two separate literatures which led us to opposing predictions concerning the direction of facial asymmetry:

1. Our original prediction, based on the lateral dominance literature was that facedness represented another lateralized motoric function like handedness and footedness, which might be controlled by the dominant cerebral hemisphere. Thus, facial expression would be right sided for right-handers and left sided for left-handers.
2. The second possibility, based on the emotional processing literature available at that time (Gainotti, 1972; H. Gardner, 1975; Heilman, Scholes, & Watson, 1975), was that facial expression of emotion might be mediated by the right hemisphere. Thus, facial expression would be left sided in right-handers, but not predictable in left-handers, as most of the literature on emotional processing was based on findings for right-handers.

Given our original prediction, and the possibility that facial asymmetry might provide another index of lateral dominance, we designed an extensive lateral dominance battery to assess preference with respect to hand, foot, and eye, and performance with respect to the dimensions of accuracy, speed, and strength (Borod, Caron, & Koff, in press). We were interested in determining which dimensions of lateral dominance might be most relevant to facial expression. The battery was quantitative rather than categorical (Crovitz & Zener, 1962; Oldfield, 1971; Palmer, 1964; Raczkowski, Kalat, & Nebes, 1974) and used behavioral measures (Benton *et al.*, 1962; Provins & Cunliffe, 1972).

If our second prediction implicating right hemisphere involvement in facial expression were supported, the relationship of facedness to lateral dominance still would be relevant. In this case, an inverse correlation between facial asymmetry and lateral dominance would suggest a complementary relationship; the absence of correlation would suggest that facedness might be independent of handedness, and a function of the right hemisphere.

Methodology

Subjects were 31 right-handed and 20 left-handed normal adults; 60% of each handedness group were female, since it had been speculated that there are sex differences with respect to emotional expression (Anastasi, 1970; Tyler, 1965). The mean age was 39, with a range from 22 to 53 years. (Facial asymmetry data were analyzed for age differences, i.e., above or below 40 years; no differences were obtained.) Handedness was assessed initially through self-report. History of familial left-handedness in a parent or a sibling was positive for 21% of right-handed and 42% of left-handed subjects.

Subjects were coached with verbal imagery and visual examples to produce appropriate facial expressions, and then videotaped making each of the expressions. Later, three observers viewed and rated each of the 459 expressions using slow motion replay to locate the film frame that demonstrated maximum or peak expression. Each expression was rated for direction and degree of facial asymmetry (i.e., extent of muscular involvement) on a 15-point scale from extreme left sided (-7) to extreme right sided ($+7$); a score of 0 was assigned when right and left sides were not detectably different from each other.

We studied eight facial expressions of emotion, including some of the basic Darwinian ones, which ranged in affective valence from positive to negative. Using the notion of Allport (1961) and Goffman (1959) regarding deliberate versus reactive expressions, we selected four that were deliberately communicative—greeting (mild smiling), clowning (silly—to amuse a child), flirtation ("come hither"), and disapproval (scolding)—and four that were more reactive—confusion (perplexed), disgust (apprehending a "bad smell"), horror (terrified), and grief (crying). In addition, we studied a ninth expression, toughness (a snarling threat), which required volitional *unilateral* facial movement for its execution.[2]

Following videotaping, an extensive lateral dominance battery (Borod, Caron, & Koff, in press) was administered to subjects. The battery included the Harris test (1958) and additional tasks to measure the dimensions of accuracy (number of errors on target tests), speed (time in seconds to complete tracing tasks), strength (pressure in kilograms exerted on a blood pressure cuff), and preference (body part used to execute a task). There were 10 handedness, 3 eyedness, and 2 footedness tasks. Ratio scores were used, and the battery provided *preference* scores for hand, foot, and eye, and *performance* scores for accuracy, speed, and strength.

---

[2]Toughness will not be discussed in this chapter, since it was elicited differently from the other facial expressions, differed from the others with respect to lateral dominance (see Borod & Caron, 1980; Borod, Caron, & Koff, 1981a), and emerged as a separate factor in a factor analysis of all nine expressions (Borod, Caron, & Koff, 1981b). The factor analysis produced two significant factors: general emotional expression (all expressions, excluding Toughness) and Toughness. A third factor emerged reflecting a positive–negative dimension.

Results and Discussion

INTERRATER RELIABILITY

Facedness was reliably rated for all expressions with interrater reliability coefficients of .83, .86, and .87, and with coefficients for individual expressions ranging from .59 to .97, with .82 as median.

DIRECTION OF FACIAL ASYMMETRY

To examine the direction of facial asymmetry during posed emotional expression, we calculated a mean total facedness score for each subject; since there were no differences by sex or handedness, data were collapsed across subjects. Overall, the left side of the face was significantly more involved than the right side (Borod & Caron, 1980). We next looked at intrasubject consistency across the eight expressions. Subjects were characterized as right- or left-faced according to the direction of the majority of the expressions. A significant number ($N = 30$) of subjects were left-faced, 13 subjects were right-faced, and 8 subjects failed to show consistent facedness ($\chi^2 = 15.64$, $df = 1$, $p < .001$) (see Figure 5.1). Among those subjects with consistent asymmetry, 70% were left-faced ($z = 2.43$, $p < .01$).

Given that our task demanded that subjects experience an emotion (e.g., anger) and then consciously produce an appropriate facial expression (e.g., disapproval), these findings seem more consistent with the prediction that facial expression is related primarily to emotion and is mediated predominantly by the right hemisphere. Facedness does not appear to be due principally to a motor effect, that is, it is not typically expressed on the right side of the body and controlled by the dominant left cerebral hemisphere. The result that facedness is significantly left sided has been corroborated by several more recent studies using composite photographs of facial expressions (Campbell, 1978; Heller & Levy, 1981; Sackeim & Gur, 1978). Unlike these composite studies, which used only right-handed subjects, our research affords the opportunity to address the relationship between facedness and handedness.

THE RELATIONSHIP BETWEEN FACIAL ASYMMETRY AND LATERAL DOMINANCE

Overall, there were no differences between right-handers and left-handers on the facedness scores (see Figure 5.2). In fact, the proportion of left- to right-faced subjects was nearly identical in each handedness group; among right-handers 70% were left-faced, and among left-handers 69% were left-faced. With respect to familial left-handedness, there were no differences for facedness nor interactions with self-reported handedness.

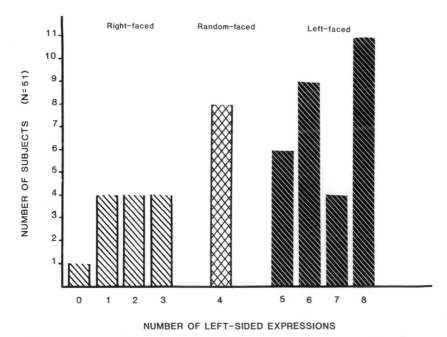

NUMBER OF LEFT–SIDED EXPRESSIONS

Figure 5.1. Number of subjects with left-sided facial asymmetry for eight expressions of emotion.

Although these findings suggested that facedness is unrelated to lateral dominance, it occurred to us that there could be a quantitative relationship wherein strongly lateralized right-handers might be more left-faced than left-handers. Such an association could result in a significant negative correlation. However, when we correlated overall facedness scores with the three

Figure 5.2. Distribution of mean facedness ratings for the eight emotional expressions by handedness group. (Scores below 0 represent left-facedness, and those above 0 represent right-facedness.) (From Borod, Caron, & Koff, 1981a.)

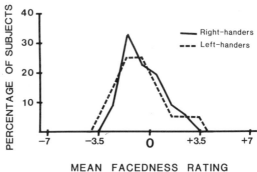

MEAN FACEDNESS RATING

performance and the three preference scores, all correlations were insignificant, except for the correlation with eye preference, which was positive (Borod, Caron, & Koff, 1981a).

Thus, facedness for emotional expression was unrelated to handedness or footedness. These findings are similar to those observed by Lynn and Lynn (1943) for spontaneous smiles as well as those observed for posed "happiness" by Campbell (1979). They also are compatible with studies of presumed right hemisphere functions, in which handedness was unrelated to behavioral laterality for face recognition (Gilbert, 1973), emotional tone perception (Safer & Leventhal, 1977), and conversion reactions (Stern, 1977). It may be the case that certain nonverbal functions are based in the right hemisphere, regardless of the localization of other lateralized operations such as hand preference.

Facedness for emotional expression, however, was related positively to eye preference, thus extending the Lynn and Lynn finding (1943) for spontaneous expression to posed expression. This positive correlation may reflect peripheral rather than central processing, since the neuroanatomy of the cranial nerves suggests some interaction and communication between the nerves innervating the face and the eyes (Gray, 1959). Eye and face dominance also differ from hand dominance in that they are measured by tasks that are less practiced and presumably less subject to shaping and cultural influences. When asked to report their preferred facial side or their dominant eye for focusing, most subjects were puzzled and indicated little awareness of these behaviors. In fact, subjects' response to "Which side of your face do you use more frequently?" was uncorrelated with the judges' ratings of facial asymmetry ($\chi^2 = .47$, $df = 2$, $p > .50$).

FACIAL ASYMMETRY IN POSITIVE AND NEGATIVE EMOTIONAL EXPRESSIONS

In view of evidence suggesting relatively greater left hemisphere involvement in positive emotion and relatively greater right hemisphere involvement in negative emotion (Ahern & Schwartz, 1979; Dimond & Farrington, 1977; Sackeim *et al.*, 1981; Schwartz, Ahern, & Brown, 1979), and our own factor analysis that produced a factor that polarized positive and negative expressions (Borod, Caron, & Koff, 1981b), we next examined the positive–negative (i.e., the pleasantness–unpleasantness) dimension of emotion.

We classified our expressions according to pleasantness. For example, greeting, clowning, and flirtation were assigned to the High Pleasant category, and horror, grief, and disgust to the Low Pleasant category. There were no overall differences in facial asymmetry with respect to different levels of pleasantness. Although these data suggested that emotional expression is not lateralized differentially along a pleasantness dimension, the only expressions that were significantly left sided (i.e., disgust, disapproval, grief, and confusion) were negatively toned (see Table 5.1). Further, those expressions that were relatively less lateralized (i.e., greeting, flirtation, and clowning) were positive in tone. The one exception was horror, which may have been closer to surprise than to fear because of the wording of our instructions. In a study just completed (Borod, Koff, & White, in press), unpleasant expressions were significantly left sided, whereas pleasant expressions were lateralized randomly, in right-handed subjects.

The explanation for this differential lateralization of emotional valence remains obscure. Perhaps some clarification can be found in the writings of Kinsbourne (1980) who has suggested that the left hemisphere may be more specialized for approach behaviors, which positive ones tend to be, whereas the right hemisphere may be more specialized for withdrawal behaviors, which negative ones tend to be.

SEX DIFFERENCES IN FACIAL ASYMMETRY

Although there were no overall sex differences for facial asymmetry, there were interactions with level of pleasantness. Females were more left faced than males for positive expressions, whereas males were more left faced than females for negative expressions. To test the hypothesis that expressions that were more difficult to pose were less intense, and therefore less lateralized, we examined both self-reported difficulty in executing each expression and the examiners' ratings of subjects' ''embarrassment'' and ''tension'' during actual filming. No sex differences were found between pleasant and unpleasant expressions.

In light of the interactions between sex and level of pleasantness, we reassessed the relationship between lateral dominance and facedness separately for males and females (Borod, Caron, & Koff, 1981b). When correlations between the 15 lateral dominance tasks and high or low pleasant expressions were examined, for males the high pleasant expressions correlated positively with measures of lateral dominance whereas low pleasant expressions correlated negatively. Just the reverse obtained for females. However, when the 15 tasks were reduced to six composite indices of preference and performance, only the data for males on the pleasant expressions correlated significantly with these measures of lateral dominance (see Table 5.2).

We believe that this finding does not speak directly to the positive–negative issue but rather relates more to the nature of the positive expressions

Table 5.1
MEANS AND STANDARD DEVIATIONS FOR EACH FACIAL EXPRESSION (WHERE SCORES LESS THAN ZERO REPRESENT LEFT-FACEDNESS), AND THE PERCENTAGE OF SUBJECTS WITH LEFT-FACEDNESS FOR EACH EXPRESSION

	Greeting	Clowning	Flirtation	Confusion	Horror	Disapproval	Disgust	Grief
Mean facedness score	− .38	− .50	− .62	− .52	− .21	− .76*	− .79*	− .52*
Standard deviation	2.00	2.50	2.40	2.30	1.70	2.20	2.10	1.80
Percentage of subjects with left facedness	57.00	62.00	61.00	65.00*	56.00	70.00*	72.00*	68.00*

*$p < .05$, using t-tests for mean scores and χ^2 tests for percentages.

Table 5.2

CORRELATIONS BETWEEN FACEDNESS SCORES FOR HIGH AND LOW PLEASANT
EXPRESSIONS AND COMPOSITE INDICES OF LATERAL DOMINANCE, BY SEX

| | | Lateral dominance scores | | | | | |
| | | Preference | | | Performance | | |
Sex	Pleasantness level	Hand	Foot	Eye	Accuracy	Speed	Strength
Males	High	.18	.39*	.31	.48*	.40*	.30
	Low	− .20	− .05	.09	− .04	− .18	.18
Females	High	− .16	− .17	.22	− .24	− .07	− .11
	Low	.11	.08	.30*	− .08	.19	.00

*$p < .05$.

that were selected for this study. The positive expressions were all communicative and approach oriented, and possibly more linguistic than emotional per se; thus our data may reflect greater left hemispheric lateralization
for linguistic behaviors in males than females, as reported by McGlone (1980)
and Inglis and Lawson (1981).

CONCLUSIONS

Left-facedness for emotional expression in general may be related to the
special role proposed for the right hemisphere in emotional processing. At
this point, there is only conjecture about how and why the right hemisphere
came to be dominant for emotional processing. One possibility is that emotional processing requires strategies and functions at, or for, which the right
hemisphere is superior, such as gestalt analysis, visuospatial organization,
pattern perception, and visual imagery. In fact, for face perception, another
putative right hemisphere function, a recent review of the literature (Sergent
& Bindra, 1981) finds support for visuoperceptual processing as the basis
for face recognition operations. Another possibility, suggested by Brown
and Jaffe (1975), is that the right hemisphere is more dominant in infancy
when the organism is responsive to emotionally laden environmental cues
(e.g., sounds, faces, somatosensory input), and that it simply retains this
primacy throughout development. In fact, head-turning in infants shows a
spontaneous right bias as early as 24 hours after birth (Michel, 1981; Turkewitz, Gordon, & Birch, 1965). Thus, from very early on, the left visual
field, the left ear, and the left side of the head may receive selectively more
exposure to the environment than the right side of the body.

While the findings of left-facedness appear to be related to the right hemisphere's role in emotion, the possibility they also could be artifacts of more peripheral asymmetries has to be considered. If the two sides of the face differed in size, for example, the expression mapped on the smaller hemiface might be experienced as more intense. Similarly, if the hemifaces differed in degree of muscle activity, the side of the face with the greater mobility might be perceived as more extensive. In a study addressing this issue (Koff, Borod, & White, 1981), right hemifaces were in fact found to be larger than left hemifaces, and a significant majority of subjects were judged to have greater left-sided facial mobility. Hemiface size and mobility were independent of sex and handedness, and unrelated to each other. Since facial movement appeared to be independent of facial morphology and lateral dominance, the interpretation that seemed most compatible was that greater left-sided facility reflects the role of the right hemisphere in emotion.

Perhaps right hemisphere specialization for emotion leads to the left hemiface being more active in the expression of emotion, so that the left hemiface might become more facile due to more practice. It is possible that facial movement developed phylogenetically in functional proximity with the human emotional system and became "parsimoniously" lateralized in the right hemisphere along with emotion. Since the face area and the arm area are adjacent in the motor cortex of each hemisphere, a similar pattern of dominance for face and arm might be expected. It is thus difficult to reconcile why the right hemisphere appears more involved in the control of facial movement while the left hemisphere is dominant for arm and hand movement.

Another piece of the puzzle concerns the role of the limbic system in asymmetries associated with emotion. Although there is ample documentation that limbic system structures are intimately involved in emotion (La-mendella, 1977; Papez, 1937), there is as yet no neuroanatomical evidence for greater or more direct limbic system connectivity to the right rather than to the left hemisphere (Geschwind, 1979; Pandya, 1979). This speculation may, of course, be borne out eventually.

ACKNOWLEDGMENTS

We are most grateful to Mary Hyde and Errol Baker for assistance in statistical analysis and to Marjorie Perlman, Marjorie Nicholas, and Priscilla Donaldson for assistance in preparing this manuscript.

REFERENCES

Agnew, D. C., & Merskey, H. Words of chronic pain. *Pain*, 1976, *2*, 73–81.

Ahern, G. L., & Schwartz, G. E. Differential lateralization for positive versus negative emotion. *Neuropsychologia*, 1979, *17*, 693–698.

Allport, G. W. *Pattern and growth in personality*. New York: Holt, Rinehart and Winston, 1961.

Anastasi, A. *Differential psychology* (3rd ed.). London: Macmillan & Co., 1970.

Bear, D. M., & Fedio, P. Quantitative analysis of interictal behavior in temporal lobe epilepsy. *Archives of Neurology*, 1977, *34*, 454–467.

Benton, A., Meyers, R., & Polder, G. Some aspects of handedness. *Psychiatria et Neurologia*, 1962, *144*, 321–337.

Berent, S. Functional asymmetry of the human brain in the recognition of faces. *Neuropsychologia*, 1977, *15*, 829–831.

Blumstein, S., & Cooper. W. Hemispheric processing of intonation contours. *Cortex*, 1974, *10*, 146–158.

Borod, J. C., & Caron, H. S. Facedness and emotion related to lateral dominance, sex, and expression type. *Neuropsychologia*, 1980, *18*, 237–242.

Borod, J. C., Caron, H. S., & Koff, E. Asymmetry of facial expression related to handedness, footedness, and eyedness: A quantitative study. *Cortex*, 1981, *17*, 381–390. (a)

Borod, J. C., Caron, H. S., & Koff, E. Asymmetries in positive and negative facial expressions: Sex differences. *Neuropsychologia*, 1981, *19*, 819–824.(b)

Borod, J. C., Caron, H., & Koff, E. Left- and right-hander compared on performance and preference measures of lateral dominance. *The British Journal of Psychology*, in press.

Borod, J. C., & Goodglass, H. Lateralization of linguistic and melodic processing with age. *Neuropsychologia*, 1980, *18*, 79–83.

Borod, J. C., & Koff, E. Asymmetries in affective facial expression: Behavior and anatomy. In N. Fox & R. Davidson (Eds.), *The psychobiology of affective development*. Hillsdale, N.J.: Erlbaum, in press. (a)

Borod, J. C., & Koff, E. Hemiface mobility and facial expression asymmetry. *Cortex*, in press. (b)

Borod, J. C., Koff, E., & White, B. Facial asymmetry in posed and spontaneous expressions of emotion. *Brain and Cognition*, in press.

Brodal, A. *The cranial nerves: Anatomy and anatomical-clinical correlations*. Oxford: Scientific Publications, 1957.

Brown, J. W., & Jaffe, J. Hypothesis on cerebral dominance. *Neuropsychologia*, 1975, *13*, 107–110.

Bruner, J., & Taguiri, R. Perception of people. In G. Lindzey (Ed.), *Handbook of psychology*. Cambridge, Mass.: Addison-Wesley, 1954.

Bryden, M. P., Ley, R. G., & Sugarman, J. H. A left-ear advantage for identifying the emotional quality of tonal sequences. *Neuropsychologia*, 1982, *20*, 83–88.

Buchtel, H., Campari, F., DeRisio, C., & Rota, R. Hemispheric differences in discriminative reaction time to facial expressions. *Italian Journal of Psychology*, 1978, *5*, 159–169.

Buck, R., & Duffy, R. J. Nonverbal communication of affect in brain-damaged patients. *Cortex*, 1980, *16*, 351–362.

Campbell, R. Asymmetries in interpreting and expressing a posed facial expression. *Cortex*, 1978, *14*, 327–342.

Campbell, R. Left-handers' smiles: Asymmetries in the projection of a posed expression. *Cortex*, 1979, *15*, 571–579.

Carmon, A., & Nachson, I. Ear asymmetry in perception of emotional nonverbal stimuli. *Acta Psychologia*, 1973, *37*, 351–357.

Chaurasia, B. D., & Goswami, H. K. Functional asymmetry in the face. *Acta Anatomica*, 1975, *91*, 154–160.

Cicone, M., Wapner, W., & Gardner, H. Sensitivity to emotional expressions and situations in organic patients. *Cortex*, 1980, *16*, 145–158.

Clark, R. G. *Manter and Gatz' essentials of clinical neuroanatomy and neurophysiology* (5th ed.). Philadelphia: F. A. Davis Co., 1975.

Crovitz, H. F., & Zener, K. A group-test for assessing hand-and-eye-dominance. *American Journal of Psychology*, 1962, *75*, 271–276.

Darwin, C. *The expression of the emotions in man and animals*. New York: D. Appleton and Company, 1890.

Davidson, R. J., Schwartz, G. E., Pugash, E., & Bromfield, E. Sex differences in patterns of EEG asymmetry. *Biological Psychology*, 1976, *4*, 119–138.

Davidson, R. J., Schwartz, G. E., Saron, C., Bennett, J., & Goleman, D. *Frontal versus parietal EEG asymmetry during positive and negative affect*. Paper presented at the meeting of the Society for Psychophysiological Research, Madison, Wisconsin, 1978.

DeJong, R. N. *The neurologic examination* (4th ed.). Hagerstown, Md.: Medical Department, Harper & Row, 1979.

Dekosky, S. T., Heilman, K. M., Bowers, D., & Valenstein, E. Recognition and discrimination of emotional faces and pictures. *Brain and Language*, 1980, *9*, 206–214.

DeRenzi, E., Faglione, P., & Spinnler, H. The performance of patients with brain damage on face recognition tasks. *Cortex*, 1968, *4*, 17–24.

DeRenzi, E., & Spinnler, H. Facial recognition in brain damaged patients. *Neurology*, 1966, *16*, 145–152.

Dimond, S. J., & Farrington, L. Emotional response to films shown to the right and left hemisphere of the brain measured by heart rate. *Acta Psychologia*, 1977, *41*, 255–260.

Dimond, S. J., & Farrington, L., & Johnson, P. Differing emotional response from right and left hemisphere. *Nature*, 1976, *261*, 689–691.

Edmonds, E. P. Psychosomatic non-articular rheumatism. *Annals of the Rheumatic Diseases*, 1947, *6*, 36–49.

Ekman, P., Friesen, W., & Ellsworth, T. *Emotion in the human face: Guidelines for research and an integration of findings*. New York: Pergamon Press, 1972.

Erlichman, H., and Weinberger, A. Lateral eye movements and hemisphere asymmetry: A critical review. *Psychological Bulletin*, 1978, *85*, 1080–1101.

Feiling, A. A case of mimic facial paralysis. *Journal of Neurology and Psychopathology*, 1927, *8*, 141–145.

Flor-Henry, P. Schizophrenic-like reactions and affective psychoses associated with temporal lobe epilepsy: Etiological factors. *American Journal of Psychiatry*, 1969, *126*, 400–403.

Fulcher, J. S. "Voluntary" facial expression in blind and seeing children. *Archives of Psychology*, 1942, *272*, 1–49.

Gainotti, G. Emotional behavior and hemispheric side of the lesion. *Cortex*, 1972, *8*, 41–55.

Galin, D., Diamond, R., & Braff, D. Lateralization of conversion symptoms: More frequent on the left. *American Journal of Psychiatry*, 1977, *134*, 578–580.

Gardner, E. *Fundamentals of neurology* (6th ed.). Philadelphia: W. B. Saunders, 1975.

Gardner, H. *The shattered mind: The person after brain damage.* New York: Alfred A. Knopf, 1975.

Gardner, H., Ling, P. K., Flamm, L., & Silverman, J. Comprehension and appreciation of humorous material following brain damage. *Brain*, 1975, *98*, 399–412.

Geffen, G., Bradshaw, J. L., & Wallace, G. Interhemispheric effects on reaction times to verbal and nonverbal visual stimuli. *Journal of Experimental Psychology*, 1971, *87*, 415–422.

Geschwind, N. Personal communication, June 15, 1979.

Gilbert, C. Strength of left-handedness and facial recognition ability. *Cortex*, 1973, *9*, 145–151.

Goffman, E. *The presentation of self in everyday life.* New York: Doubleday, 1959.

Gray, H. The cranial nerves. In C. M. Gass (Ed.), *Anatomy of the human body.* Philadelphia: Lea and Febiger, 1959.

Haggard, M. P., & Parkinson, A. M. Stimulus task factors as determinants of ear advantages. *Quarterly Journal of Experimental Psychology*, 1971, *23*, 168–177.

Halliday, J. Psychological factors in rheumatism. *British Medical Journal*, 1937, *1*, 264–269.

Harman, D. W., & Ray, W. J. Hemispheric activity during affective verbal stimuli: A EEG study. *Neuropsychologia*, 1977, *15*, 457–460.

Harris, A. J. *Harris tests of lateral dominance: Manual of directions.* New York: The Psychological Corporation, 1958.

Hécaen, H. Clinical symptomatology in right and left hemispheric lesions. In V. B. Mountcastle (Ed.), *Interhemispheric relations and cerebral dominance.* Baltimore: Johns Hopkins University Press, 1962.

Hécaen, H., & Angelergues, D. Agnosia for faces. *Archives of Neurology*, 1962, *7*, 92–100.

Heilman, K. M., Scholes, R., & Watson, R. T. Auditory affective agnosia: Disturbed comprehension of affective speech. *Journal of Neurology, Neurosurgery, and Psychiatry*, 1975, *38*, 69–72.

Heilman, K. M., & Valenstein, E. *Clinical neuropsychology.* New York: Oxford University Press, 1979.

Heller, W., & Levy, J. Perception and expression of emotion in right-handers and left-handers. *Neuropsychologia*, 1981, *19*, 263–272.

Hilliard, R. D. Hemispheric laterality effects on a facial recognition task. *Cortex*, 1973, *9*, 246–258.

Hirsch, S. Left, right, and identity. *Archives of General Psychiatry*, 1966, *14*, 84–88.

Hiscock, M. Effects of examiner's location and subjects' anxiety on gaze laterality. *Neuropsychologia*, 1977, *15*, 409–416.

Inglis, J., & Lawson, J. S. Sex differences in the effects of unilateral brain damage on intelligence. *Science*, 1981, *212*, 693–695.

Izard, C. D. *The face of emotion.* New York: Appleton-Century-Crofts, 1971.

Kahn, E. A. Facial expression. *Clinical Neurosurgery*, 1964, *12*, 9–22.

Karch, G. R., & Grant, C. W. Asymmetry in perception of the sides of the human face. *Perceptual and Motor Skills*, 1978, *47*, 727–734.

Kenyon, F. E. Hypochondriasis: A clinical study. *British Journal of Psychiatry*, 1964, *110*, 478–488.

Kimura, D. Left–right differences in the perception of melodies. *Quarterly Journal of Experimental Psychology*, 1964, *16*, 355–358.

King, F. L., & Kimura, D. Left-ear superiority in dichotic perception of vocal nonverbal sounds. *Canadian Journal of Psychology*, 1972, *26*, 111–116.

Kinsbourne, M. *The attempt to find an organizing principle for the specialized function of each hemisphere.* Paper presented at the Society for Research in Development Symposium, "The development of emotion and cerebral asymmetry," Tarrytown, New York, October, 1980.

Knox, K. *An investigation of nonverbal behavior in relation to hemisphere dominance.* Unpublished M. A. thesis, University of California, San Francisco, 1972.

Koff, E., Borod, J., & White, B. Asymmetries for hemiface size and mobility. *Neuropsychologia,* 1981, *19,* 825–830.

Kolb, B., Milner, B., & Taylor, R. *Analysis of affective behavior in patients with lateralized cortical excisions: A consideration of both lesion site and side.* Unpublished paper, 1979.

Kuypers, H. G. J. M. Corticobulbar connections to the pons and lower brainstem in man. *Brain,* 1958, *81,* 364–390.

Lamendella, J. T. The limbic system in human communication. In H. Whitaker & H. A. Whitaker (Eds.), *Studies in neurolinguistics.* New York: Academic Press, 1977.

Landis, I. Studies of emotional reactions, I: A preliminary study of facial expression. *Journal of Experimental Psychology,* 1924, *7,* 325–341.

Lang, E. M., & Schenkel, R. Geigy Documenta: Goam, das Basler Gorillakind, Basel (1960–1961). Cited in K. Poeck, Pathophysiology of emotional disorders associated with brain damage. In P. J. Vincken & G. W. Bruyn (Eds.), *Handbook of clinical neurology* (Vol. 3), New York: Wiley, 1969.

Ley, R. G. *Asymmetry of hysterical conversion symptoms.* Paper presented at the Canadian Psychological Association, Ottawa, Ontario, 1978.

Ley, R. G., & Bryden, M. P. Hemispheric differences in processing emotions and faces. *Brain and Language,* 1979, *7,* 127–138.

Libby, W. L., & Yaklevich, D. Personality determinants of eye contact and direction of gaze aversion. *Journal of Personality and Social Psychology,* 1973, *27,* 197–206.

Lindzey, G., Prince, B., & Wright, H. K. A study of facial asymmetry. *Journal of Personality,* 1952, *21,* 68–84.

Lynn, J. G., & Lynn, D. R. Face–hand laterality in relation to personality. *Journal of Abnormal and Social Psychology,* 1938, *33,* 291–322.

Lynn, J. G., & Lynn, D. R. Smile and hand dominance in relation to basic modes of adaptation. *Journal of Abnormal and Social Psychology,* 1943, *38,* 250–276.

Mackie, R. E. The importance of the "left." *American Journal of Psychotherapy,* 1967, *21,* 112–115.

McGlone, J. Sex differences in human brain asymmetry: A critical survey. *The Behavioral and Brain Sciences,* 1980, *3,* 215–263.

McKeever, W. F., & Dixon, M. F. Right-hemisphere superiority for discriminating memorized from nonmemorized faces: Affective imagery, sex, and perceived emotionality effects. *Brain and Language,* 1981, *12,* 246–260.

Michel, G. Right-handedness: A consequence of infant supine head-orientation preference? *Science,* 1981, *212,* 685–687.

Milner, B. Cited in discussion in G. F. Rossi, & G. Rosadini. Experimental analysis of cerebral dominance in man. In C. H. Millikan & F. L. Darley (Eds.), *Brain mechanisms underlying speech and language,* New York: Grune & Stratton, 1967.

Monrad-Krohn, G. H. On the dissociation of voluntary and emotional innervation in facial paresis of central origin. *Brain,* 1924, *47,* 22–35.

Moscovitch, M., & Olds, J. *Right-hemisphere superiority in controlling the production of spon-*

taneous facial expressions. Paper presented at the meeting of the International Neuropsychology Society, Holland, June, 1979.

Myers, R. F. Comparative neurology of focalization and speech: Proof of a dichotomy. *Annals of the New York Academy of Sciences,* 1976, *280,* 745–757.

Oldfield, R. C. The assessment and analysis of handedness. *Neuropsychologia,* 1971, *9,* 97–113.

Palmer, R. D. Development of a differential handedness. *Psychological Bulletin,* 1964, *62,* 257–272.

Pandya, D. Personal communication, May 3, 1979.

Papez, J. W. A proposed mechanism of emotion. *Archives of Neurology and Psychiatry,* 1937, *38,* 725–743.

Perria, L., Rosadini, G., & Rossi, G. F. Determination of side of cerebral dominance with amobarbital. *Archives of Neurology,* 1961, *4,* 173–181.

Poeck, K. Pathophysiology of emotional disorders associated with brain damage. In P. J. Vinken & G. W. Bruyn (Eds.), *Handbook of clinical neurology* (Vol. 3). New York: Wiley, 1969.

Provins, K. A., & Cunliffe, P. The relationship between EEG activity and handedness. *Cortex,* 1972, *8,* 136–146.

Raczkowski, D., Kalat, J. W., & Nebes, R. Reliability and validity of some handedness questionnaire items. *Neuropsychologia,* 1974, *12,* 43–47.

Rizzolatti, G., Umilta, G., & Berlucchi, G. Opposite superiorities of the right and left cerebral hemispheres in discriminative reaction time to physiognomical and alphabetical material. *Brain,* 1971, *95,* 61–78.

Roberts, L. Central brain mechanisms in speech. In E. C. Carterette (Ed.), *Brain function, Vol. 3: Speech, language and communication.* Berkeley: University of California Press, 1966.

Ross, E. D., & Mesulam, M. Dominant language functions of the right hemisphere? Prosody and emotional gesturing. *Archives of Neurology,* 1979, *36,* 144–148.

Sackeim, H., Greenberg, M., Weiman, A., Gur, R., Hungerbuhler, J., & Geschwind, N. Functional brain asymmetry in the expression of positive and negative emotions: Lateralization of insult in cases of uncontrollable emotional outbursts. *Archives of Neurology,* 1982, *39,* 210–218.

Sackeim, H. A., & Gur, R. C. Lateral asymmetry in intensity of emotional expression. *Neuropsychologia,* 1978, *16,* 473–481.

Safer, M., & Leventhal, H. Ear differences in evaluating emotional tones of voice and verbal content. *Journal of Experimental Psychology: Human Perception and Performance,* 1977, *3,* 75–82.

Satz, P., Achenbach, K., & Fennell, E. Correlations between assessed manual laterality and predicted speech laterality in normal population. *Neuropsychologia,* 1967, *5,* 295–310.

Schlanger, B., Schlanger, P., & Gerstman, L. J. The perception of emotionally toned sentences by right hemisphere damaged and aphasic subjects. *Brain and Language,* 1976, *3,* 396–403.

Schwartz, G. E., Ahern, G. L., & Brown, S.L. Lateralized facial muscle response to positive and negative emotional stimuli. *Psychophysiology,* 1979, *16,* 561–571.

Schwartz, G. E., Davidson, R. J., & Maer, F. Right hemisphere lateralization for emotion in the human brain: Interactions with cognition. *Science,* 1975, *190,* 286–288.

Seidman, L., & Mirsky, A. F. *Hemispheric dysfunction and personality in temporal lobe epi-*

lepsy. Paper presented at the meeting of the International Neuropsychology Society, San Francisco, February, 1980.

Seinen, M., & Van Der Werff, J. J. The perception of asymmetry in the face. *Nederlands Tijdschrift voor de Psychologie en Haar Grensgebieden*, 1969, *24*, 551–558.

Sergent, J., & Bindra, D. Differential hemispheric processing of faces: Methodological considerations and reinterpretation. *Psychological Bulletin*, 1981, *89*, 541–554.

Spiller, W. G. Loss of emotional movements of the face with preservation or slight impairment of voluntary movement in partial paralysis of the facial nerve. *American Journal of the Medical Sciences*, 1912, *143*, 390–393.

Stern, D. Handedness and the lateral distribution of conversion reactions. *Journal of Nervous and Mental Diseases*, 1977, *164*, 122–128.

Strauss, E., & Kaplan, E. Lateralized asymmetries in self-perception. *Cortex*, 1980, *6*, 283–293.

Stringer, R., & May, P. *Attributional asymmetries in the perception of moving, static, chimeric and hemisected faces*. Internal report, Katholieke Universiteit, Nijmegen, 1980.

Suberi, M., & McKeever, W. F. Differential right hemisphere memory storage of emotional and nonemotional faces. *Neuropsychologia*, 1977, *15*, 757–768.

Tembrock, G. Grundzüge der Schimpansen-Psychologie, Berlin: Verlag Naturkundliche Korrespondenz, 1949. Cited in K. Poeck, Pathophysiology of emotional disorders associated with brain damage. In P. J. Vincken & G. W. Bruyn (Eds.), *Handbook of clinical neurology* (Vol. 3), New York: Wiley, 1969.

Terzian, H. Behavioral and EEG effects of intracarotid sodium amytal injection. *Acta Neurochirurgica*, 1964, *12*, 230–239.

Tschiassny, K. Eight syndromes of facial paralysis and their significance in locating the lesion. *Annals of Otology, Rhinology and Laryngology*, 1953, *62*, 677–691.

Tucker, D. M. Lateral brain function, emotion, and conceptualization. *Psychological Bulletin*, 1981, *89*, 19–46.

Tucker, D. M., Roth, R. S., Arneson, B. A., & Buckingham, V. Right hemisphere activation during stress. *Neuropsychologia*, 1977, *15*, 697–700.

Tucker, D. M., Watson, R. T., & Heilman, K. M. Discrimination and evocation of affectively intoned speech in patients with right parietal disease. *Neurology*, 1977, *27*, 947–950.

Turkewitz, G., Gordon, E., & Birch, H. Head turning in the human neonate: Spontaneous patterns. *The Journal of Genetic Psychology*, 1965, *107*, 143–158.

Tyler, L. E. *The psychology of human differences* (3rd ed.). New York: Appleton-Century-Crofts, 1965.

van Gelder, R. Personal communication, June 6, 1981.

Wechsler, A. F. The effect of organic brain disease on recall of emotionally charged versus neutral narrative texts. *Neurology*, 1973, *23*, 130–135.

Wolff, W. The experimental study of forms of expression. *Character and Personality*, 1933, *2*, 168–173.

Wolff, W. *The expression of personality: Experimental depth psychology*. New York: Harper & Row, 1943.

Woodworth, R. S., & Schlosberg, H. *Experimental psychology*. New York: Holt, Rinehart and Winston, 1954.

6

Right Hemispheric Involvement in Imagery and Affect[1]

M. P. BRYDEN
ROBERT G. LEY

"Left hemisphere . . . language, . . . left hemisphere . . . language,
. . . ." has been something of a mantra resonating from the labs of
researchers investigating cerebral laterality and cognitive functions. Count-
less descriptions of these research endeavors have been introduced by some
variant of the statement, "It is generally agreed that the left cerebral hemisphere in normal, dextral adults is relatively superior to the right hemisphere
in processing auditory and visual representations of language and its con-
stituents." Most readers of this chapter are well familiar with unilateral experimental procedures, such as tachistoscopic and dichotic listening
techniques, and findings of right visual field (RVF) and right ear advantages
(REA) for recognizing words, letters, or nonsense syllables. Although variables such as sex, handedness, and cognitive strategy can attenuate the
strength of the association, the relationship between the left hemisphere
and verbal or linguistic "things" is a well-established one. In fact, in a
research domain often beset by elusive and nonreplicable effects, the as-

[1]Preparation of this chapter was aided by a grant from the Natural Sciences and Engineering
Research Council of Canada to M. P. Bryden.

111

COGNITIVE PROCESSING IN
THE RIGHT HEMISPHERE

sociation between the left hemisphere and language processes has provided a touchstone for other experimental inquiries into the functional division of skills between the left and right hemispheres.

Much less is known about language functions of the right hemisphere. However, recent evidence suggests a right hemispheric involvement in emotion and imagery and indicates a possible way in which language depends upon the right hemisphere. This chapter briefly reviews previous research and describes two recent experiments which support a hypothesis of right hemispheric mediation of emotional, imageable language. This evidence suggests that the generalization of a left hemispheric specialization for language is an overly inclusive one which fails to take into account the role of the right hemisphere in some language-related tasks.

LATERALIZATION OF EMOTIONAL PROCESSES

Although some controversy exists as to the relative contribution of each hemisphere to the perception of emotion, the majority of experimental studies with normal subjects have found a right hemispheric superiority for processing a diversity of emotional stimuli including speech, music, and facial expressions. Dichotic listening procedures have shown left ear advantages (LEA) for recognizing nonverbal, human sounds with affective components, such as laughing, crying, and shrieking (Carmon & Nachson, 1973; King & Kimura, 1972). Left ear advantages also exist for identifying the affective tone of spoken passages (Haggard & Parkinson, 1971; Ley & Bryden, 1981; Safer & Leventhal, 1977). One of the most convincing experiments of this sort showed a LEA for recognizing the emotional intonation (happy, sad, angry) of spoken sentences, and a simultaneous REA for recognizing the verbal content of the same sentences (Ley & Bryden, 1981). Such a dissociation of hemispheric effects makes it most likely that the findings are due to differential lateralization of affective and semantic functions, rather than to varying subject strategy effects. Evidence also supports the involvement of the right hemisphere in assessing the affective content of musical passages. Tonal sequences, evoking both positive and negative moods, are rated more accurately and judged more emotional when listened to on the left ear (Beaton, 1979; Bryden, Ley, & Sugarman; 1982).

Experiments employing lateral tachistoscopic presentation of human faces have confirmed a specialized right hemispheric involvement in the perception of emotional stimuli. Photographs and drawings of faces expressing different emotions are more quickly and accurately identified when they are presented to the left visual field (LVF) (Ley & Bryden, 1979; Safer, 1981; Suberi & McKeever, 1977). In these experiments, separate LVF superiorities for judging the emotional expression and identity of the stimulus characters provides some support for the notion that the emotion recognition effect is independent of the more general right hemispheric superiority for processing faces.

The dichotic and tachistoscopic studies reviewed here have largely investigated the lateralization of emotion *perception*. Evidence also exists that the right hemisphere may be disproportionately involved in emotion *expression*. A number of experiments have found that emotions are expressed more intensely on the left side of the face (Borod & Caron, 1980; Moscovitch & Olds, 1982; Sackheim, Gur, & Saucy, 1978). In short, the left half of the face is more emotional than the right, giving some credence to the oftheard description of "two-faced" people.

LATERALIZATION OF IMAGERY PROCESSES

Despite some unanswered questions about whether positive and negative affects are equally dependent upon the right hemisphere, a relatively comprehensive description of cerebral laterality and emotion is emerging from numerous investigations. Considerably less is known about the lateralization of imagery processes. Nevertheless, data from varied sources converge on the proposition that imagery is a right hemispheric function.

Some initial support for this proposition can be culled from the clinical domain. For instance, cessation of visual dreaming and deterioration of imagery during waking periods is commonly reported following right hemispheric posterior parietal lesions (Humphrey & Zangwill, 1951). It will also be remembered that patients in Penfield's dramatic brain stimulation studies most frequently described dreamlike, visual illusions coincident with electrical stimulation of the right temporal lobe (Penfield & Perot, 1963). Likewise, performance decrements have been shown in a nonverbal recall task involving visual imagery following right hemisphere ECT, while performance was preserved for recall tasks not mediated by imagery strategies (Cohen, Berent, & Silverman, 1973). Similarly, Jones-Gotman and Milner (1978) found that patients with right temporal lobectomies were impaired in recalling pairs of image-linked words.

Electroencephalographic studies of normal subjects have confirmed a relationship between imagery and the right hemisphere. For example, Robbins and McAdam (1974) found alpha suppression, and hence general activation, to be greatest over the right hemisphere when subjects were asked to form "pictures in their mind" of scenic post cards. Similarly, both Morgan, McDonald, and MacDonald (1971) and Davidson and Schwartz (1976) demonstrated an EEG alpha asymmetry over the right hemisphere during questions that required visualizing various scenes. The latter study is particularly germane to the thesis of this chapter as right hemispheric activation was greatest when subjects were required to visualize personally relevant, emotional events. It would seem that highly imageable, emotional experiences were especially potent in arousing right hemispheric processes.

Thus, despite the varying quantity and quality of evidence, a putative case can be made for a functional relationship between the right hemisphere and processes involving imagery (see Ley, 1982).

RIGHT HEMISPHERIC MEDIATION OF CONCRETE OR IMAGEABLE LANGUAGE

Several studies of dyslexics with localized left hemisphere damage have found that the patients' vocabulary for concrete or imageable nouns was retained, whereas grammatical, functional, abstract, and nonimageable items were lost (e.g., Patterson & Marcel, 1977). Although concreteness and imageability are highly correlated, Richardson's (1975a, 1975b) studies of dyslexic patients imply that imageability is the more important dimension. Richardson hypothesized that printed words generate images which can then be responded to or identified.

Recognition studies of laterally presented words varying in concreteness or imageability with normal dextral subjects have produced conflicting results. Ellis and Shepherd (1974) found a RVF superiority for abstract as opposed to concrete nouns, with concrete nouns being better identified than abstract ones when presented in the LVF. They suggested that concrete nouns could directly access the lexicon in the right hemisphere, most likely by an evoked image, whereas abstract nouns presented in the LVF were processed in the left hemisphere by a less direct, phonological route. Marcel and Patterson (1978) showed that word imageability affected LVF but not RVF presentations. Although a number of studies have found similar LVF effects for concrete or high imagery words (Hines, 1976, 1977; Day, 1977), other related studies have failed (Orenstein & Meighan, 1976; McFarland & Ashton, 1978; Schmuller & Goodman, 1979). In a review of right hemisphere language, Bradshaw (1980) concluded that "a number of clinical and neurological findings support the concept of direct lexical access being possible, via the right hemisphere for high-frequency, concrete or imageable items; the left hemisphere's phonological mechanisms would be more adapted for the analysis and interpretation of low-frequency, abstract or nonimageable material [p. 182]." Although Bradshaw recommends cautious interpretation of this data base, it can safely be said that provisional evidence exists for right hemispheric reading and futhermore that such reading may be mediated by imagery.

It has seldom been considered that right hemisphere language functions might be mediated by the emotional, as well as by the imageable, attributes of words. Such a hypothesis seems intuitively plausible in light of indications that the right hemisphere has a special role in processing emotional information. Some rudimentary right hemisphere language functions have also been inferred from the verbal behavior of severe aphasics, who despite massive language impairment might at times curse prolifically, or have other emotion-infused linguistic outbursts (Gardner, 1976). Similarly, limited language functions have also been ascribed to the right hemispheres of certain split-brain patients (see, e.g., patient P.S. in Gazzaniga & LeDoux, 1978). Thus, some observations exist of right hemispheric language productions, which may be occasioned by the emotional attributes of the language, or perhaps by the emotional state of the individual.

HEMISPHERIC PRIMING EFFECTS

The majority of studies with normal adults that have attempted to assess the capacities of the right hemisphere have involved comparisons between stimuli presented to the left hemisphere and the same stimuli presented to the right hemisphere. Thus, most of the investigations of right hemisphere language capacity have compared words presented in the left visual field to the same words presented in the right visual field (e.g., Day, 1977; Schmuller & Goodman, 1979). With visual presentation, there are difficulties in choosing an appropriate way of displaying the words, and controlling for sequential constraints within the particular words being used (Bryden, 1982). Because of these considerations, we carried out experiments using a rather different approach, that of determining whether different types of material had different priming effects on a standardized task.

Kinsbourne (1973, 1975) had proposed that many laterality effects in normals can be accounted for in terms of attentional biases. In one experiment (Kinsbourne, 1970), for example, he presented a rectangle with a gap in it to one side or the other of fixation. When the task was simply one of detecting the gap, no visual field differences were observed. However, when the subjects also had to remember a list of words while engaging in the task, they were more accurate in the RVF. Kinsbourne suggested that thinking of or rehearsing verbal material activates the left hemisphere, and leads to a turning of the head and eyes to the right, a biasing of attention to the right, and an increased sensitivity to stimuli on the right side of the body. Conversely, spatial thought leads to a bias of attention to the left side of space, and a concomitant increase in sensitivity to stimuli on the left. In support of his theory, Kinsbourne (1972) has reported that people tend to look to the left when asked questions that involve visualization of spatial relations, and to the right when asked questions that involve verbal thought.

More recent evidence has cast some doubts on Kinsbourne's theory. Many of his original experiments have proven very difficult to replicate (e.g., Gardner & Branski, 1976; Boles, 1979), and the elementary predictions that follow from the model are often not substantiated (e.g., Allard & Bryden, 1979). Nevertheless, Kinsbourne's theories have focused attention on procedures that would serve to prime or activate one hemisphere, and thereby bias attention. Some rather interesting results have emerged from this concern.

We have carried out two experiments designed to see whether different types of words led to different priming effects. The two experiments were essentially identical in design, except that one employed a face recognition task, and the other a dichotic listening task. In each experiment, six groups of eight subjects were initially tested on a laterality task. The subjects were then given a word list to study for 5 minutes and were told that they would be asked to recall the words at a later time. Then, while holding the words in memory, the subjects were retested on the laterality task to see if any changes in performance could be observed. Finally, they were asked to recall the words they had committed to memory.

In the first study, the laterality task involved the tachistoscopic identification of cartoon drawings of human faces. These stimuli had previously been shown to exhibit a left visual field effect (Ley & Bryden, 1979). In the second experiment, the laterality task involved the dichotic presentation of simple consonant–vowel pairs, using the six stop consonants (/ba, pa, da, ta, ga, ka/). This material had been shown to yield a robust right ear advantage (Studdert-Kennedy & Shakweiler, 1970). Thus, the first experiment involved a visual right hemispheric task, and the second an auditory left hemispheric task.

Six different word lists were constructed, varying in imagery and in affective value. Each word list consisted of 20 nouns of similar type. For example, the high imagery–positive affect list included words like *friend* and *home*, the high imagery–negative affect list words like *corpse* and *snake*, and the high imagery–neutral affect list words like *pencil* and *acrobat*. Comparable low imagery lists were constructed with positive affect words (e.g., *devotion, freedom*), negative affect words (*malice, greed*), and neutral words (*typical, average*).

Ratings of imagery and affective value had previously been obtained for all of these words by asking a large group of subjects to rate the words according to the procedure employed by Paivio, Yuille, and Madigan (1968).

The data of primary interest concern the changes in performance on the laterality tasks from the initial tests to the retests when the word list was being held in memory. In the initial tests, as expected, LVF superiority was found with the face recognition task, and a REA with the dichotic syllables (Figures 6.1 and 6.2). In both of the studies, the word lists had essentially identical effects. When compared to neutral words, affectively loaded words led to a performance shift to the left. Likewise, high imagery words, as compared to low imagery words, also led to a shift to the left. These two effects were statistically independent in the sense that there was no three-way side by imagery by affective value interaction in either study. Thus, in the face recognition study the LVF effect found in the initial testing was enhanced by the study of high imagery words, and by the study of affectively loaded words. The LVF advantage became particularly large with af-

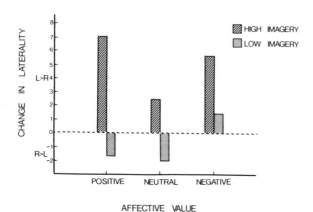

Figure 6.1. Changes in lateralization on a face recognition task from initial testing to testing under memory load, as a function of imagery level and affective value of the words in memory. Scores are changes in L–R difference scores. Values where L > R indicate that performance in LVF increased more than performance in RVF.

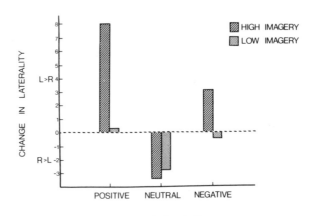

Figure 6.2. Changes in lateralization on a verbal dichotic listening task from initial testing to testing under memory load, as a function of imagery level and affective value of the words in memory. Scores are changes in L–R difference scores. Values where L > R indicate that performance on left ear increased more than performance on right ear.

fectively positive or negative high imagery words. In the dichotic experiment, the normal REA was attenuated by the same factors, shifting to a slight LEA when emotional high imagery words were studied. It should be noted that the right hemisphere improvement cannot result from the word list overloading left hemispheric systems: Word recall varied only with imagery, yet the right hemisphere improvement was also influenced by affect.

THE ROLE OF THE RIGHT HEMISPHERE IN IMAGERY AND AFFECT

These experiments provide two important pieces of information. First, they corroborate the notion that the right hemisphere has a special role in dealing with emotion (Ley & Bryden, 1979; Bryden, Ley, & Sugarman, 1982). Second, the data also indicate that the right hemisphere plays a role in dealing with high imagery words.

There are two ways in which these data can be considered, one emphasizing the priming effect, and the other attempting to provide a more general explanation of imagery and emotion effects in laterality studies.

Perhaps these results are specific to the priming task, and provide a means for extending Kinsbourne's (1973, 1975) attentional bias model. The findings are at variance with an elementary interpretation of Kinsbourne's model: Remembering a list of high imagery or emotional words has the effect of priming the *right* hemisphere, rather than the left. Therefore, Kinsbourne cannot be correct in the general assertion that verbal thinking activates the left hemisphere. Rather, under certain conditions verbal material may also activate the right hemisphere. By this argument, the cumulative effect of studying a list of high imagery or high affect words is to produce a generalized activation which is sufficient to prime the right hemisphere and make it more receptive to incoming information. Such an interpretation does not imply that words have affective or imagery components, but merely that prolonged study of a set of similar words will lead to the activation of some general concept of "high imagery" or "positive affects."

If the priming interpretation is correct, one might expect that studying an affectively positive or affectively negative word list would lead to at least a mild mood change. In the dichotic study, we attempted to assess this possibility by administering a shortened form of the Rorschach (Cards II, IV, and IX) and a mood adjective checklist (Nowlis, 1965). Neither measure provided any evidence for a mood shift on the part of our subjects, although it may have been that the measures were not sufficiently sensitive to pick up any shift.

An alternative view of the data from these two experiments would suggest that the study time serves to activate the internal lexical representations of the words on the study list, and that these lexical representations have both left and right hemispheric components. Although it would seem logical to assume that *all* words have a major left hemispheric lexical representation, both high imagery words and emotional words might have significant right hemispheric components. Paivio (1971, 1975), for example, has mustered a great deal of evidence to indicate that words are encoded both verbally and pictorially. It is possible that the pictorial encoding postulated by Paivio has its basis in a right hemispheric component to the lexical representation of high imagery words. As right hemispheric processes have also been implicated in the perception of emotional stimuli, it would also seem plausible to assume that emotional words had a right hemispheric component to their lexical representation.

By this argument, the presentation of a high imagery word or an emotional word would immediately activate its lexical representation, including the right hemispheric component. If this right hemispheric activation persists for any length of time, the priming effects noted in our experiments can be accounted for. Further, any presentation of a high imagery word or an emotional word would be expected to activate both left and right hemispheric components in the lexical representation. As a result, we would expect to find that the usual right visual field superiority for word recognition in tachistoscopic laterality experiments would be reduced or reversed with high imagery words or with highly emotional words. Day (1977) has found a reduced RVF effect for high imagery words in a lexical decision task, and Graves, Landis, and Goodglass (1981) have reported that affect is a more important determinant of recognition in the LVF than in the RVF.

It should be noted that this proposal does not necessarily imply that for right hemispheric processes to be activated recognition of the word must have reached a conscious level. Zajonc (1980), for example, has proposed that affective responses to stimuli have an immediacy and potency that permits affect to be registered in the absence of cognitive awareness of the stimulus. Perhaps this is one reason why Day (1977) was able to show a reduced RVF effect for high imagery words in a lexical decision task, where one need not be cognitively aware of the specific words employed, whereas Schmuller and Goodman (1979) failed to find an imagery effect in a word recognition task, where the specific words had to be identified.

Of the two alternatives, the latter speculations concerning a right hemispheric component to the internal lexical representations of high imagery and emotional words seem more attractive to us, since they account for a wider range of data. However, one must remember that imagery effects are often hard to observe (Bradshaw, 1980), and that the specific role of the right hemisphere in emotion is not yet established (cf. Ahern & Schwartz, 1979; Tucker, Stenslie, Roth, & Shearer, 1980). Nevertheless, the idea of a right hemispheric component to the lexical representation suggests that future research should focus on techniques for further assessing the linguistic capacities of the right hemisphere.

REFERENCES

Ahern, G. L., & Schwartz, G. E. Differential lateralization for positive versus negative emotion. *Neuropsychologia*, 1979, *17*, 693–698.

Allard, F., & Bryden, M. P. The effect of concurrent activity on hemispheric asymmetries. *Cortex*, 1979, *15*, 5–17.

Beaton, A. A. Hemisphere function and dual task performance. *Neuropsychologia*, 1979, *17*, 629–636.

Boles, D. Laterally biased attention with concurrent verbal load: Multiple failures to replicate. *Neuropsychologia*, 1979, *17*, 353–362.

Borod, J. C., & Caron, H. S. Facedness and emotion related to lateral dominance, sex and expression type. *Neuropsychologia*, 1980, *18*, 237–242.

Bradshaw, J. L. Right hemisphere language: Familial and nonfamilial sinistrals, cognitive deficits and writing hand position in sinistrals, and concrete–abstract, imageable–nonimageable dimensions in word recognition. A review of interrelated issues. *Brain and Language*, 1980, *10*, 172–188.

Bryden, M. P. The behavioral assessment of lateral asymmetry: Problems, pitfalls, and partial solutions. In R. N. Malatesha & L. C. Hartlage (Eds.), *Neuropsychology and cognition* (Vol. 2). The Hague, The Netherlands: Martinus Nijhoff, 1982.

Bryden, M. P., Ley, R. G., & Sugarman, J. H. A left-ear advantage for identifying the emotional quality of tonal sequences. *Neuropsychologia*, 1982, *20*, 83–87.

Carmon, A., & Nachson, I. Ear asymmetry in perception of emotional nonverbal stimuli. *Acta Psychologica*, 1973, *37*, 351–357,

Cohen, B. D., Berent, S., & Silverman, A. J. Field dependence and lateralization of function in the human brain. *Archives of General Psychiatry*, 1973, *28*, 165–167.

Davidson, R. J., & Schwartz, G. E. Patterns of cerebral lateralization during cardiac biofeedback versus the self-regulation of emotion: Sex differences. *Psychophysiology* 1976, *13*, 62–68.

Day, J. Right hemisphere language processing in normal right-handers. *Journal of Experimental Psychology: Human Perception and Performance*, 1977, *3*, 518–528.

Ellis, H. D., & Shepherd, J. W. Recognition of abstract and concrete words presented in left and right visual fields. *Journal of Experimental Psychology*, 1974, *103*, 1035–1036.

Gardner, E. B., & Branski, D. M. Unilateral cerebral activation and perception of gaps: A signal detection analysis. *Neuropsychologia*, 1976, *14*, 43–53.

Gardner, H. *The shattered mind*. New York: Vintage Books, 1976.

Gazzaniga, M. S., & LeDoux, J. E. *The integrated mind*. New York: Plenum, 1978.

Graves, R., Landis, T., & Goodglass, H. Laterality and sex differences for visual recognition of emotional and non-emotional words. *Neuropsychologia*, 1981, *19*, 95–102.

Haggard, M. P., & Parkinson, A. M. Stimulus and task factors in the perceptual lateralization of speech signals. *Quarterly Journal of Experimental Psychology*, 1971, *23*, 168–177.

Hines, D. Recognition of verbs, abstract nouns and concrete nouns from the left and right visual half-fields. *Neuropsychologia*, 1976, *14*, 211–216.

Hines, D. Differences in tachistoscopic recognition between abstract and concrete words as a function of visual half-field and frequency. *Cortex*, 1977, *13*, 66–73.

Humphrey, M. E., & Zangwill, O. L. Cessation of dreaming after brain injury. *Journal of Neurology, Neurosurgery, and Psychiatry*, 1951, *14*, 322–325.

Jones-Gotman, M., & Milner, B. Right temporal lobe contribution to image-mediated verbal learning. *Neuropsychologia*, 1978, *16*, 61–71.

King, F. L., & Kimura, D. Left-ear superiority in dichotic perception of vocal nonverbal sounds. *Canadian Journal of Psychology*, 1972, *26*, 111–116.

Kinsbourne, M. The cerebral basis of lateral asymmetries in attention. *Acta Psychologica*, 1970, *33*, 193–201.

Kinsbourne, M. Eye and head turning indicate cerebral lateralization. *Science*, 1972, *176*, 539–541.

Kinsbourne, M. The control of attention by interaction between the cerebral hemispheres. In S. Kornblum (Ed.), *Attention and performance, IV*. New York: Academic Press, 1973.

Kinsbourne, M. The mechanism of hemispheric control of the lateral gradient of attention. In P. M. A. Rabbitt & S. Dornic (Eds.), *Attention and performance, V*. New York: Academic Press, 1975.

Ley, R. G. Cerebral laterality and imagery. In A. A. Sheikh (Ed.), *Imagery: Current theory, research, and application*. New York: Wiley, 1982.

Ley, R. G., & Bryden, M. P. Hemispheric differences in recognizing faces and emotions. *Brain and Language*, 1979, 7, 127–138.

Ley, R. G., & Bryden, M. P. Consciousness, emotion, and the right hemisphere. In R. Stevens & G. Underwood (Eds.), *Aspects of consciousness*, (Vol. 2). London: Academic Press, 1981.

Marcel, A. J., & Patterson, K. E. Word recognition and production: Reciprocity in clinical and normal studies. In J. Requin (Ed.), *Attention and performance VII*. Hillsdale, N.J.: Lawrence Erlbaum Associates, 1978.

McFarland, K., & Ashton, R. The influence of brain lateralization of function on a manual skill. *Cortex*, 1978, *14*, 102–111.

Morgan, A. H., McDonald, P. J., & MacDonald, H. Differences in bilateral alpha activity as a function of experimental task with a note on lateral eye movements and hypnotizability. *Neuropsychologia*, 1971, *9*, 459–469.

Moscovitch, M., & Olds, J. Asymmetries in spontaneous facial expressions and their possible relation to hemispheric specialization. *Neuropsychologia*, 1982, *20*, 71–81.

Nowlis, V. Research with the Mood Adjective Check List. In S. Tompkins & C. Izard (Eds.), *Affect, cognition, and personality*. New York: Springer, 1965.

Orenstein, H. B., & Meighan, W. B. Recognition of bilaterally presented words varying in concreteness and frequency: Lateral dominance or sequential processing? *Bulletin of the Psychonomic Society*, 1976, 7, 179–180.

Paivio, A. *Imagery and verbal processes*. New York: Holt, 1971.

Paivio, A. Perceptual comparisons through the mind's eye. *Memory and Cognition*, 1975, *3*, 635–647.

Paivio, A., Yuille, J. C., & Madigan, S. A. Concreteness, imagery, and meaningfulness values of 925 nouns. *Journal of Experimental Psychology Monograph Supplements*, 1968, *76*, (1, Pr. 2).

Patterson, K. E., & Marcel, A. J. Aphasia, dyslexia, and the phonological coding of written words. *Quarterly Journal of Experimental Psychology*, 1977, *29*, 307–318.

Penfield, W., & Perot, P. The brain's record of auditory and visual experience. *Brain*, 1963, *86*, 595–696.

Richardson, J. The effect of word imageability in acquired dyslexia. *Neuropsychologia*, 1975, *13*, 281–288. (a)

Richardson, J. Further evidence on the effect of word imageability in dyslexia. *Quarterly Journal of Experimental Psychology*, 1975, *27*, 445–449. (b)

Robbins, K. L., & McAdam, D. W. Interhemispheric alpha asymmetry and imagery mode. *Brain and Language*, 1974, *1*, 189–193.

Sackheim, H. A., Gur, R. C., & Saucy, M. C. Emotions are expressed more intensely on the left side of the face. *Science*, 1978, *202*, 434–436.

Safer, M. A. Sex and hemisphere differences in access to codes for processing emotional expressions and faces. *Journal of Experimental Psychology: General*, 1981, *110*, 86–100.

Safer, M., & Leventhal, H. Ear differences in evaluating emotional tones of voice and verbal content. *Journal of Experimental Psychology: Human Perception and Performance*, 1977, *3*, 75–82.

Schmuller, J., & Goodman, R. Bilateral tachistoscopic perception, handedness, and laterality. *Brain and Language*, 1979, *8*, 81–91.

Studdert-Kennedy, M., & Shankweiler, D. Hemispheric specialization for speech perception. *Journal of the Acoustical Society of America*, 1970, *48*, 579–594.

Suberi, M., & McKeever, W. Differential right hemispheric memory storage of emotional and nonemotional faces. *Neuropsychologia,* 1977, *15,* 757–768.

Tucker, D. M., Stenslie, C. E., Roth, R. S., & Shearer, S. L. Right frontal lobe activation and right hemisphere performance decrement during a depressed mood. *Archives of General Psychiatry,* 1980, *38,* 169–174.

Zajonc, R. B. Feeling and thinking: Preferences need no inferences. *American Psychologist,* 1980, *35,* 151–175.

Hemispheric EEG Asymmetries
Related to Cognitive Functioning
in Children[1]

R. W. THATCHER
R. McALASTER
M. L. LESTER
R. L. HORST
D. S. CANTOR

This volume focuses on the unique and distinctive contributions of the right hemisphere to human cognitive processes. This body of knowledge is derived largely from the approach of observing patients who have had surgical removal or isolation of diseased brain tissue for medical reasons; that is, from studying the pattern of behavioral deficits of individuals following removal of all or part of the right hemisphere, or following callosal resection (Gazzaniga, 1970). Many insights concerning lateralization of function in the nervous system have been gained from these studies. However, inferring mechanisms of function in the intact brain from the results of experiments using subjects with missing or disconnected brain tissue has serious limitations.

Several of these limitations have recently been summarized by Kinsbourne (1974). Kinsbourne emphasizes that the pattern of functional dominance in the intact brain appears to be maintained by within-hemisphere and between-hemisphere interactions. This inference is borne out by clinical

[1]This research was supported by USDA grant HRD–0200 and NIH/MBRS Grant RR08079–09 to R. W. Thatcher, principal investigator.

COGNITIVE PROCESSING IN
THE RIGHT HEMISPHERE

observation and by research on functional deficits incurred from localized brain injury, as well as by the factors that influence recovery after these injuries. For example, the apparent paradox of focal lesions within a hemisphere producing deficits that are not found after removal of the entire lobe strongly suggests a role for interhemispheric inhibitory interactions in functional dominance. Similarly, it is well established that the younger an individual at the time of brain injury, the more likely is functional recovery. This indicates that the functioning of different regions of the brain becomes more specialized over development. An ontogeny of functional cerebral differentiation, perhaps based on the development of within- and between-hemispheric patterns of inhibition and disinhibition, may occur.

Studies of subjects with split hemispheres or only one functional hemisphere cannot contribute to an understanding of these interhemispheric interactions. In addition, most studies of hemispheric functioning rely on neuropsychological tests and behavioral evaluations. These tests emphasize product rather than process. That is, they measure only overt responses, the product of a complex of internal processes, without attempting to measure these internal processes directly.

In contrast to neuropsychological and psychometric assessments, there are several "functional" tests of hemispheric processing which, although limited in other ways, are capable of "real time" evaluation of these mediating brain processes during rest or during the performance of specific cognitive tasks. These tests include EEG (e.g., John, 1977), evoked potentials (e.g., Dustman, Schenkenberg, & Beck, 1976), measures of regional cerebral blood flow (e.g., Ingvar & Schwartz, 1974), and the Positron Emission Tomography (PET) scan (e.g., Schwartz, 1981). Each of these assessment techniques possesses the capability of studying processes intermediate between input and output, and all may also be used with intact subjects.

Electrophysiological studies of cognitive and perceptual function have been widely used to assess brain function, and it is generally accepted that sensory input and high level information processing can influence scalp electrical activity. Furthermore, many EEG and evoked potential studies have demonstrated hemispheric asymmetries (e.g., Thatcher & John, 1977; Thatcher, 1977). The functional significance of these hemispheric asymmetries, however, is largely unknown. As reviewed elsewhere (Thatcher, 1977; Thatcher & Maisel, 1979), there are two general types of electrophysiological interhemispheric asymmetries. One type is amplitude asymmetry, which may occur independent of waveshape (Galin & Ornstein, 1972; Morrell & Morrell, 1965; Morrell & Salamy, 1971; Teyler, Harrison, Roemer, & Thompson, 1973); and the other type is asymmetry of wave form which may occur independent of amplitude (Brown, Marsh, & Smith, 1973; Buchsbaum & Fedio, 1969, 1970; Cohn, 1971; Thatcher & John, 1975). The latter type of asymmetry can be assessed using the measure "coherence" (Glaser & Ruchkin, 1976). To comprehensively evaluate EEG asymmetries between different scalp regions, measures of both amplitude and waveform asymmetry are required.

Clinical electroencephalographers, however, usually consider only amplitude asymmetries in their use of the EEG for diagnostic purposes. Generally, an EEG amplitude in one hemisphere that is at least twice that of the other is assumed to indicate organic pathology (Kiloh, McComas, & Osselton, 1972; Gibbs & Gibbs, 1964). This standard, of a 2–1 ratio in amplitude, is also used in evoked potential assessment of organic pathology (Kooi & Bagchi, 1964; Oosterhuis, Ponsen, Jonkman, & Magnus, 1969). A comparable standard for waveshape asymmetries does not exist, due in part to difficulties inherent in reliably judging waveshape asymmetry by eye, and in part to the fact that computer measures of coherence have not been standardized on a large normative data base in an adequate fashion.

The data reported in the present study are the initial results of a longer term effort to provide such a normative perspective. The studies cited earlier suggest that measures of hemispheric EEG asymmetries are promising candidates for both providing information about the interplay of the brain hemispheres throughout normal development, and providing information that is of diagnostic utility for children functioning abnormally. Two approaches seem necessary, however, if this promise is to be realized. One is to describe empirically how the complementary measures of coherence and amplitude asymmetry change with age in a large normative population of children. The other, which to some extent justifies the first, is to further explore the strength of the relationships between these measures of EEG asymmetry and measures of behaviorally relevant cognitive functioning.

Toward this latter end, we focus here on the extent to which measures of coherence and amplitude asymmetry, in the resting EEG recorded from children with eyes closed, are related to a standardized psychometric measure of cognitive ability. To best describe the shapes and strengths of these relationships, regression analyses were performed, relating the psychometric measure to measures of EEG asymmetry in different frequency bands and from different pairs of scalp electrodes. In addition, these relationships were also viewed in terms of the way children are typically grouped for academic purposes. Moreover, to determine the extent to which the relationships between cognitive abilities and EEG asymmetries between scalp sites are specific to interhemispheric pairings, we also examined measures of asymmetry between pairs of scalp sites within the same hemisphere.

METHODS

Subjects

A total of 200 children were tested. From this group, the data of 9 children were omitted from the analysis, including those of one child who had suffered severe neurological damage, one who died from a brain tumor 6 months after testing, one with an unreliable WISC-R test, two who were outliers in age, and four whose EEGs were lost due to technical problems. The 191 subjects included in this study (88 female, 103 male) were aged 5–16. All children were enrolled in the public school systems of the rural Eastern Shore of Maryland. Subjects were recruited by newspaper advertisements as well as through cooperative arrangements with the Somerset County Board of Education.

Psychometric and Behavioral Tests

The Wechsler Intelligence Scale for Children (WISC-R) was administered to subjects aged 6–16, and the Wechsler Pre-School and Primary Scale of Intelligence (WPPSI) was administered to the 5-year-olds. These two tests are considered equivalent measures of intelligence for these age ranges. An eight-item short form of the WISC-R and WPPSI was used. The following WPPSI subtests were selected as the most nearly equivalent to those used on the WISC-R: information, arithmetic, vocabulary, digit span (sentences for the WPPSI), picture completion, block design, coding (animal house for the WPPSI), and mazes. In addition, the Wide Range Achievement Test (WRAT) was administered to test the three primary areas of school achievement (reading, spelling, and arithmetic). Level I was administered to children aged 5–11; Level II was administered to children aged 12 and older. All children were given an eight-item "laterality" test consisting of three tasks to determine eye dominance, two tasks to determine foot dominance, and three tasks to determine hand dominance. Scores ranged from −8 (representing strong sinistral preference), to +8 (representing strong dextral preference). Most of the analyses in this study were performed on all subjects, without regard to their laterality scores. However, some analyses were performed on groups of children who were considered to be dextral or sinistral dominant. Dextral dominant children were defined as having a laterality score of $+2$ or greater, sinistral dominant children were defined as having a laterality score of -2 or less.

Academic Group Classifications

For some analyses, the children were divided into five distinct groups based on their WISC-R and WRAT scores. The criteria for grouping were selected to reflect Federal Law 94–142 diagnostic criteria for school achievement classification and candidacy for special education. Although the WISC-R and WRAT tests (or equivalent tests) are invariably used as part of a diagnostic assessment, these tests alone are typically not sufficient to classify a child as learning disabled or in need of special education. Thus, no attempt was made to label children as "learning disabled"; rather, academically relevant groups were established based solely on each child's WISC-R and WRAT scores for purposes of testing whether or not our EEG coherence and amplitude asymmetry measures varied among these groups. The groups were as follows: 1—"Gifted" (IQ $>$ 130, WRAT $>$ 89 on all three subtests, $N = 18$); 2—"Normal" (IQ 90–129, WRAT $>$ 89 on all three subtests, $N = 91$); 3—"Borderline Normal" (IQ 84–89, WRAT $>$ 89 on all three subtests, $N = 31$); <4—"Low Achievers (LA)" (IQ $>$ 84, WRAT $<$ 89 on one, two, or three subtests, $N = 34$); 5—"Very Low Achievers (VLA)" (IQ $<$ 84; WRAT $<$ 89 on all three subtests, $N = 17$). There were no children with IQs less than 84 who had WRAT scores greater than 89.

Electrophysiological Data Analyses

Grass silver disk electrodes were applied to the 19 scalp sites of the International 10/20 system (Jasper, 1958). A transorbital eye channel (electro-oculogram or EOG) was used to measure eye movements. All scalp recordings were referenced to linked ear lobes. Amplifier bandwidths were nominally .5–30 Hz, the outputs being 3 dB down at these frequencies. The EEG activity was digitized on line by a PDP 11/03 data acquisition system. An on-line artifact rejection routine was used which excluded segments of EEG if the voltage in any channel exceeded a preset limit determined at the beginning of each session to be typical of the subject's resting EEG and EOG.

One minute of eyes-closed artifact-free EEG was obtained at a digitization rate of 100 Hz with the subject's eyes closed. The EEG segments were analyzed by a PDP 11/70 computer and plotted by a Versatec printer–plotter. Each subject's EEG was then visually examined and edited to eliminate any artifacts that may have passed through the on-line artifact rejection process.

A two-dimensional recursive filter analysis was performed on the edited EEG samples for the following frequency bands: delta (.5–3.5 Hz), theta (3.5–7.0 Hz), alpha (7.0–13 Hz), and beta (13–22 Hz). Coherence (i.e., the ratio of the square of the cross spectrum to the product of the autospectrum, see Glaser & Ruchkin, 1976) was computed for each frequency band for seven interhemisphere electrode pairs (O1–O2, P3–P4, T5–T6, T3–T4, C3–C4, F3–F4, and F7–F8; $4 \times 7 = 28$ variables), for five intrahemisphere electrode pairs on the left side of the head (O1–P3, P3–C3, T3–T5, T3–F7, and C3–F3; $4 \times 5 = 20$ variables), and for five intrahemisphere electrode pairs on the right side of the head (O2–P4, P4–C4, T4–T6, T4–F8, and C4–F4; $4 \times 5 = 20$ variables). Amplitude asymmetry measures were computed from the absolute power (μV^2) in each frequency band for the same intra- and interhemisphere electrode pairs as for coherence. The formula for amplitude asymmetry was (left − right/left + right) for the interhemisphere comparisons and (posterior derivation − anterior derivation/posterior + anterior derivation) for intrahemisphere comparisons.

Statistical Analyses

BMDP Biomedical Statistical Programs (Dixon & Brown, 1979) were used for all analyses. Distributions and descriptive statistics were computed for each variable, using BMDP2D and BMDP7D. These measures included histograms, arithmetic means, standard deviations, variance, skewness, kurtosis, and the coefficient of variation. These analyses revealed that all variables approximated the normal distribution. Polynomial regression (BMDP5R) analyses were conducted with full scale IQ regressed on each of the coherence and amplitude asymmetry variables. These analyses indicated which EEG variables were systematically related to full scale IQ and whether the relationships were linear or nonlinear. Stepwise multiple regression analyses (BMDP2R) were then performed with full scale IQ as the dependent variable, and age, sex, and subsets of the coherence or amplitude asymmetry measures as independent variables. These analyses examined the extent to which EEG variables accounted for IQ with the effects of age and sex regressed out, and after adjusting for covariance among the EEG predictor variables. To better view the present effects in the context of academically relevant groupings of the subjects, analyses of variance (BMDP7D) were used to compare the academic groups defined earlier on each of the coherence and amplitude asymmetry measures.

RESULTS

Relations between Coherence and Full Scale IQ

The full scale IQ scores for the sample population were normally distributed with mean = 107.37, standard deviation = 17.39, skewness = −.3703, and a range from 44 to 150. The results of the polynomial regression analyses (BMDP5R) using each coherence variable as the independent variable and full scale IQ as the dependent variable showed numerous statistically significant relationships. The t values for all linear and quadratic regressions that were significant at the $p < .05$ level or better can be found in Table 7.1.

Of the 28 regression analyses using coherence measures obtained from interhemisphere electrode pairs, 21 (75%) were significant at the $p < .05$ level. Of the 20 left hemisphere coherence variables, 9 (45%) were significantly related to IQ at the $p < .05$ level; and of the 20 right hemisphere variables, 12 (60%) were likewise significant. Of the total number of significant relationships between IQ and coherence measures, 81% were adequately described solely by a linear function, while 11.9% of the regressions exhibited both significant linear and quadratic terms. Only 7.1% of the relationships were quadratic with no significant linear effect. Strikingly, in every instance of a significant linear effect, an inverse relationship was found. That is, as coherence increased, full scale IQ decreased. Several representative examples of these relationships are presented in Figure 7.1.

Of course, the large number of regressions performed were not independent, since the EEG waveforms recorded with different scalp derivations were no doubt influenced to some extent by the same underlying neural generators. The apparent pattern of the results was that more right hemisphere than left hemisphere coherence variables were significantly related to full scale IQ, and more interhemisphere than intrahemisphere variables were likewise related. However, these trends could reflect differing covariances among these subsets of EEG variables, rather than regional brain differences in the extent to which full scale IQ is related to EEG activity. To examine this possibility, stepwise multiple regression analyses were performed. Full scale IQ was the dependent variable and, in three separate analyses, all in-

Table 7.1
t VALUES RESULTING FROM POLYNOMIAL REGRESSION ANALYSES WITH FULL SCALE IQ AS THE DEPENDENT VARIABLE AND EACH EEG MEASURE AS THE INDEPENDENT VARIABLE[a]

Amplitude asymmetry						Coherence					
Interhemisphere			Intrahemisphere			Interhemisphere			Intrahemisphere		
Variable	Linear	Quadratic	Variable	Linear	Quadratic	Variable	Linear	Quadratic	Variable	Linear	Quadratic
Delta			**Delta**			**Delta**			**Delta**		
O1–O2	—	—	P3–O1	—	2.00	O1–O2	−2.17	—	P3–O1	−2.61	—
P3–P4	—	2.18	C3–P3	—	—	P3–P4	−3.68	−2.95	C3–P3	−3.34	—
T5–T6	—	—	T3–T5	—	—	T5–T6	−3.72	—	T3–T5	—	—
T3–T4	—	—	F3–C3	—	—	T3–T4	−5.28	—	F3–C3	—	—
C3–C4	—	—	T3–F7	—	—	C3–C4	−4.11	—	T3–F7	—	—
F3–F4	—	2.96				F3–F4					
F7–F8	—	—	P4–O2	—	2.32	F7–F8	—	—	P4–O2	−2.62	−2.75
			C4–P4	—	—				C4–P4	—	—
			T4–T6	—	—				T4–T6	−3.03	—
			F4–C4	2.63	—				F4–C4	—	−2.54
			T4–F8	—	—				T4–F8	−3.20	—
Theta			**Theta**			**Theta**			**Theta**		
O1–O2	—	—	P3–O1	—	—	O1–O2	−2.69	−2.35	P3–O1	−3.04	—
P3–P4	—	—	C3–P3	—	2.20	P3–P4	−3.71	—	C3–P3	−3.71	—
T5–T6	—	—	T3–T5	—	—	T5–T6	−3.04	—	T3–T5	−2.12	—
T3–T4	2.05	—	F3–C3	—	—	T3–T4	−3.22	—	F3–C3	—	−2.28
C3–C4	—	—	T3–F7	2.33	—	C3–C4	−2.29	—	T3–F7	—	—
F3–F4	—	—				F3–F4					
F7–F8	—	—	P4–O2	—	—	F7–F8	—		P4–O2	−2.69	—
			C4–P4	−2.59	—				C4–P4	—	—
			T4–T6	—	—				T4–T6	−2.68	—

			F4–C4	—	—				F4–C4	—	—
			T4–F8	—	—				T4–F8	− 3.22	—
Alpha			Alpha			Alpha			Alpha		
O1–O2	—	—	P3–O1	—	—	O1–O2	− 3.58	—	P3–O1	− 3.11	—
P3–P4	—	—	C3–P3	—	—	P3–P4	− 4.58	—	C3–P3	—	—
T5–T6	—	—	T3–T5	—	—	T5–T6	− 2.50	—	T3–T5	—	—
T3–T4	—	− 2.19	F3–C3	—	—	T3–T4	—	—	F3–C3	—	—
C3–C4	—	—	T3–F7	—	—	C3–C4	—	—	T3–F7	—	—
F3–F4	—	—				F3–F4	− 1.96	—			
F7–F8	2.27	—	P4–O2	—	—	F7–F8	− 2.94	—	P4–O2	− 2.90	—
			C4–P4	—	—				C4–P4	—	—
			T4–T6	—	—				T4–T6	—	—
			F4–C4	—	—				F4–C4	—	—
			T4–F8	—	—				T4–F8	—	—
Beta			Beta			Beta			Beta		
O1–O2	—	—	P3–O1	—	—	O1–O2	− 3.57	—	P3–O1	− 2.99	—
P3–P4	—	—	C3–P3	—	—	P3–P4	− 4.63	− 2.26	C3–P3	− 2.97	—
T5–T6	—	− 2.30	T3–T5	—	—	T5–T6	− 4.00	—	T3–T5	—	—
T3–T4	—	—	F3–C3	—	—	T3–T4	—	− 2.46	F3–C3	—	—
C3–C4	—	—	T3–F7	—	—	C3–C4	− 2.94	—	T3–F7	—	—
F3–F4	—	—				F3–F4	—	—			
F7–F8	2.54	—	P4–O2	—	—	F7–F8	− 2.55	—	P4–O2	− 2.73	− 2.93
			C4–P4	—	—				C4–P4	− 2.16	—
			T4–T6	—	—				T4–T6	− 3.57	—
			F4–C4	—	—				F4–C4	—	—
			T4–F8	—	—				T4–F8	− 3.30	—

[a]On the left half of the table are the results of regression analyses using amplitude asymmetry variables, both intra- and interhemispheres. The values in the right half of the table are from the regressions using coherence variables intra- and interhemispheres. Variable names are based on the International 10–20 system for electrode placement. Only t values of $p < .05$ are represented here.

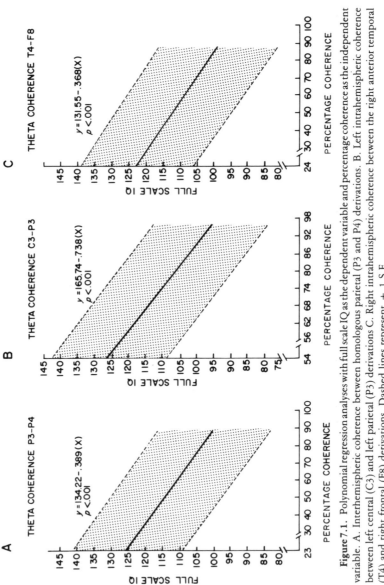

Figure 7.1. Polynomial regression analyses with full scale IQ as the dependent variable and percentage coherence as the independent variable. A. Interhemispheric coherence between homologous parietal (P3 and P4) derivations. B. Left intrahemispheric coherence between left central (C3) and left parietal (P3) derivations C. Right intrahemispheric coherence between the right anterior temporal (T4) and right frontal (F8) derivations. Dashed lines represent ± 1 S.E.

Table 7.2

RESULTS OF MULTIVARIATE REGRESSION ANALYSES WITH FULL SCALE IQ AS THE DEPENDENT VARIABLE AND COHERENCE AS THE INDEPENDENT VARIABLES, AFTER REGRESSING OUT THE EFFECTS OF AGE AND SEX[a]

	Multivariate R	Multivariate R^2	Multivariate F	Power at $p < .05$
Interhemispheric	.610	.3721	3.460***	.99
Left intrahemispheric	.4766	.2272	1.800**	.96
Right intrahemispheric	.4522	.2045	1.564*	.93

[a]The total N for these analyses were less than 196 because a pairwise deletion procedure was used. The degrees of freedom were 20/116.

*** $p < .0005$ one tailed.

** $p < .025$ one tailed.

* $p < .05$ one tailed.

terhemisphere coherence variables, all left hemisphere coherence variables, or all right hemisphere coherence variables were entered as predictors. The order in which these predictor variables were entered into the regression equations was determined by their ability to account for the variance in IQ. that remained after each step, with the unentered variables at each step being adjusted for their partial correlation with the variables previously entered. To determine the extent to which the apparent relation of EEG coherence variables to IQ could have been confounded by IQ differences in our sample across age or sex, these two variables were forced into each regression equation as independent variables at the first two steps.

In addition to regressing out the possible confounding effects of age and sex, our interest was in comparing the ability of the three sets of coherence variables to predict full scale IQ. Therefore, an equal number of variables were entered into the regression equations for each of the three variable sets. All 20 left and right hemisphere coherence variables were entered, and 20 of the 28 interhemisphere coherence variables were entered into the regression equation.[2]

[2]Another way to compare the strengths of the three variable sets is to restrict entry of variables into the regression equation by setting the F-to-enter greater or equal to $p < .05$.

With this procedure six interhemisphere variables were entered, accounting for 25.24% of the variance of full scale IQ and a multiple F significant at $p < .0001$, while only two left hemisphere variables were entered ($R^2 = .125$ and $p < .005$) and one right hemisphere variable ($R^2 = .0711$ and $p < .005$). These results are consistent with the pattern observed when 20 variables were entered, that is, interhemisphere variables were the strongest predictor of full scale IQ with little difference in the strength of prediction between left and right hemisphere variables.

As seen in Table 7.2, strong significant effects were present even after the effects of age and sex were regressed out. Further, there were virtually no differences in the extent to which left and right hemisphere variables predicted IQ (22.72% and 20.45% of the variance of full scale IQ was accounted for by left and right hemisphere variables respectively), and the interhemisphere variables were yet more strongly related to IQ (37.21% of the variance accounted for) than were either of the intrahemisphere subsets of coherence variables. The multivariate Fs for the analyses involving the left and right hemisphere variables were significant at $p < .025$ and $p < .05$ respectively; the multivariate F for the analysis involving interhemisphere variables was significant at $p < .0005$.

Statistical power analyses provide another index with which to evaluate the strengths of the present effects. The effect sizes (Cohen, 1977) based on the percentage variance of full scale IQ accounted for by the interhemisphere variables show a 99% probability of replicating this effect at $p < .05$ if another sample of the same size used here were to be examined. The probability of similarly replicating the left and right hemisphere effects was 96% and 93% respectively.

Relations between Amplitude Asymmetries and Full Scale IQ

Statistically significant polynomial regressions were also observed when full scale IQ was regressed on each amplitude asymmetry variable (see Table 7.1). Of the 28 regression analyses using interhemisphere amplitude asymmetry measures as the independent variables, 7 (25%) were significant at the $p < .05$ level. Of the 20 analyses using right hemisphere variables, 3 (15%) were significant at the $p < .05$ level, and of the 20 analyses using left hemisphere variables, 3 were likewise significant.

An interesting pattern was noted in the interhemisphere amplitude asymmetry measures. In every instance of a significant linear relationship between IQ and an interhemisphere amplitude asymmetry, the slope of the regression line was positive. Furthermore, inspection of the scatter plots from these analyses revealed that practically all subjects had positive amplitude asymmetry scores (amplitude asymmetry can range from large negative values, indicating amplitude on the right side of the head greater than that on the left side of the head, to large positive values, indicating amplitude on the left greater than that on the right). This trend suggests that the larger the amplitude asymmetry (with left side greater than right) the greater the full scale IQ. Although four of the seven significant relationships between IQ and interhemisphere variables were quadratic, with no significant linear terms (an example is presented in Figure 7.2C), a further observation suggests that these trends were consistent with the conclusion based on the linear effects. Polynomial regression analyses restricted to the 163 subjects who were dextral dominant (i.e., subjects with laterality scores of +2 or greater) failed to produce any quadratic functions, yielding only linear relationships (with left hemisphere amplitude greater than right). This finding suggests that the direction of amplitude asymmetry between interhemisphere scalp sites varied as a function of behavioral, and by inference hemispheric, laterality. Moreover, it strengthens the generalization that the greater the amplitude asymmetry, regardless of which side of the head displays the largest amplitude, the greater the IQ.

Stepwise multiple regression analyses similar to those performed with the coherence variables were conducted with the various subsets of amplitude asymmetry variables. Of interest were the abilities of the interhemisphere, left hemisphere, and right hemisphere subsets of variables to account for full scale IQ after the effects of age and sex were regressed out. Twenty EEG variables were allowed to enter the regression equations for each variable set. As shown in Table 7.3, the interhemisphere variables accounted for 21.92% of the variance of full scale IQ with a multiple F significant at $p < .025$ and the right intrahemisphere variables accounted for 20.64% of the variance with the multiple F significant at $p < .05$. The left hemisphere variables, although accounting for 18.92% of the variance, were not significant ($p < .1$).

Table 7.3
RESULTS OF MULTIVARIATE REGRESSION ANALYSES WITH FULL SCALE IQ AS THE DEPENDENT VARIABLE AND AMPLITUDE ASYMMETRY AS THE INDEPENDENT VARIABLES, AFTER REGRESSING OUT THE EFFECTS OF AGE AND SEX[a]

	Multivariate R	Multivariate R^2	Multivariate F	Power at $p < .05$
Interhemispheric	0.4682	0.2192	1.695**	0.95
Left intrahemispheric	0.4350	0.1892	1.431 NS	—
Right intrahemispheric	0.4543	0.2064	1.580*	0.94

[a]The total N for these analyses were less than 196 because a pairwise deletion procedure was used. The degrees of freedom were 20/116.

** $p < .025$ one tailed.
* $p < .05$ one tailed.

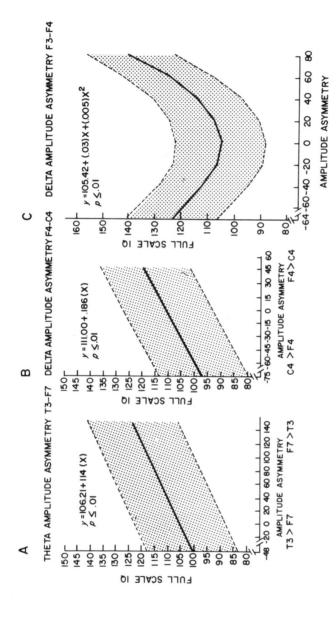

Figure 7.2. Polynomial regression analyses with full scale IQ as the dependent variable and amplitude asymmetry as the independent variable. A. Left intrahemispheric amplitude asymmetry between the left anterior temporal (T3) and left frontal (F7) derivations. Negative abscissa values represent T3 amplitude greater than F7, and positive abscissa values represent F7 amplitude greater than T3. B. Right intrahemispheric amplitude asymmetry between the right frontal (F4) and right central (C4) derivations. Negative abscissa values represent C4 greater amplitude than F4, and positive abscissa values represent F4 greater amplitude than C4. C. Interhemispheric amplitude asymmetry between homologous frontal (F3 and F4) derivations. Negative abscissa values represent right hemisphere (F4) greater amplitude than left hemisphere (F3), and positive abscissa values represent left hemisphere (F3) greater amplitude than the right hemisphere (F4). Dashed lines represent ± 1 S.E.

Discrimination between Academic Groups Based on EEG Coherence

To better view the relationships between EEG coherence variables and full scale IQ in the context of differences among our academically relevant grouping of children, analyses of variance (BMDP7D) were used to compare each coherence measure among the five groups. The Welch and Brown–Forsythe statistics, which are insensitive to heteroscedasticity, were used. Of the 28 interhemisphere coherence variables, 15 were significantly different among the groups at the $p < .05$ level. Of the left hemisphere coherence variables, 4 out of 20, and of the right hemisphere variables, 6 out of 20, differed significantly among the groups. This represents a total of 25 out of 68 (36.7%) significant effects. Examples of the means and standard errors across groups for several representative inter- and intrahemispheric variables are shown in Figure 7.3.

A clear increase in coherence can be observed from gifted to normal to borderline to low to very low achieving groups. The overall F was significant in each case.

To ensure that these trends in EEG asymmetries could not have been caused by systematic differences in the artifacting of the EEG, which might have resulted, for example, if children of differing IQ generated different amounts or types of movement artifact during data acquisition, we compared a number of features of the edited EEG among the academic groups of children. The indices examined were the total duration of EEG that remained after editing, number of segments edited out, average duration of EEG segments, and number of EEG segments < 1 sec. Analyses of variance (BMDP7D) showed that none of these features differed significantly among the groups of children.

Discrimination between Academic Groups Based on Amplitude Asymmetries

Analyses of variance (BMDP7D) were similarly conducted between academic groups for each of the amplitude asymmetry variables. Of the 68 such analyses, 3 were significant at $p < .05$ (alpha and beta T3–F7 and delta T3–T4) and 3 were significant at $p < .01$ (theta T3–F7, theta T3–T4, and theta C4–P4). Although only a few significant effects were obtained, some consistency in the direction of the effects was seen. In comparison to the normal and gifted subjects, the very low achievement children exhibited less of an amplitude difference between anterior and posterior scalp sites within

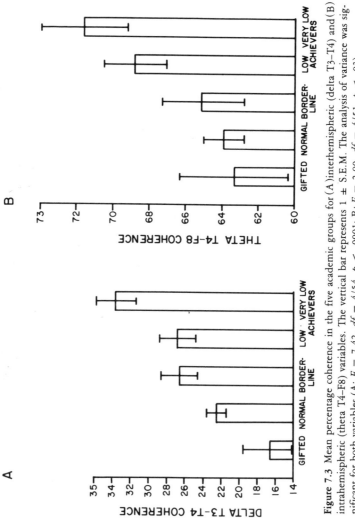

Figure 7.3 Mean percentage coherence in the five academic groups for (A) interhemispheric (delta T3–T4) and (B) intrahemispheric (theta T4–F8) variables. The vertical bar represents 1 ± S.E.M. The analysis of variance was significant for both variables (A: $F = 7.42$, $df = 4/54$, $p < .0001$; B: $F = 2.90$, $df = 4/51$, $p < .03$).

a hemisphere. An example of the anterior–posterior amplitude differences between groups can be seen in Figure 7.4.

DISCUSSION

The results of the present study show that measures of EEG coherence and amplitude asymmetry between pairs of scalp sites in children are related to the children's performance on tests of cognitive functioning. The two complementary measures of similarity—coherence and amplitude—each showed numerous instances, across EEG frequencies and scalp site pairings, of a statistically significant relationship to full scale IQ. These relationships were manifest not only when full scale IQ was regressed on each EEG asymmetry variable, but also when the EEG measures were compared among groups of the children that were formed on the basis of their IQ and achievement test performance.

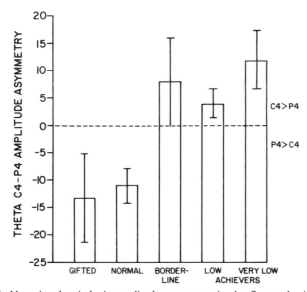

Figure 7.4. Mean intrahemispheric amplitude asymmetry in the five academic groups of children for one pair of scalp sites (right central and parietal). Negative numbers represent posterior (P4) amplitude greater than anterior (C4), whereas positive numbers represent anterior (C4) amplitude greater than posterior (P4). The horizontal dashed line represents zero asymmetry. The vertical bars represent $1 \pm$ S.E.M. The analysis of variance was statistically significant ($F = 4.89$, $df = 4/53$, $p < .002$).

Although they were recorded from the same paired scalp sites, many more coherence measures than amplitude asymmetry measures were systematically related to IQ. Consistent with this observation were the results of stepwise multiple regressions of IQ in which the covariance among EEG predictor variables was adjusted for. Variables were chosen for these regression equations in a stepwise manner from, in separate analyses, the interhemisphere, left hemisphere, and right hemisphere electrode pairings. Despite the fact that all such analyses showed statistically significant effects, subsets of coherence variables in combination accounted for more of the variance in full scale IQ than subsets of the amplitude asymmetry variables. Moreover, the same regression analyses indicated that these effects were not due to a confounding with age or sex.

A primary interest, of course, was whether or not there would be hemispheric differences in the extent to which EEG measures were related to IQ. The between-hemisphere coherence variables were, in combination, stronger predictors of IQ (37.2% of the variance accounted for) than were either of the subsets of within-hemisphere variables (approximately 20% of the variance accounted for in the case of both left and right within-hemisphere pairings). There were no consistent left versus right hemisphere differences for either coherence or amplitude asymmetry variables in the strength or direction of relations to full scale IQ. It is important to note that the failure to find such differences does not seem to be due to a high proportion of sinistrals in the present population. The vast majority (85.3%) of the children appeared to be dextral dominant in that they scored 2 or more on our measure of laterality. Furthermore, preliminary analyses of only this group likewise showed no significant differences between the within-hemisphere measures from the left and right sides of the head in their abilities to predict full scale IQ. Interpretation of the present results, however, must be restricted to the full scale IQ, as preliminary analyses of individual WISC-R subtests indicate that hemispheric asymmetries may be present for certain subtests. It will be remembered that there were apparent hemispheric differences in the direction of some amplitude asymmetry measures. Some variables showed a quadratic, U-shaped relationship to IQ, with the base of the U falling around zero (i.e., no amplitude asymmetry). However, when only the dextral dominant subjects were examined, these relationships all became linear, with positive regression slopes. This finding suggested that these subjects had interhemisphere asymmetries in the opposite direction from the relatively few subjects in our sample who were sinistral dominant and, therefore, that the direction of the relationship between amplitude asymmetries and full scale IQ may reflect left- versus right-handedness.

It is somewhat surprising that EEG asymmetries in the resting EEG, recorded with eyes closed, should be so strongly related to measures of cognitive functioning that were obtained separately. It remains to be seen whether or not similar asymmetries exist while children are engaged in an active task. Nonetheless, preliminary analyses of some evoked potential data, recorded from the same children and scalp sites as the present EEG data, provide additional evidence that the similarity of the waveshape recorded from interhemispheric pairs of electrodes is related to IQ. Averaged evoked potentials were elicited by blank-field and patterned visual stimuli that were passively observed by the children (methodological details and more extensive analyses of these results will be presented elsewhere). Cross-correlations between homologous pairs of electrodes over the two hemispheres were calculated for each of several latency epochs and regressed against IQ in a manner similar to the EEG variables presented here. Trends consistent with the present analyses of EEG coherence variables were found. More statistically significant relationships between evoked potential correlation coefficients and full scale IQ were obtained (12 of 36) than would have been expected by chance, and these relationships all showed greater interhemispheric correlation to be associated with lower IQ.

Whether the EEG asymmetries recorded here are in any sense causally related to the children's cognitive abilities is impossible to say, as neither the functional significance of scalp-recorded EEG activity nor its relationship to underlying cellular activity is well understood. Nevertheless, our findings must be taken into account by any comprehensive theory of brain function. In general, the implication of these relationships between EEG asymmetries and intelligence would seem to be that the resting EEG reflects a readiness or capacity to effectively process information.

Some further speculation may be in order, for the sake of integrating the coherence and amplitude asymmetry effects observed here and providing a hypothesis to guide the interpretation of future results. Following this premise, the trends in the present data suggest an explanation based on the concepts of information theory (Shannon, 1948). In order to code information, the elements of a system must be capable of assuming different states. Moreover, to the extent that a system contains redundancies it is less capable of carrying information. It may be reasonable to view similarities in the EEG recorded simultaneously at a pair of scalp sites as indicative of a state of redundancy in the brain. In other words, when the underlying generators that contribute to the EEG seen at the two sites are coherent with one another, there is less capacity for coding the information that may become available from the outside world or from other groups of cells. In physiological terms, a state of maximal coherence and minimal amplitude asymmetry represents a state of minimal differentiation.

Within this framework, high coherence and low amplitude asymmetry between the EEG seen at pairs of scalp sites can be viewed as reflecting redundancy or minimal differentiation in the brain and thus a lowered capacity for processing information. The relationships between IQ and EEG asymmetry in the present study are consistent with this view. Specifically, the greater the child's EEG coherence between sites over the two hemispheres or within a given hemisphere, the lower was the child's IQ. Similarly, the less the amplitude asymmetry between two sites, the lower was the IQ. These data therefore appear to support the notion that, with organically intact children, increased dissimilarity in EEG activity between pairs of scalp sites is positively correlated with cerebral differentiation and the mental capacity for processing information.

This theoretical explanation is, of course, highly speculative and not as yet supported by deductive evidence. Furthermore, it is possible that such a relationship will hold only for a limited range of an EEG parameter. As the clinical literature has noted pronounced EEG asymmetries in patients with organic pathologies such as strokes, tumors, and senile dementia, the present results may pertain only to intact subjects without gross organic disorders.

Seen in the context of our long-term objectives, the present results are encouraging. That relationships between measures of EEG asymmetries and cognitive abilities have been demonstrated suggests the value of formulating standardized norms that will characterize these measures throughout development. Our goal in this work is not to develop an electrophysiological intelligence test. Instead, we wish to explore the possibility of using EEG and evoked potential measures to identify the operating characteristics or dynamic ranges of brain function. If reliable and replicable electrophysiological correlations to intelligence can be obtained, then it may be possible to optimize the physiological parameters, for example, through interventions involving diet, minimization of exposure to toxins, environmental enrichment, or education. In so doing, beneficial changes in a child's ability to function behaviorally might be produced.

Currently, analyses of the topographic distributions of EEG coherence and amplitude asymmetry are being examined in our laboratory. In addition, these measures are being related to children's performance on various subtests of the WISC-R as well as other measures of intellectual development. A comparison between asymmetry measures obtained in passive conditions, as in the present study, and those revealed when children perform active processing tasks is also of interest. Such analyses and new data may yield more detailed information about the functional significance of the present results.

ACKNOWLEDGMENTS

We gratefully acknowledge the assistance of Rebecca Walker, Judy Leasure, and Faye Leatherbury in many aspects of this study. The computer software for data acquisition and analysis was provided by Neurometrics, Inc.

REFERENCES

Brown, W. S., Marsh, J. T., & Smith, J. C. Contextual meaning effects on speech evoked potentials. *Behavioral Biology*, 1973, *9*, 755–761.

Buchsbaum, M., & Fedio, P. Visual information and evoked responses from the left and right hemisphere. *Electroencephalography and Clinical Neurophysiology*, 1969, *36*, 266–272.

Buchsbaum, M., & Fedio, P. Hemispheric differences in evoked potentials to verbal and nonverbal stimuli in the left and right visual fields. *Physiology and Behavior*, 1970, *5*, 207–210.

Cohen, J. *Statistical power analysis for the behavioral sciences*. New York: Academic Press, 1977.

Cohn, R. Differential cerebral processing of noise and verbal stimuli. *Science*, 1971, *172*, 599–601.

Dixon, W., & Brown, M. *Biomedical Computer Programs P-Series*. Berkeley and Los Angeles: University of California Press, 1979.

Dustman, R., Schenkenberg, T., & Beck, E. The development of the evoked response as a diagnostic and evaluative procedure. In R. Karrer (Ed.), *Developmental psychophysiology of mental retardation*. Springfield, Ill.: Charles C. Thomas, 1976.

Galin, D., & Ornstein, R. Lateral specialization of cognitive mode: An EEG study. *Psychophysiology*, 1972, *13*, 45–50.

Gazzaniga, M. S. *The bisected brain*, New York: Appleton-Century-Crofts, 1970.

Gevins, A. S., Doyle, J. C., Cutillo, B. A., Schaffer, R. E., Tannehill, R. S., Ghannam, J. H., Gilcrease, V. A., & Yeager, C. L. Electrical potentials in human brain during cognition: New method reveals dynamic patterns of correlation. *Science*, 1981, *213*, 918–922.

Gibbs, F. A., & Gibbs, E. L. *Atlas of encephalography, Vol. 3: Neurological and psychological disorders*. Cambridge, Mass.: Addison-Wesley, 1964.

Glaser, E. M., & Ruchkin, D. S. *Principles of neurobiological signal analysis*. New York: Academic Press, 1976.

Ingvar, D. H., & Schwartz, M. S. Blood flow patterns induced in the dominant hemisphere by speech and writing. *Brain*, 1974, *97*, 274–288.

Jasper, H. H. The ten–twenty electrode system of the International Federation. *Electroencephalography and Clinical Neurophysiology*, 1958, *10*, 371–375.

John, E. R. *Functional neuroscience, Vol. 2, Neurometrics: Clinical applications of quantitative electrophysiology*. Hillsdale, N. J.: Lawrence Erlbaum Associates, 1977.

John, E. R., Karmel, B., Corning, W., Easton, P., Brown, D., Ahn, H., John, M., Harmony, T., Prichep, L., Toro, A., Gerson, I., Bartlett, F., Thatcher, R., Kaye, H., Valdes, P., & Schwartz, E. Neurometrics: Numerical taxonomy identifies different profiles of brain functions within groups of behaviorally similar people. *Science*, 1977, *196*, 1393–1410.

Kiloh, L. G., McComas, A. J., & Osselton, J. W. *Clinical electroencephalography*. London.: Butterworth, 1972.

Kinsbourne, M. Mechanisms of hemispheric interaction in man. In M. Kinsbourne & L. Smith (Eds.), *Hemispheric disconnection and cerebral function*. Springfield, Ill.: Charles C. Thomas, 1974.

Kooi, K. A., & Bagchi, B. K. Visual evoked responses in man: Normative data. *Annals of the New York Academy of Science*, 1964, *112*, 254–269.

Morrell, F., & Morrell, L. Computer aided analysis of brain electrical activity. In L. D. Proctor & W. R. Adey (Eds.), *The analysis of central nervous system and cardiovascular data using computer methods*. Washington, D.C.: NASA, U.S. Government Printing Office, 1965.

Morrell, L. K., & Salamy, J. G. Hemispheric asymmetry of electrocortical response to speech stimuli, *Science*, 1971, *174*, 164–166.

Oosterhuis, H. J., Ponsen, L., Jonkman, E. J., & Magnus, O. The average visual response in patients with cerebrovascular disease. *Electroencephalography and Clinical Neurophysiology*, 1969, *27*, 23–24.

Schwartz, E. L. Positron emission tomography studies of human visual cortex. *Society for Neuroscience 11th Annual Meeting, Abstract 118.11*.

Shannon, C. E. A mathematical theory of communication. *Bell Systems Technical Journal*, 1948, *27*, 379–423.

Teyler, T., Harrison, T., Roemer, R., & Thompson, R. Human scalp recorded evoked potential correlates of linguistic stimuli. *Journal of the Psychonomic Society Bulletin*, 1973, *1*, 333–334.

Thatcher, R. W., & John, E. R. Information and mathematical quantification of brain states. In N. Burch & H. L. Altshuler (Eds.), *Behavior and brain electrical activity*. New York: Plenum Press, 1975.

Thatcher, R. W., & John, E. R. *Functional neuroscience: Foundations of cognitive processes*. Hillsdale, N. J.: Lawrence Erlbaum Associates, 1977.

Thatcher, R. W. Evoked potential correlates of hemispheric lateralization during semantic information processing, In S. Harnad (Ed.), *Lateralization of the nervous system*. New York: Academic Press, 1977.

Thatcher, R. W., & Maisel, E. B. Functional landscapes of the brain: An electrotopographic perspective. In H. Begleiter (Ed.), *Evoked brain potentials and behavior*. New York: Plenum Press, 1979.

PART III

STUDIES OF
BRAIN-DAMAGED SUBJECTS

Selective Impairment of
Semantic-Lexical Discrimination
in Right-Brain-Damaged Patients

GUIDO GAINOTTI
CARLO CALTAGIRONE
GABRIELE MICELI

Studies conducted in split-brain patients have consistently shown that the right hemisphere possesses a far greater capability to comprehend language than to produce it in either the oral or the written modality (Gazzaniga & Sperry, 1967; Sperry & Gazzaniga, 1967; Gazzaniga, 1970; Zaidel, 1976, 1977, 1978). Furthermore, these investigations have shown that the disconnected right hemisphere, although surprisingly able to understand the meaning of single words (Zaidel, 1976, 1978), performs very poorly on tasks requiring phonemic analysis (Springer & Gazzaniga, 1975; Levy & Trevarthen, 1977; Zaidel, 1974, 1978) and seems to possess only a limited syntactic capability (Gazzaniga, 1970; Gazzaniga & Hillyard, 1971; Zaidel, 1978). These data are of great interest, as they suggest that the structure of right hemisphere language is particular and that the linguistic skills of the right hemisphere cannot be considered as a faded but faithful reproduction of the left hemisphere linguistic competence (Zaidel, 1978). It must be acknowledged, on the other hand, that extreme caution is necessary in drawing general models about the hemispheric representation of language from data obtained in split-brain patients, as these patients, owing to their early brain damage because of epileptic seizures, might have a cerebral organi-

COGNITIVE PROCESSING IN
THE RIGHT HEMISPHERE

zation of functions different from that found in normal subjects (Searleman, 1977; Gazzaniga & LeDoux, 1978). Models based on data from split-brain patients should, therefore, be confirmed by results obtained in normal subjects (studied by means of special behavioral or neurophysiological procedures) and by data obtained in other forms of brain pathology.

Three forms of cerebral pathology have been of particular interest from this point of view:

1. Subjects submitted after childhood to a left hemispherectomy (Smith, 1966; Gott, 1973; Burklund & Smith, 1977)
2. Patients affected by extensive and long-standing lesions of the left hemisphere and in particular patients showing the syndrome of the so-called deep dyslexia (Marshall & Newcombe, 1973; Coltheart, Patterson, & Marshall, 1980)
3. Patients suffering from lesions restricted to the right hemisphere

We have conducted investigations along this last line of research. In what follows, we shall report the results of these studies and discuss them in light of other data, particularly that obtained in split-brain patients.

LANGUAGE DISORDERS ASSOCIATED WITH RIGHT HEMISPHERE DAMAGE

Eisenson (1962) and Critchley (1962) were the first authors to claim that right hemisphere lesions, although producing no clinically apparent aphasia, may nevertheless give rise to subtle linguistic deficits. As these deficits are more apparent in tasks requiring the use of abstract concepts, Eisenson (1962) assumed that the right hemisphere might be involved in "super- or extraordinary language functions." Such claims were criticized by other authors (e.g., Lenneberg, 1967) who maintained that more economical interpretations could also account for the findings obtained by Eisenson and Critchley. Nonetheless, a variety of other language disturbances in right-damaged patients were subsequently described by Marcie, Hécaen, Dubois, and Angelergues (1965), who reported (*a*) phonological errors on repetition tasks in patients with frontorolandic lesions of the right hemisphere, and (*b*) a general tendency to perseverate on both oral tasks (of lexical choice and of grammatical transformation) and writing tasks (with frequent iterations of strokes and letters).

Even more relevant to the problem of right hemisphere language organization are data obtained by Lesser (1974) in studying various aspects of language comprehension in right- and left-brain-damaged patients. Lesser (1974) found that right-brain-damaged patients in fact score significantly worse than normal controls on a test of semantic-lexical discrimination, although obtaining normal scores on a phonological and a syntax test. These data are well in line with the model of right hemisphere language organization drawn from the study of split-brain patients, but can be submitted to a certain criticism, as the author did not control for the influence of associated variables (such as unilateral spatial neglect and general mental deterioration) that could in part account for the semantic confusion of her right-brain-damaged patients. For example, patients studied by Lesser were requested to point to the picture corresponding to a word pronounced aloud by the examiner, selecting it from an array of spatially arranged figures. Now it has been shown by various authors (Gainotti, 1968; Jones, 1969; Oxbury, Campbell, & Oxbury, 1974) that in such a multiple choice test situation, right-brain-damaged patients tend to ignore the responses lying on the left half of the page, pointing only to pictures on the right half. Semantic-lexical errors obtained by right-brain-damaged patients could therefore be due more to the influence of unilateral spatial neglect than to a specifically semantic impairment. Furthermore, it has been shown by Archibald and Wepman (1968) that the subtle language disturbances of right-brain-damaged patients are generally observed in a context of widespread mental deterioration. Now, since semantic confusion is a common feature of general cognitive impairment (Tissot, Richard, Duval, & Ajuriaguerra, 1967; Irigaray, 1973), we cannot dismiss a priori the possibility that semantic-lexical errors of right-brain-damaged patients are primarily due to a certain degree of general mental deterioration. As Lesser had not controlled for the influence of unilateral spatial neglect and of widespread cognitive impairment, we thought it useful to reconsider the meaning of semantic disorders of language comprehension in right-brain-damaged patients. Thus, our first study (Gainotti, Caltagirone, & Miceli, 1979) was designed to determine the following:

1. Whether results obtained by Lesser, and in particular the semantic-lexical impairment of right-brain-damaged patients, could be confirmed by administering to normal controls and right-brain-damaged patients a test constructed to study simultaneously both the phonemic and the semantic aspects of auditory language comprehension
2. Whether semantic errors observed in right-brain-damaged patients are due to a proper linguistic impairment or are, at least in part, attributable to the influence of unilateral spatial neglect

3. Whether these errors are due to the lesion of the right hemisphere per se or are mainly to the concomitant effect of a widespread mental deterioration.

GENERAL METHODOLOGY

All the investigations reported in this chapter were conducted on large groups of unselected right-brain-damaged patients, suffering either from cerebro-vascular disease or from brain tumor. Although no selection was made in forming the groups, ambidextrous or left-handed patients, subjects of a very low sociocultural level, and patients with clinical, EEG, or neuroradiological evidence of bilateral brain damage were excluded. Control subjects suffered either from psychoneurosis or from nervous system lesions located below the level of the cervical spine. Special care was taken to ensure that there were no significant differences between normal controls and right-brain-damaged patients with respect to age, sex, and education.

Relationship between Semantic Discrimination Errors, Lesion of the Right Hemisphere, and Associated Variables

The impairment of the semantic system at the receptive level was investigated in our first study (Gainotti, Caltagirone, & Miceli, 1979) by administering to 110 right-brain-damaged patients and to 94 normal controls a test of auditory language comprehension (the *Verbal Sound and Meaning Discrimination Test*), which had proved in previous studies (Gainotti, Caltagirone, & Ibba, 1975; Gainotti, 1976) to be useful for evaluating the degree of semantic disintegration in aphasia. The test consists of 20 simple, concrete depictable nouns, which are read aloud by the examiner one at a time, while the patient looks at a card containing 6 pictures, arranged in two vertical columns, on the right and on the left half of the sheet. One of the pictures on the card corresponds to the stimulus word; the name of the object represented in a second picture is phonemically very similar to the correct word; and the object represented in a third picture is semantically very similar. The objects represented in the remaining three pictures have no relation to the stimulus word from either the semantic or the phonemic point of view. Patients are requested to point to the picture corresponding to the word read aloud by the examiner. If, instead of giving the correct response, they point to the phonemically similar alternative, this is considered a phonemic discrimination error; if they select the semantically related picture, this is considered a semantic discrimination error. As the main purpose of our investigation was to study the meaning of semantic discrimination errors shown by right-brain-damaged patients, we focused our attention on this type of error throughout our research. However, as data obtained by Lesser (1974) had suggested a marked discrepancy between the clear impairment observed at the semantic level and a lack of impairment at the phonemic level, the incidence of phonemic discrimination errors was also looked at in the first part of this study.

In the second part of this study, the influence of unilateral spatial neglect and of widespread mental impairment on semantic discrimination errors was more specifically investigated. The *influence of unilateral spatial neglect* was evaluated by distinguishing between semantic errors obtained on items in which the correct picture was placed on the right versus the left half of the card. It was reasoned that, as right-brain-damaged patients tend to ignore items lying on the left half of the sheet, unilateral spatial neglect should have no deleterious effect on the items in which the correct response is placed on the right half. Semantic discrimination errors made on this part of the test should, therefore, be considered as due to semantic disintegration proper and not to inattention for the items lying on the half sheet contralateral to the hemispheric locus of lesion. Finally, in order to determine whether semantic discrimination errors are mainly due to the lesion of the right hemisphere per se or to the *influence of a concomitant general cognitive impairment,* all right-brain-damaged patients received a *mental deterioration battery,* which has been shown capable of discriminating at a satisfactory level normal controls from demented patients (Caltagirone, Gainotti, Masullo, & Miceli, 1979). The battery is composed both of verbal and of visuospatial tasks and was constructed to test intelligence, memory, and constructive capabilities in focal and diffuse brain-damaged patients.

RESULTS

Number of Semantic and of Phonemic Errors Obtained by Normal Controls and by Right-Brain-Damaged Patients. Phonemic discrimination errors were rather infrequent both in normal controls (NC) and in right-brain-damaged patients (RBP), whereas semantic discrimination errors were much more frequent. The mean number of phonemic errors was, in fact, .38 in NC and .57 in RBP, whereas the mean number of semantic discrimination errors was 1.38 in NC and 2.67 in right-brain-damaged patients. As the distribution of scores did not allow the use of parametric tests, the statistical value of these differences was checked by means of the Mann–Whitney U

Test. The statistical testing showed that the number of phonemic errors does not discriminate NC from RBP at a significant level ($z = .425$; $p = .33$) whereas the number of semantic errors clearly distinguishes the former group from the latter ($z = 5,46$; $p < .001$).

As phonemic discrimination errors were so infrequent both in NC and in RBD, they were eliminated from further analysis, and the meaning of semantic discrimination errors was more carefully investigated.

Influence of Unilateral Spatial Neglect and of General Mental Deterioration upon Semantic Discrimination Errors.   When the influence of unilateral spatial neglect was ruled out, by taking into account only the items of the test for which the correct response was placed on the right half of the sheet, no significant difference remained between NC and RBP: The mean number of semantic errors decreased slightly (from 1.38 to .90) in NC, proportionally to the reduced number of items taken into account, but much more dramatically (from 2.67 to 1.19) in RBP, showing that most of the semantic errors obtained on this test by right-brain-damaged patients are due to unilateral spatial neglect and not to a real semantic impairment. Furthermore, when a distinction was made between "deteriorated" and "nondeteriorated" patients (on the basis of the results obtained on the mental deterioration battery), nondeteriorated right-brain-damaged patients obtained a mean number of semantic errors only slightly greater than that obtained by normal controls (1.82 versus 1.38), whereas patients affected by a general mental deterioration made a much higher number ($\bar{x} = 4.66$) of semantic discrimination errors.

The significance of the differences observed among normal controls, nondeteriorated and deteriorated right-brain-damaged patients was tested by means of the Mann–Whitney U Test. This analysis revealed a mild but significant difference between NC and nondeteriorated RBP ($z = 2.06$; $p < .0394$) and a much more significant difference between patients affected by a diffuse mental impairment and normal controls ($z = 6.96$; $p < .001$) or nondeteriorated RBP ($z = 5.83$; $p < .001$).

DISCUSSION

To summarize in few lines the results of our first study, we can say that our findings confirm Lesser's (1974) claim of a significant and rather selective impairment of the semantic level of integration of language in right-brain-damaged patients, but at the same time cast some doubts on the specificity of the relationship existing between semantic discrimination errors and right hemisphere damage: Both unilateral spatial neglect and general cognitive impairment seemed in part responsible for the semantic discrimination errors shown by right-brain-damaged patients, even if not all the signs of semantic impariment shown by RBP could be attributed to the influence of these associated variables.

This puzzling situation was further complicated by the possibility that the very low number of phonemic discrimination errors obtained by both NC and RBP on the Verbal Sound and Meaning Discrimination Test might be due, at least in part, to methodological factors. Thus, given that in our test phonemic and semantic errors were in competition (for each item the subject could point only to the phonemically or to the semantically related alternative), it is possible that the low number of phonemic discrimination errors was due to the masking effect of the more powerful semantic alternatives over the phonemic ones. As a matter of fact, since in a word comprehension task identification of meaning is probably the critical factor, orienting the analysis of the phonological structure of the intended word, it seems logical that semantic discrimination errors may dominate and eventually mask phonemic discrimination errors. On the other hand, the influence of the semantic level of language over the phonemic one cannot be avoided by using phonemic discrimination tests similar to the one used by Lesser (1974). As has been pointed out by Basso, Casati, and Vignolo (1977), these procedures inevitably involve the semantic level as well as the phonemic one.

It was therefore decided to again investigate the problem of the selectivity of semantic-lexical impairment of right-brain-damaged patients, by studying phonemic disorders with a testing technique based on the use of nonsense verbal material, and semantic disorders with two tests of semantic-lexical discrimination based on auditory and on visual data. To study more closely the influence of right hemisphere damage per se on semantic discrimination impairment, special care was taken to rule out the influence of unilateral spatial neglect, by constructing tests of semantic discrimination in which no activity of lateral visual exploration was required of the patients.

Selective Impairment of Semantic-Lexical Discrimination in Right-Brain-Damaged Patients

Three main factors distinguished our second study (Gainotti, Caltagirone, Miceli, & Masullo, 1981) from the first one:

1. Semantic and phonemic discrimination were studied by means of independent tests constructed with the aim of examining in isolation the semantic and the phonemic levels of language.
2. The deleterious influence of unilateral spatial neglect was ruled out

by presenting the multiple choice alternatives arranged in a vertical array, so that no activity of lateral visual exploration was requested of the patients.

3. In addition to a task of *auditory language comprehension,* a task of *reading comprehension* was also used to study semantic-lexical discrimination at the receptive level. Zaidel (1978) has shown that, in the disconnected right hemisphere the auditory lexicon is much richer than the visual lexicon. So, it seemed useful to determine whether semantic-lexical errors observed after right hemisphere damage are more evident when lexical representation is accessed through the auditory rather than the visual modality.

In order to resolve these questions, 50 right-brain-damaged patients and 39 control subjects were given (*a*) two tests of semantic-lexical discrimination (the auditory language comprehension and the reading comprehension tests), (*b*)a phoneme discrimination test, and (*c*) the mental deterioration battery used in our previous study. The tests of auditory language comprehension and reading comprehension were both multiple choice tests requiring the patient to point to the picture corresponding to the stimulus word, by selecting it from among three semantically similar alternatives arranged in a vertical column in the middle of the response plate. However, in the auditory language comprehension test the stimulus word was pronounced aloud by the examiner, whereas in the reading comprehension test it was written in large characters at the bottom of the column formed by the multiple choice pictures. Both tests consisted of 20 items. The maximum score obtainable on each test was, therefore, 20.

The phoneme discrimination test used in this second study has been described in detail elsewhere (Miceli, Caltagirone, Gainotti, & Payer-Rigo, 1978). It is based on the capability of the patient to discriminate, under normal listening conditions, whether two nonsense syllables, pronounced aloud by the examiner, are identical or different. Stimuli are the syllables *prin, trin, krin, brin, drin,* and *grin,* which in Italian are meaningless and which are contrasted only for the features of voice, and/or place of articulation of the initial stop consonant. In the test, each syllable is paired with itself and with every other syllable; each pair of different syllables is presented twice and each pair of identical syllables three times. Thus, the test comprises 48 randomly ordered pairs of syllables, of which 30 are different and 18 are identical. One point is given for each pair correctly judged as identical or different. The maximum score obtainable is, then, 48.

The mental deterioration battery has already been described, in conjunction with our first study, where it was used to make a broad distinction between "deteriorated" and "nondeteriorated" patients. Of the right-brain-damaged patients in the present study, 11 were considered as showing a widespread cognitive impairment, whereas the remaining 39 were judged as nondeteriorated.

RESULTS

Errors Obtained on the Tests of Semantic and of Phonemic Discrimination by Right-Brain-Damaged Patients and Normal Controls. The mean number of errors obtained by normal controls and by right-brain-damaged patients on the tests of auditory language comprehension, of reading comprehension, and of phoneme discrimination are reported in Table 8.1. Because the distribution of scores again did not allow the use of parametric tests, the significance of the differences observed between normal controls and right-brain-damaged patients (taken as a whole and subdivided into "deteriorated" and "nondeteriorated") was controlled by means of the Mann–Whitney U test.

The first statistical control concerned the differences observed between normal subjects and right-brain-damaged patients taken as a whole on the

Table 8.1

MEAN NUMBER OF ERRORS OBTAINED ON THE SEMANTIC AND PHONEMIC DISCRIMINATION TESTS BY NORMAL CONTROLS AND BY DETERIORATED AND NONDETERIORATED RIGHT-BRAIN-DAMAGED PATIENTS

	Normal controls ($N = 39$)		Right-brain-damaged patients ($N = 50$)	
Semantic tests				
Auditory language			Deteriorated (y_1)	
comprehension	$x = .36$	$y = 1.35$	($N = 11$)	$y_1 = 2.78$
			Nondeterior. (y_2)	
			($N = 39$)	$y_2 = .95$
Reading			Deteriorated	
comprehension	$x = .40$	$y = .99$	($N = 11$)	$y_1 = 2.45$
			Nondeterior.	
			($N = 39$)	$y_2 = .58$
			Deteriorated	
Phoneme discrimination test	$x = 1.51$	$y = 2.82$	($N = 11$)	$y_1 = 5.73$
			Nondeterior.	
			($N = 39$)	$y_2 = 1.74$

tests of semantic and of phonemic discrimination. This difference reached a high level of statistical significance on the semantic tests of auditory language comprehension ($z = 3.720; p < .001$) and of reading comprehension ($z = 3.001; p < .002$), but did not reach the level of statistical confidence on the test of phoneme discrimination ($z = 1.441; p = .077$).

The next step consisted of checking the significance of the differences observed between normal controls, nondeteriorated and deteriorated right-brain-damaged patients. The difference between RBP showing signs of general cognitive impairment and the other two groups—normal controls and nondeteriorated right-brain-damaged patients—reached on each test a very high level of statistical significance. This finding is not surprising as the data reported in Table 8.1 show that patients affected by a general mental deterioration are much more severely impaired than any other group both on the semantic and on the phonemic discrimination tests. On the other hand, when normal controls were compared with nondeteriorated right-brain-damaged patients, a much more selective pattern of impairment emerged. As a matter of fact, a highly significant level of confidence was obtained only for the semantic test of auditory language comprehension ($z = 2.544; p < .005$); the difference between the two groups just barely failed to reach the significance level on the test of reading comprehension ($z = 1.621; p = .054$) and was far from significant on the test of phoneme discrimination ($z = 0.907; p = .166$).

Comparison between the Number of Semantic Errors Obtained in the Auditory and in the Visual Modality. Data reported in Table 8.1 seem to show that the number of semantic errors made by right-brain-damaged patients is higher when the lexical representation is accessed through the auditory modality than when it is accessed through the visual modality. The significance of this difference was controlled both in the whole sample of RBP and in the subgroups of nondeteriorated and deteriorated RBP, by means of the Wilcoxon test. The level of statistical significance was never reached, but the tendency to make more errors on the test of auditory language comprehension than on the test of reading comprehension was consistent in each comparison undertaken within the right-brain-damaged patients, whereas an analogous trend was not observed within the normal controls.

DISCUSSION

The main results of our second investigation can be summarized as follows:

1. Right-brain-damaged patients scored significantly worse than normal controls on two multiple choice tests of semantic discrimination, in which special care had been taken to minimize the effects of unilateral spatial inattention.
2. No significant difference was found in contrast, when results obtained on a phonemic discrimination test were analyzed.
3. Most of the semantic errors obtained by RBP were due to the influence of a general mental deterioration, but some seemed attributable to the lesion of the right hemisphere per se and not to the effect of associated variables. When a separate analysis of the scores obtained by deteriorated and nondeteriorated RBP was undertaken, a significant difference was still found between nondeteriorated right-brain-damaged patients and normal controls.
4. The number of semantic errors was slightly higher when the lexical representation was accessed through the auditory than when accessed through the visual modality, but this difference did not reach the level of statistical significance.

Results of this second investigation seemed, therefore, to show that right hemispheric lesions selectively impair semantic-lexical discrimination and that this impairment is in part due to the lesion of the right hemisphere per se and not to the effect of associated variables (such as unilateral spatial neglect and/or general mental deterioration).

However, it has been observed (e.g., Hécaen, personal communication) that defective performances of right-brain-damaged patients on tasks of semantic discrimination using pictorial material as multiple choice responses could be in part due to the subtle visuoperceptual disability that is often produced by lesions of the right hemisphere. Furthermore, it has been observed (Goldblum, personal communication) that if a true semantic-lexical impairment underlies the semantic discrimination errors of right-brain-damaged patients, then such an impairment should also be manifested in the verbal output of these patients, in the form of semantic paraphasic substitutions. Although very few data on this problem are available in the neurolinguistic literature, some findings reported by Oldfield (1966) could be in line with the hypothesis of a semantic-lexical impairment of right-brain-damaged patients not limited to the receptive level. Oldfield found a significant difference between the response latencies of normal controls and right-brain-damaged patients, when submitted to a test of visual naming. However, as the data reported by Oldfield gave only indirect support to the hypothesis of a semantic impairment of right-brain-damaged patients, we thought it useful to control more directly the criterion proposed by Goldblum, by administering a task of confrontation naming to large groups of normal controls and right-brain-damaged patients. Hence, our third study was designed to investigate the following:

1. Whether right-brain-damaged patients show significantly more errors than normal controls on a test of visual naming
2. Whether the errors of these patients are due to a true semantic-lexical disorder or to a visuoperceptual confusion.

Naming Errors on Confrontation of Right-Brain-Damaged Patients: The Influence of Visual and of Semantic Disturbances

The influence of visuoperceptual disabilities and of semantic-lexical disorders on scores obtained by right-brain-damaged patients submitted to a task of confrontation naming was studied by administering to 65 RBP and to 74 NC, 20 simple colored figures, very similar from the pictorial point of view to the figures used in the tests of auditory language comprehension and reading comprehension. It was reasoned that if errors made by right-brain-damaged patients on tests of semantic-lexical discrimination are due mainly to visuoperceptual disturbances, then instances of visual confusion should also be observed when patients are requested to name a pictorially similar visual material. If, on the contrary, semantic discrimination disturbances are chiefly due to properly lexical (and not to visuoperceptual) defects, then one should observe instances of semantic paraphasia in the course of a confrontation naming test. Because it can be difficult to decide if the wrong response produced by a patient on a test of visual naming is due to a visuoperceptual disorder or to a true semantic-lexical impairment, great care was taken to avoid the intrusion of uncontrolled subjective factors (such as a priori personal expectations) in the analysis of naming errors. Thus, it was decided to pool all the responses produced by normal controls and by right-brain-damaged patients and considered wrong by five blind judges. The same judges were also requested to distinguish the wrong responses into three main categories: (*a*) those probably due to a visual disorder; (*b*) those probably due to a semantic confusion; and (*c*) those related to the stimulus by both perceptual and semantic links. For example, when the stimulus was the picture of an apple, the response "a ball" was considered as due to a *visual impairment,* "a pear" as a *semantic confusion,* and "a peach" as a *visual–semantic response.*

In addition to errors that fell into one of these three categories, some responses seemed to bear no obvious visual or semantic link to the stimulus (*unrelated responses,* e.g., "a door"); yet others consisted in giving, instead of the specific name of the stimulus object, the name of the class (e.g., "a fruit") to which the object belonged (*generic responses*). However, as unrelated responses and generic responses were rather uncommon within the right-brain-damaged patients, and as they were not very relevant to the specific aim of our investigation, they were not taken into separate account in our study. Besides the total number of wrong responses, only the following three categories of naming errors were, therefore, specifically taken into account:

1. Visually (and nonsemantically) related errors
2. Semantically (and nonvisually) related errors
3. Visually and semantically related naming errors

The following hypotheses were advanced:

- If semantic discrimination errors committed by right-brain-damaged patients on tasks of auditory language comprehension and of reading comprehension are due chiefly to visuoperceptual disorders, then these patients should present mainly visual and visual–semantic errors on the naming task.
- If, on the contrary, these errors are due chiefly to a true semantic-lexical impairment, then right-brain-damaged patients should present mainly semantic and visual–semantic errors on the task of confrontation naming.

RESULTS

Incidence of the Various Types of Naming Errors in Normal Controls, Deteriorated and Nondeteriorated Right-Brain-Damaged Patients. As in our previous studies, results obtained on the mental deterioration battery were used to make a broad distinction between deteriorated and nondeteriorated right-brain-damaged patients: Of 65 RBP, 14 were considered as deteriorated, the other 51 as nondeteriorated. Seventy-four normal controls were also used.

Table 8.2 reports the number of NC, of nondeteriorated RBP, and of deteriorated RBP who presented one or more incorrect responses of the various types on the test of visual naming. Data reported in Table 8.2 show that deteriorated RBP obtain the highest incidence of naming errors, both when the overall number of wrong responses is considered and when separate account is taken of visual errors and of semantic confusions. Results

Table 8.2
NUMBER OF NORMAL CONTROLS AND OF RIGHT-BRAIN-DAMAGED PATIENTS
SHOWING ONE OR MORE INCORRECT RESPONSES

	Number of subjects showing naming error		
Category of naming errors	Normal controls ($N = 74$)	Deteriorated RBP ($N = 14$)	Nondeteriorated RBP ($N = 51$)
Semantic errors	4 (5.4%)	10 (71.0%)	9 (17.6%)
Visual errors	4 (6.7%)	9 (64.0%)	7 (13.8%)
Visual–semantic errors	5 (6.7%)	2 (14.3%)	13 (25.5%)
Total number of wrong responses	19 (26.0%)	12 (86.0%)	24 (47.0%)

obtained on confrontation naming are therefore very similar to those observed on the tasks of auditory language comprehension and of reading comprehension, since in any case most errors made by right-brain-damaged patients are due to the influence of a concomitant general mental impairment. Furthermore, data reported in Table 8.2 suggest that both visuoperceptual disorders and semantic-lexical confusions can account for the semantic discrimination errors shown by deteriorated right-brain-damaged patients. If we analyze the types of naming errors made by nondeteriorated RBP, we see that these patients produce mainly visual–semantic and purely semantic errors and that only a relatively small number of their wrong responses can be classified as purely visual. From the statistical point of view, the difference between NC and nondeteriorated RBP was significant when separate account was taken of the visuosemantic errors ($\chi^2 = 7.15$; $p <$ .01), just failed to reach the level of statistical confidence when the purely semantic errors were considered ($\chi^2 = 3.64$; $p \leq .10$), and was far from significance when the purely visual errors were taken into account ($\chi^2 = 0.98$; $p = $ n.s.).

These findings clearly argue against the hypothesis that semantic discrimination errors of right-brain-damaged patients may be due to a purely visuoperceptual disorder and rather point to the existence in these patients of a true semantic-lexical impairment.

GENERAL DISCUSSION

We must be cautious before attributing to the loss of a specific linguistic capacity of the right hemisphere the subtle language disturbances that can be observed in studies conducted on large groups of right-brain-damaged patients. We must, for example, acknowledge that inasmuch as the exact nature of the relationships between handedness and language lateralization remains unclear (Searleman, 1977) the exclusion from these studies of left-handed and ambidextrous patients does not guarantee that all the subjects had a "normal" representation of language at the level of the left hemisphere. Furthermore, even if special care is taken to exclude patients with EEG, clinical, or neuroradiological evidence of bilateral brain damage, we cannot rule out the possibility that some patients might have, in addition to an obvious right hemisphere damage, a small, subclinical lesion of the left hemisphere. Such possibilities could lead us to attribute to a disrupted linguistic capacity of the right hemisphere disturbances that are in reality due to the existence of a diffuse representation of language or to the presence of a bilateral brain damage. However, even proceeding with the cautiousness suggested by these considerations, it must be acknowledged that the pattern of impairment shown by right-brain-damaged patients studied in the present investigations seems fairly selective and that it draws a sort of mirror image of the linguistic capabilities described as characteristic of the intact right hemisphere. In fact, data obtained in split-brain patients (Zaidel, 1974, 1976, & 1978) and in subjects submitted after the childhood to a left ("dominant") hemispherectomy (Smith, 1966; Gott, 1973; Burklund & Smith, 1977) have consistently shown that the *intact right hemisphere* (*a*) possesses a high capability to understand the meaning of single words, (*b*) performs very poorly on tasks requiring phonemic analysis, and (*c*) has an auditory lexicon that is richer than its visual lexicon. Conversely, results of the investigations reported here have shown that *right-brain-damaged patients:* (*a*) score significantly worse than normal controls on various tasks of semantic-lexical discrimination even when the influence of associated variables (such as unilateral spatial neglect or general cognitive impairment) is ruled out; (*b*) do not perform worse than normal controls when the number of phonemic errors obtained on two different tests of word comprehension and of nonsense syllables discrimination is taken into account; (*c*) tend to commit a higher number of semantic errors when the lexical representation is accessed through the auditory modality than when it is accessed through the visual (reading) modality. Furthermore, the hypothesis of a selective semantic impairment of right-brain-damaged patients was confirmed by the results obtained on the confrontation naming task, in which naming errors due to a semantic-lexical confusion were carefully distinguished from errors due to a visuoperceptual disorder. In fact, non-deteriorated right-brain-damaged patients showed an incidence of pathological responses higher than normal controls when semantic and visual–

semantic responses were considered, but did not differ from control subjects when purely visual errors were considered. These results clearly suggest that semantic discrimination errors of right-brain-damaged patients are due to true semantic-lexical disorders and not to more peripheral visuoperceptual disabilities.

It must be acknowledged, on the other hand, that the hypothesis of a causal relationship between disruption of the right hemisphere linguistic competence and subtle language disturbances observed in the present investigations can be criticized on theoretical grounds. Given the dominance of the left hemisphere for all types of linguistic functions, it might be predicted that in right-brain-damaged patients the intact left hemisphere would assume entirely the functions that in a normal brain it shares with the right hemisphere. The lesion of the right hemisphere should therefore have a very limited effect upon the performance obtained on a verbal task, irrespective of the level of competence that the normal right hemisphere could have for that task.

How, then, might we reconcile the results of our research with the substance of this objection? In our opinion, a possible solution might be to assume that, when it is submitted to a task demanding complex linguistic discrimination (as was the case in our investigations) the brain makes use of each useful contribution and enlists the support both of the major linguistic competence of the left hemisphere and of the supplementary linguistic capabilities of the right hemisphere. If this assumption is correct, we should find a mild but nonhomogeneous pattern of impairment in right-brain-damaged patients submitted to various tasks of linguistic discrimination. No impairment should be found on tasks for which the right hemisphere is incompetent, whereas a mild impairment should be found on tasks to which the right hemisphere can bring a useful contribution. This prediction is quite consistent with the discrepancy observed by Lesser (1974), by Coughlan and Warrington (1978), and by ourselves in the present investigations, between the results obtained by right-brain-damaged patients on lexical-semantic versus phonemic discrimination tasks: Right hemispheric lesions consistently affected semantic-lexical discrimination (in accordance with the semantic-lexical capabilities of the right hemisphere) but did not hamper phonemic discrimination (in accordance with the inability of the right hemisphere to perform tasks requiring a phonemic analysis).

An alternative and more reductive explanation of these findings would be to attribute the semantic-lexical errors of right-brain-damaged patients to a high-level cognitive defect, rather than to a specifically linguistic impairment (Coughlan & Warrington, 1978) and to assume that this high-level cognitive defect would impair semantic discrimination more than phonemic discrimination. Results of the investigations reported here cannot rule out this hypothesis, as on one hand, they have shown that nondeteriorated right-brain-damaged patients are significantly more impaired than normal controls on various tasks of semantic discrimination, but, on the other hand, they have shown that most semantic errors of right-brain-damaged patients are under the influence of a general mental deterioration. It is therefore possible that the subtle semantic impairment of our "nondeteriorated" right-brain-damaged patients was attributable to the influence of a mild, subclinical form of mental deterioration. A strategy that could perhaps be used to solve this difficult question, by disentangling the cognitive from the properly linguistic factors, involves distinguishing between two parts of the lexicon, namely, between abstract versus concrete words. It has been claimed (e.g., Ellis & Shepherd, 1974; Hines, 1976; Day, 1977; McFarland, McFarland, Bain, & Ashton, 1978) that concrete words are represented at the level of the right hemisphere, whereas abstract words are not. Thus, if we administer to right-brain-damaged patients tests involving the discrimination of both concrete and abstract words, it should be possible to make the following predictions:

- If semantic discrimination errors of right-brain-damaged patients are due to disruption of the specific lexical competence of the right hemisphere, discrimination of concrete words should be more impaired than discrimination of abstract words.
- If, on the contrary, semantic errors of right-brain-damaged patients are due to a high-level cognitive defect and not to the disruption of a specific lexical competence, discrimination of abstract words should be more impaired than discrimination of concrete words.

In any event, although the exact meaning of the findings obtained in the investigations reported here remains speculative, the results of our investigations consistently show that right hemisphere lesions produce a selective disorder of the semantic level of language. This finding supports the assumption of a relative autonomy of lexical representation from the phonological and syntactic structures and suggests that the neural mechanisms underlying phonology, syntax, and lexical-semantics may be, at least in part, independent.

REFERENCES

Archibald, Y. M., & Wepman, J. M. Language disturbance and nonverbal cognitive performance in eight patients following injury to the right hemisphere. *Brain,* 1968, *91,* 117–130.

Basso, A., Casati, G., & Vignolo, L. A. Phonemic identification defect in aphasia. *Cortex*, 1977, *13*, 84–95.

Burklund, C. W., & Smith, A. Language and the cerebral hemispheres. Observations of verbal and nonverbal responses during 18 months following left ("dominant") hemispherectomy. *Neurology*, 1977, *27*, 627–633.

Caltagirone, C., Gainotti, G., Masullo, C., & Miceli, G. Validity of some neuropsychological tests in the assessment of mental deterioration. *Acta Psychiatrica Scandinavica*, 1979, *60*, 50–56.

Coltheart, M., Patterson, K. E., & Marshall, J. C. *Deep dyslexia*. London: Routledge and Kegan Paul, 1980.

Coughlan, A. D., & Warrington, E. K. Word-comprehension and word-retrieval in patients with localized cerebral lesions. *Brain*, 1978, *101*, 163–185.

Critchley, M. Speech and speech-loss in relation to the duality of the brain. In V. B. Mountcastle (Ed.), *Interhemispheric relations and cerebral dominance*. Baltimore: Johns Hopkins University Press, 1962.

Day, J. Right-hemisphere language processing in normal right-handers. *Journal of Experimental Psychology: Human Perception and Performance*, 1977, *3*, 518–528.

Eisenson, J. Language and intellectual modifications associated with right cerebral damage. *Language and Speech*, 1962, *5*, 49–53.

Ellis, H. D., & Shepherd, J. W. Recognition of abstract and concrete words presented in right and left visual field. *Journal of Experimental Psychology*, 1974, *103*, 1035–1036.

Gainotti, G. Les manifestations de négligence et d'inattention pour l'hémiespace. *Cortex*, 1968, *4*, 64–91.

Gainotti, G. The relationship between semantic impairment in comprehension and naming in aphasic patients. *British Journal of Disorders of Communication*, 1976, *11*, 71–81.

Gainotti, G., Caltagirone, C., & Ibba A. Semantic and phonemic aspects of auditory language comprehension in aphasia. *Linguistics*, 1975, *154/155*, 15–29.

Gainotti, G., Caltagirone, C., & Miceli, G. Semantic disorders of auditory language comprehension in right brain-damaged patients. *Journal of Psycholinguistic Research*, 1979, *8*, 13–20.

Gainotti, G., Caltagirone, C., Miceli, G., & Masullo, C. Selective semantic-lexical impairment of language comprehension in right brain-damaged patients. *Brain and Language* 1981, *13*, 201–211.

Gazzaniga, M. S. *The bisected brain*. New York: Appleton-Century-Crofts, 1970.

Gazzaniga, M. S., and & Hillyard, S. Language and speech capacity of the right hemisphere. *Neuropsychologia*, 1971, *9*, 273–280.

Gazzaniga, M. S., & LeDoux, J. E. *The integrated mind*. New York: Plenum Press, 1978.

Gazzaniga, M. S., & Sperry, R. W. Language after section of the cerebral commissures. *Brain*, 1967, *90*, 131–138.

Gott, P. S. Language after dominant hemispherectomy. *Journal of Neurology, Neurosurgery and Psychiatry*, 1973, *36*, 1082–1088.

Hines, D. Recognition of verbs, abstract nouns and concrete nouns from the left and right visual half fields. *Neuropsychologia*, 1976, *14*, 211–216.

Irigaray, L. *Le langage des déments*. The Hague: Mouton, 1973.

Jones, A. C. Influence of mode of stimulus presentation on performance in facial recognition tasks. *Cortex*, 1969, *5*, 290–301.

Lenneberg, E. H. *Biological foundations of language*. New York: Wiley, 1967.

Lesser, R. Verbal comprehension in aphasia: An English version of three Italian tests. *Cortex*, 1974, *10*, 247–263.

Levy, J., & Trevarthen, C. Perceptual, semantic and phonetic aspects of elementary language processes in split-brain patients. *Brain*, 1977, *100*, 105–118.

Marcie, P., Hécaen, H., Dubois, J., & Angelergues R. Les réalisations du langage chez les malades atteints de lésions de l'hémisphère droit. *Neuropsychologia*, 1965, *3*, 217–245.

Marshall, J. C., & Newcombe, F. Patterns of paralexia: A psycholinguistic approach. *Journal of Psycholinguistic Research*, 1973, *2*, 175–199.

McFarland, K., McFarland, M. L., Bain, J. D., & Ashton, R. Ear differences of abstract and concrete word recognition. *Neuropsychologia*, 1978, *16*, 555–561.

Miceli, G., Caltagirone, C., Gainotti, G., & Payer-Rigo, P. Discrimination of voice versus place contrasts in aphasia. *Brain and Language*, 1978, *6*, 47–51.

Oldfield, R. C. Things, words and the brain. *Quarterly Journal of Experimental Psychology*, 1966, *18*, 340–353.

Oxbury, J. M., Campbell, D. C., & Oxbury, S. M. Unilateral spatial neglect and impairment of spatial analysis and visual perception. *Brain*, 1974, 97, 551–564.

Searleman, A. A review of right hemisphere linguistic capabilities. *Psychological Bulletin*, 1977, *84*, 503–528.

Smith, A. Speech and other functions after left (dominant) hemispherectomy. *Journal of Neurology, Neurosurgery and Psychiatry*, 1966, *29*, 467–471.

Sperry, R. W., & Gazzaniga, M. S. Language following surgical disconnection of the hemispheres. In C. H. Millikan & F. L. Darley (Eds.), *Brain mechanisms underlying speech and language*, New York: Grune & Stratton, 1967.

Springer, S. P., & Gazzaniga, M. S. Dichotic testing of partial and complete split-brain subjects. *Neuropsychologia*, 1975, *13*, 341–346.

Tissot, R., Richard, J., Duval, F., & Ajuriaguerra, J. de Quelques aspects du langage des démences dégénératives du grand âge. *Acta Neurologica Belgica*, 1967, 67, 911–923.

Zaidel, E. Language, dichotic listening and the disconnected hemispheres. Paper presented at the Conference on Human Brain Function, U.C.L.A., Sept. 27, 1974.

Zaidel, E. Auditory vocabulary of the right hemisphere following brain bisection or hemidecortication. *Cortex*, 1976, *12*, 191–211.

Zaidel, E. Unilateral auditory language comprehension on the token test following cerebral commissurotomy and hemispherectomy. *Neuropsychologia*, 1977, *15*, 1–18.

Zaidel, E. Auditory language comprehension in the right hemisphere following cerebral commissurotomy and hemispherectomy: A comparison with child language and aphasia. In A. Caramazza & E. B. Zurif (Eds.), *Language acquisition and language breakdown: Parallels and divergencies*. Baltimore: Johns Hopkins University Press, 1978.

9

Missing the Point:
The Role of the Right Hemisphere
in the Processing of
Complex Linguistic Materials[1]

HOWARD GARDNER
HIRAM H. BROWNELL
WENDY WAPNER
DIANE MICHELOW

On December 31, 1974, Associate Justice William O. Douglas, long one of the most impressive and vigorous members of the United States Supreme Court, suffered a stroke. At first, it appeared that Douglas would recover quickly and resume his place on the Court. Overly optimistic news reports indicated that "the stroke has not affected the Justice's brain [sic]"; other accounts dwelled on the fact that the Justice was still able to talk and, be-

[1]This chapter reports research conducted over the past several years at the Aphasia Research Center, Department of Neurology, Boston University School of Medicine, and the Boston Veterans Administration Medical Center. The research was supported by the National Institute of Neurological Diseases, Communication Disorders, and Stroke (NS 11408), the Veterans Administration, and Harvard Project Zero. Earlier versions of this chapter were presented at the International Neuropsychology Symposium, Dubrovnik, Yugoslavia, June 1979; the Academy of Aphasia, San Diego, October 1979; and the Conference on Cognitive Processes and the Right Hemisphere, New York University, October 1980. In addition, much of the research reported here was described in more preliminary form in Wapner, Hamby, and Gardner, "The Role of the Right Hemisphere in the Processing of Complex Linguistic Materials," *Brain and Language*, 1981, *14*, 15–33. We thank the editor of that journal, Prof. Harry Whitaker, and Academic Press for permission to adapt portions of that article.

cause the stroke had affected the left side of his body, was still able to write with his preferred hand.

As months passed, however, it became increasingly clear that Justice Douglas was seriously impaired and would not be able to resume his full duties on the bench. Rumors circulated, documenting surprising behaviors uncharacteristic of a distinguished jurist. It became a question of when, rather than whether, Justice Douglas would resign.

With the publication of a number of articles and books, in particular that by Woodward and Armstrong (1979), more facts have come to light about Douglas's last months on the Court and the period following his resignation in November 1975. For all public purposes, Douglas acted as if he were fine, as if he could soon assume full work on the Court. He insisted on checking himself out of the hospital where he was receiving rehabilitation and then refused to return. He responded to seriously phrased queries about his condition with offhanded quips: "Walking has very little to do with the work of the Court [Woodward & Armstrong, 1979, 381]"; "If George Blanda can play, why not me? [p. 385]." He insisted in a press release that his arm had been injured in a fall, thereby baldly denying the neurological cause of his paralysis. Occasionally, he acted in a paranoid fashion, claiming, for example, that the Chief Justice's quarters were his and that he was the Chief Justice. During sessions of the Court, he dozed, asked irrelevant questions, and sometimes rambled on.

Finally, after considerable pressure from many quarters over a long period of time, Douglas did resign. But in the sad dénouement to this saga, the Justice refused to accept that he was no longer a member of the Court. He came back to his office, buzzed for his clerks, and, in general, tried to inject himself into the flow of business. He took aggressive steps to assign cases to himself, asked to participate in, author, and even publish separately his own opinions, and he requested that a tenth seat be placed at the Justices' bench. As Chief Justice Burger put it, he was like an old firehouse dog— "too old to run along with the trucks, but his ears prick up just the same [p. 399]." Only after each of the Justice's brethren, including his close friend Brennan, signed a letter in which they explicitly asked him to desist from interfering with the business of the Court, did Justice Douglas retreat from the scene. He continued to ail for the last years of his life, and died amid great honors and tributes on January 19, 1980.

Understandably, there was little discussion in the American press about the causes of Justice Douglas's bizarre reactions and behaviors. In addition to the propriety of such silence, it is impossible to determine in any single case *why* an individual behaves in an unfathomable manner. It might have been that Douglas was becoming senile, that he was reflecting (or emphasizing) aspects of his personality—always difficult, proud, narcissistic—which had been in evidence earlier. In our own view, however, it is most likely that Justice Douglas's behavioral patterns were a direct consequence of his stroke—a massive infarct in the right cerebral hemisphere which left him paralyzed and in great pain for several years.

To suggest that bizarre thoughts, words, and actions are consequent to injury to the right, or nondominant, hemisphere would have seemed an extreme statement some decades ago. For many years after the initial documentation of lateralized representation of language in the human brain (e.g., Broca, 1861), little attention was paid to the higher cognitive sequelae of injury to the right hemisphere. In the wake of more intensive study of the higher cortical functions during and after World War II, evidence began to accumulate that the right hemisphere was dominant for certain functions, in particular those involved in visuospatial processing (Critchley, 1953; Hécaen, 1962; Piercy, 1964; Zangwill, 1960) and in musical processing (Milner, 1962; Wertheim & Botez, 1961). There were also suggestions of a right hemisphere superiority for a "holistic" mode of processing information (Bever & Chiarello, 1974; Bogen, 1969abc; Galin, 1974; Ornstein, 1972). Even these functions, however, were often considered somewhat apart from the most important higher cognitive problem solving functions, which continued to be associated with the left cerebral hemisphere (de Reuck & O'Connor, 1964; Lebrun & Hoops, 1974; Luria, 1966).

The reason for this bias in the neuropsychological literature is readily identified. Language has almost universally been considered the most central human cognitive capacity; and, more so than any other function, language seems (in normal right-handers) to be lateralized to the left cerebral cortex. When individuals become aphasic, following damage to the dominant hemisphere, they almost always show deficits in a range of problem-solving tasks, including those which are not primarily verbal (de Ajuriaguerra & Hécaen, 1964; Head, 1926; Luria, 1966). Thus, although hardly ever tested in a thorough manner, the idea persisted that an individual's cognitive competence is closely linked to the intactness of his left hemisphere, as did the corollary assumption that individuals with right hemisphere damage, their language apparently intact, are not seriously compromised in their ability to understand situations, solve problems, and make their way in the world.

Over the last 20 years, however, much more attention has been paid to the performance by right-hemisphere-injured patients (hereafter, right hemisphere patients) both in formal psychological testing and in informal bedside interactions. These lines of study have yielded an impression of a patient population which, in its own ways, is significantly impaired across a range of capacities. Investigators have described significant impairments in the abilities to express emotions (Ross & Mesulam, 1979) and to detect the emotional aspects of other individuals' expressions and communication (Cicone, Wapner, & Gardner, 1980; Tucker, Watson, & Heilman, 1977); the right hemisphere also seems to be dominant for emotional appropriateness (Gardner, 1975; Geschwind, 1976). In addition, atypical senses of humor have been reported for these patients (Gardner, Ling, Flamm, & Silverman, 1975). There is also considerable documentation of anasagnosia following right hemisphere injury: Patients with such injury are far more likely than left-hemisphere-injured patients to deny their illness, to ignore paralyzed limbs, to claim that they are fine, or to confabulate a spurious cause of their illness, as did Justice Douglas (Weinstein & Kahn, 1955).

Even the most hallowed sanctuary for the left hemisphere—that of language competence—has recently been challenged. Superficially, to be sure, the language of right hemisphere patients seems unexceptional. Such patients have seemingly normal syntax and phonology, and they often can carry on a reasonable conversation. However, closer inspection reveals that such patients often seem to lack a full understanding of the context of an utterance, the presuppositions entailed, the affective tone, or the point of a conversational exchange. They appear to have difficulties in processing abstract sentences, in reasoning logically, and in maintaining a coherent stream of thought—all findings relevant to a documentation of right hemisphere involvement in linguistic processing (cf. Caramazza, Gordon, Zurif, & DeLuca, 1976; Eisenson, 1962; Lezak, 1979).

Experiments in our laboratory have documented further difficulties. Right hemisphere patients are impaired in discerning the connotations of common words (Gardner & Denes, 1973), appreciating antonymic contrasts (Gardner, Silverman, Wapner, & Zurif, 1978; Michelow, Brownell, Masson, Wapner, & Gardner, 1982), and interpreting figures of speech (Winner & Gardner, 1977). In addition, the spontaneous speech of such patients is often excessive and rambling: Their comments may be off-color and their humor primitive and inappropriate; they tend to focus on insignificant details or make tangential remarks; and the usual range of intonation is frequently lacking (Gardner, 1975; Geschwind, 1976; Heeschen & Reischies,

1979; Ross & Mesulam, 1979; Weinstein, 1971). Thus, although less intimately involved with the traditional building blocks of language, the right hemisphere seems pivotal in the processing of extra- or paralinguistic facets of language—facets which contemporary students of language would designate as part of pragmatics or the discourse function of language (Bates, 1976; Foldi, 1982; Sadock, 1974; Searle, 1969).

These various lines of clinical and experimental research dictate the hypothesis that the right hemisphere plays a far more central role in the processing of linguistic materials than had hitherto been suspected. As of yet, however, these various hints have not been followed up systematically within a coordinated program of research. And so it is not known to what extent these various symptoms and syndromes tend to cooccur or to be associated with specific anatomical loci; nor is it known whether, in dealing with language, the right hemisphere plays an especially crucial role in handling specific kinds of content (e.g., those dealing with spatial or emotional information), in employing a particular style of processing (e.g., holistic), in processing information at a certain level of abstraction (e.g., logical reasoning), or in some as yet unspecified fashion.

To secure systematic information on the linguistic functions served at least in part by the right hemisphere, our research group has developed and administered tests of complex linguistic processing to groups of right-hemisphere-damaged subjects, as well as to a number of control groups. Together, these tests make it possible to assess subjects' abilities to understand, integrate, and recall connected discourse in the forms of narrative (i.e., stories of varying types and lengths), jokes, and joke-like linguistic pieces such as puns or puzzles. By conducting this inquiry, which deliberately taps complex linguistic competence from a number of angles, we hope to discover whether certain basic principles can account for the pattern of results recently observed with right hemisphere patients.

In this chapter, we give an interim report of results, amplifying and refining findings reported in our first account of this program of research (Wapner, Hamby, & Gardner, 1981). In addition to providing quantitative data, we have given considerable attention to the type and quality of responses that have typically emerged. To the extent possible, we have indicated which findings characterize the gamut of right hemisphere patients, and which seem restricted to subpopulations. Because of their pronounced language deficits, it has not proved possible to use aphasic patients as a brain-damaged control group in all phases of the study; however, whenever possible, comparison to the performance of aphasic subgroups has been included. In addition, we report results obtained with normal middle-aged and normal aging populations.

TESTS AND PREDICTIONS

1. Stories with Different Contents. The ability of patients to recall story content and to integrate particular story elements has been tested through the administration of four stories. One story concerns a farmer and his lazy hired hand who will not fix a leaking barn; a second concerns a grocer who is robbed; the third describes a fireman and a little girl who has secretly climbed aboard a fire engine just before a fire breaks out; and a fourth describes a fishing trip.

Each story has been composed in such a way that it can be elaborated upon through the insertion of certain additional elements: spatial elements, emotional elements, or noncanonical (bizarre) elements. Each patient hears the first three stories with a different element added in each story. Thus, the spatial version of the Grocer Story includes sentences detailing spatial relations in the story (e.g., "The large moving van concealed the front of a police station"). The noncanonical version of the Farmer Story includes bizarre sentences (e.g., "The farmer decided to give the hired hand a raise"). In the emotional version of the Fireman Story, the bare narrative is elaborated with words and phrases that convey the emotional states of characters explicitly or implicitly (e.g., "The little girl began crying, her heart pounding as she crept in"). The fourth story, The Fishing Trip, includes a spatial, a noncanonical, and a emotional element. After hearing each story, the patient is asked to retell the story in as much detail as possible; he is then asked a set of questions about the main points of the story and the particular elements that have been inserted into the narrative. If a subject answers incorrectly, four answers are read to him and he is asked to select the most appropriate response.

2. Story Recall and Interpretation. To further examine right hemisphere patients' abilities to deal with the many facets of narrative processing, a longer, more fable-like story (The Silver Hammer) has been presented to subjects. Following presentations, subjects are asked to retell the story as accurately as possible. Their spontaneous recall is recorded, transcribed, and then scored on the following dimensions:

A. *Overall Output.* The measure of overall output is a count of both correctly and incorrectly assigned traits and actions produced by a subject during recall.

B. *Confusions*. This measure is a count of the incorrectly assigned traits and actions produced by a subject.

C. *Main Events*. A subject's score on this dimension reflects his recall of a set of six main events which together provide a basic structure for the story.

D. *Confabulations*. This measure is based on statements produced during recall having no obvious relevance to the story, that is, statements other than those included in the measure of overall output.

E. *Sequencing Errors*. A sequencing error is counted each time a subject "backtracks" or violates the temporal ordering of events while retelling the story.

F. *Moral Abstraction*. Success on this variable requires that a subject produce, when asked by the experimenter, an accurate version of the Golden Rule, which is considered the correct moral for the stimulus story.

3. Sentence Arrangement Task. A sentence arrangement task has been administered in which subjects are presented with seven sentences written on individual cards, randomly ordered, and then asked to arrange them into a coherent narrative (cf. Delis, 1980): Content type is varied; some sets of sentences describe temporal, some spatial, and some categorical sequences (e.g., kinship relations). It was hypothesized that right hemisphere subjects would show deficits on spatial and emotional stimuli but not on categorical items (cf. Veroff, 1978). In this paradigm, memorial factors are kept to a minimum. Hence, a more direct examination of patients' sequencing and integrating abilities is possible.

4. Humor Appreciation. To investigate whether the inappropriate humor responses observed in right hemisphere patients could be documented in a formal testing situation, a study was designed specifically to measure humor appreciation in a linguistic modality. This task requires that subjects listen to tape recordings of jokes and joke-like short passages, and then to rate how funny each item is on a scale of 0, (not at all funny) to 5 (very funny). To determine if patients are lured or deceived by the superficial features of jokes, that is, *trappings*, the stimulus items included a set of short story jokes using, for example, unusual person names (Mr. McGillicuddy rather than Mr. Smith) and place names (Timbuktoo rather than Chicago). To test patients' abilities to distinguish funny from unfunny content, stimuli also varied (orthogonally) with respect to *funniness*. To construct the unfunny short story items, punch lines were removed from jokes (selected from the same pool as the funny items) and replaced with straightforward, matter-of-fact resolutions to the jokes' premises.

In addition, several other question and answer item types were studied in less detail. These types included puns (e.g., "What happened to the girl who swallowed a spoon? She couldn't stir"); tricks (e.g., "Why do birds fly south for the winter? It's too far to walk"); puzzles (e.g., "What speaks in every language in the world but never went to school? An echo"); and foils (e.g., "Why do clouds move? The wind pushes them"). These different categories of items were included both to test right hemisphere patients' reactions to different linguistic forms (e.g., puns versus puzzles) and to examine patients' relative funniness ratings within each type.

In addition to the expectations already noted, a number of additional hypotheses were examined in one or more of the tasks:

1. Basic Linguistic Processing. In the story recall tasks, right hemisphere patients should use appropriate phonology and syntax. In addition, such patients should exhibit no difficulty in processing and recalling elementary details of the story and categorical (as opposed to emotional or spatial) forms of information.

2. Integration of Narrative Materials. Consistent with their tendencies to focus on isolated details, make tangential or inappropriately personal remarks, and miss the overall point of a discussion right hemisphere patients should have difficulty correctly ordering segments of a story and inferring the moral of a story. In addition, they should exhibit deficits in distinguishing major themes from minor details, and in excluding personal details and confabulations from their recountings. Finally, owing to difficulties in logical inference and integration of disparate elements, such patients should be impaired in their ability to detect incongruities in a narrative.

3. Humor. Reflecting their apparent difficulties in integrating materials, and in exhibiting appropriate emotional responses, right hemisphere patients should exhibit anomalous mirth responses and aberrant funniness ratings.

Subjects

The subject group of principal interest was composed of patients with unilateral right brain damage. These subjects (both males and females) were drawn from the neurological wards of the Boston Veterans Administration Medical Center, the New England Rehabilitation Hospital, the Braintree Hospital, and the Massachusetts Rehabilitation Hospital. All subjects were right-handed adults who were less than 65 years of age. Diagnoses of unilateral right brain disease were based on clinical signs (e.g., hemiplegia, sensory loss, visual field cuts) and, in most cases, CT scans. With two exceptions, all subjects suffered brain damage as a result of stroke. These patients were further classified whenever possible into one of four groups: (*a*) those with lesions restricted to the prerolandic, *anterior* region of the minor hemisphere; (*b*) those with equivalently sized perirolandic or *central* lesions; (*c*) those with large or *extensive* lesions that included anterior (frontal), parietal, and temporal areas; and (*d*) those patients with lesions restricted to the postrolandic or *posterior* region.

In addition, three groups of control patients drawn from the same general population were tested. The first control group included normal adults of less than 65 years of age with no history of neurological disorders. The second group was composed of right-handed adult aphasic patients less than 65 years of age who had suffered unilateral left-sided brain damage from strokes. Diagnoses were based on clinical signs and confirmed in all cases by CT scans. These aphasic subjects were further subdivided into the following three groups: (*a*) those with purely anterior lesions who were nonfluent with relatively good comprehension; (*b*) those with lesions restricted to the posterior (i.e., temporoparietal) region who were fluent aphasics; and (*c*) anomic patients, again with posterior lesions. Diagnoses of aphasias were made on the basis of the Boston Diagnostic Aphasia Examination (Goodglass & Kaplan, 1972).

A population of aging adults was included as a third control group. These aging subjects had no history of neurological disorder, and ranged in age from 65 to 85 years. This group was included for two reasons. First, it has been hypothesized that as people age, right hemisphere functions deteriorate more rapidly than left hemisphere abilities (see Albert & Kaplan, 1980, for a critical discussion of this hypothesis). Therefore, it is important to confirm that patterns discerned in the performance of the right hemisphere patients are a result of acute onset of right brain damage and not of the normal aging process. In addition, even if the "right hemisphere aging" hypothesis is not substantiated, findings obtained with an aging population should permit tentative conclusions on an important question: Which difficulties on the battery might be obtained with any group performing in a suboptimal fashion, and which difficulties are restricted to or highlighted in individuals with documented focal injury in the right hemisphere?

Procedure

Subjects were tested individually in experimental sessions lasting approximately 30 minutes. If an individual subject participated in more than one task, testing was spread out over days, one session per day. For practical reasons, it was not possible to test all patients on all tasks. All subject groups were tested on the battery of narrative tests; the sole exception was the sentence arrangement task, on which no aging subjects were tested. Only right hemisphere patients and normal controls were tested on the verbal humor task.

RESULTS AND DISCUSSION

Basic Linguistic Processing

Right hemisphere patients exhibited no obvious difficulty in using appropriate phonology and syntax. However, their recall showed qualitative differences from that produced by normal subjects. Whereas normal controls characteristically paraphrased the stories, right hemisphere patients often repeated segments of prose essentially as given, without recoding it into more concise or abstract form. The only other pronounced abnormality was the flat mode of delivery which characterized many right hemisphere patients' retellings of stories and answers to questions (Ross, 1981).

Narrative Ability

Analysis of subjects' recall of the short passages that included spatial, emotional, and noncanonical elements revealed that, contrary to expectation, spatial elements in the stimulus paragraphs did not prove particularly troublesome. However, responses to the emotional and noncanonical (bizarre) versions invite further comment.

The emotional elements proved relatively difficult to master. Moreover, many of the errors produced by right hemisphere subjects on the emotional items triggered inappropriate embellishments. That is, when a patient attributed an incorrect emotion to the character under consideration, the patient went on to elaborate a reason for the emotion that the character was feeling. For example, in the Fireman Story, one patient said that the little girl "didn't express any opinion or feelings except being excited. She didn't wet her panties, she didn't kiss anybody around . . . and she didn't hug anybody."

Though often at variance with the emotions implied in the stories, the emotions stated by the patients were typically ones that could logically have been involved. Characteristically, the patients made inferences about how a character *could* have felt but not how he/she actually felt. This finding is consistent with results from an earlier study of emotional sensitivity among right hemisphere patients (Cicone, Wapner, & Gardner, 1980). There, as in the present study, patients often designated an emotion other than the one actually portrayed but then produced a reasonable explanation (or confabulation) for the stated emotion. Such findings suggest that the patient's ability to make logical inferences about the emotional sphere (as in the spatial sphere) is less impaired than the ability to marshall this logic in order to appreciate a particular story or scene is compromised. Possibly this result may reflect a kind of functional dissociation between the ability to make logical inferences about emotions and the ability to attribute emotions appropriately to situations. In other words, patients can activate appropriate routines for inference, but tend to invoke them inappropriately.

More dramatic were the right hemisphere patients' difficulties in reacting appropriately to the noncanonical (or bizarre) story elements. Normal and aging controls and anterior aphasics typically found these elements funny, as they were clearly at variance with the rest of the story and, to some extent, with stories in general. Individuals in all these control groups looked puzzled when they heard the noncanonical sentences read to them; in recall, they characteristically omitted, regularized, or challenged the jarring elements. Although posterior aphasics made a great number of errors on the noncanonical elements, their errors consisted primarily of transforming the bizarre sentences into logical, more appropriate versions of events. Because these patients may have been uncertain of having accurately heard the sentence, or because they simply could not comprehend enough of the sentence to appreciate its incongruity, they tended to report the events as they *should* have unfolded.

In sharp contrast, the right hemisphere patients recalled these elements as they had been presented and accepted them, frequently adding explanations to justify their inclusion in the story. For example, asked why, in one story, a lazy hired hand had received a raise, patients were quick to justify the sentence. Four typical responses were: "The cost of living is up"; "Maybe he thought he wasn't paying him enough"; "...to encourage him to work a little harder"; "He thought he was such a good worker he'd give him a raise."

Indeed, one patient felt such a need to justify these noncanonical elements that, even after acknowledging his puzzlement, he proceeded to figure out a way in which they *could* make sense. Thus, in The Fishing Trip, the father tells his son never to bring a flashlight on a boat although he has just been rescued because he had such a flashlight on board; at first the patient said it was "nonsensible" but then he continued, "he was trying to collect his son's insurance." Similarly, in the story where the farmer gives his hired hand a raise after finding him asleep in a haystack, his job left undone, the patient realized this was "inconsistent with the rest of the story," yet went on to justify it: "The guy quits—no discussion or any-thing—the farmer meets him and raises his wages. 'Say hey, Joe—if you're gonna quit, I'm raising your wages; it won't cost me a cent, you won't be here!' "

Such rationalizing behavior may have been rooted in different causes. In some circumstances, or for some patients, the subject fails to appreciate that the noncanonical elements were far-fetched and thus was unable to appre-ciate their incongruity with the rest of the story. In other instances, the subject may have sensed that the elements were in some way incongruous, and yet felt the need to justify them, if necessary confabulating in order to create a link. One gets the feeling that at one level the noncanonicity was appreciated, but that, for some as yet undetermined reason, the patient at the same time felt the urge (or was unable to inhibit the temptation) to provide a rationalization for the seemingly discordant element. Whatever the reason for this peculiar behavioral profile, right hemisphere patients in this study regularly accepted and justified the noncanonical elements, whereas posterior aphasics changed or normalized the elements, and all other subjects tended to omit, reject, or normalize them.

As already noted, the most obvious control group for the right hemi-sphere patients—that of aphasic patients—is not wholly appropriate for this investigation. Thus, findings from our other control group of aging subjects assume added importance.

As opposed to the younger control group, our aging subjects showed many similarities to the right hemisphere subjects, for example, making personal remarks and embellishments, and exhibiting deficits in recalling elements of stories. Yet, the quality of responses and errors is generally dif-ferent. For example, our right hemisphere patients rarely displayed word finding difficulty whereas this was common among the aging patients. Also, when an aging patient made personal remarks, those remarks, unlike those of the right hemisphere patients, were often of a moralistic nature, and seldom caused the subject to drift away from the main point of the story. And whereas the aging subjects were quick to point out that they did not remember something and to ask for aid, the right hemisphere patients al-most never indicated a lack of confidence about their responses.

Subjects' spontaneous recall of the longer, fable-like story (The Silver Hammer) was scored on the several measures outlined earlier. Table 9.1 contains the means for each of the major subject groups, and Tables 9.2

Table 9.1

MEAN PERFORMANCE BY MAJOR SUBJECT GROUPS ON STORY ("SILVER HAMMER") RECALL TASK

	Dimensions					
Subject group	Overall output	Confu-sions	Main events correctly recalled	Confab-ulations	Sequencing errors	Moral abstractions[a]
Right hemisphere (N = 16)	14.7	3.2	3.8	1.8	1.5	.50
Normals (N = 10)	20.6	1.5	5.1	.4	.5	.70
Aging (N = 9)	17.7	2.1	3.9	1.9	1.1	.44
Left hemisphere (N = 11)	9.0	.3	3.1	.3	.4	.30

[a]Entries indicate proportion of subjects in each group producing the correct moral.

and 9.3 contain, respectively, the means for the right and left hemisphere subgroups. In many respects, the right hemisphere subjects performed poorly relative to the normal controls and also relative to the aging controls. First, with respect to overall output, normal controls produced the most information, followed, in descending order, by aging subjects, right hemisphere subjects, and left hemisphere subjects. The mean number of main events correctly recalled by each subject also presents a picture of right hemisphere subjects' impaired functioning as well as an interesting comparison with aphasic subjects' performance. Normal subjects recalled most main events, followed by aging and right hemisphere subjects, and aphasics recalled the fewest main events. Looking at the aphasics' performance across the two measures, one sees that the low output is associated with adequate recount-

Table 9.2

MEAN PERFORMANCE BY RIGHT HEMISPHERE SUBGROUPS ON STORY ("SILVER HAMMER") RECALL TASK

	Dimensions					
Right hemisphere subgroup	Overall output	Confu-sions	Main events correctly recalled	Confab-ulations	Sequencing errors	Moral abstractions[a]
Right anterior (N = 1)	11.0	7.0	.0	1.0	1.0	.00
Right posterior (N = 5)	12.8	2.4	3.8	2.2	1.4	.60
Right central (N = 8)	16.9	3.3	4.3	1.9	1.6	.86
Right extensive (N = 2)	12.5	3.0	3.5	.5	1.5	.00

[a]Entries indicate proportion of subjects in each subgroup producing the correct moral.

Table 9.3

MEAN PERFORMANCE BY APHASIC SUBGROUPS ON STORY ("SILVER HAMMER")
RECALL TASK

Aphasic subgroup	Dimensions					
	Overall output	Confu- sions	Main events correctly recalled	Confab- ulations	Sequencing errors	Moral abstractions[a]
Left anterior (N = 5)	5.8	.2	1.8	.0	.2	.00
Left posterior (N = 3)	11.3	.3	4.3	.3	.0	.33
Anomic (N = 3)	12.0	.3	4.0	.7	1.0	.67

[a]Entries indicate proportion of subjects in each subgroup producing the correct moral.

ing of main events. Indeed, the posterior aphasics performed comparably to the right hemisphere group on this measure, based on oral language production, despite their documented language disorders. This result speaks well for aphasics' appreciation of narrative; in the face of reduced production or comprehension, what resources are available to these subjects are devoted to central information.

The remaining four indices document more profound areas of impaired functioning for right hemisphere patients. First, these subjects made the most sequencing errors; normal controls and aphasics made the fewest sequencing errors, while aging subjects made intermediate numbers of errors. Right-lesioned patients also produced the most confused story renderings, followed by aging subjects, and by normal and aphasic subjects. Right hemisphere subjects were also given to considerable confabulation, though no more than the aging subjects.

Finally, right hemisphere patients were markedly deficient in their abilities to extract the correct moral from the story. After recall, when asked for a moral, only half of the right hemisphere patients produced a good paraphrasing of the Golden Rule, compared to 70% of the normal controls. The aphasics and aging subjects also performed poorly on the task, although perhaps for different reasons. The errors of the right-brain-damaged subjects tended to involve either simply repeating the plot or giving a literal response such as "keep clean" or "take care of your tools."

The sentence arrangement task revealed that right hemisphere patients were markedly impaired in their ability to organize sentences into coherent narratives. They performed significantly worse than the non-brain-damaged control group, and their performance was on a par with that of the aphasic patients. Specifically, the orderings produced by normals were completely correct on 78% of the trials, those for right hemisphere patients on 45% of the trials, and those for aphasics on 40% of the trials. Thus, although right hemisphere individuals were relatively unimpaired in basic linguistic processing, they exhibited clear impairments in organizing linguistic information at the narrative level. As in the recall task results described earlier, there were no important effects due to passage type; subjects performed equivalently on the temporal, spatial, and categorical items. In general, then, the right hemisphere subjects' poor performance on this integrative, linguistic task shows that the deficits obtained on testing complex linguistic ability were probably not due solely to memory limitations.

Humor Appreciation

The humor-rating task, in which subjects rated the funniness of different linguistic segments, produced provocative results that clearly distinguished right hemisphere patients from normal controls. The means of these two groups are shown in Table 9.4.

Overall, there was no significant effect of *trapping*, nor was there any important group difference in mean ratings given by normal controls and right hemisphere subjects. There was, not surprisingly, a large effect of funniness; the funny items were rated as being substantially funnier than the unfunny items. More interestingly, though, was the pattern of results shown in Table 9.4. The normal controls made a far clearer distinction between the funny and unfunny items than did the right hemisphere patients. Put another way, the right hemisphere subjects responded similarly to the normals on truly humorous items; but, exposed to the unfunny items, right-lesioned subjects treated them as more humorous than did the normals. (This interaction effect was highly reliable statistically.)

A separate analysis was performed on subjects' responses to item types

Table 9.4
MEAN FUNNINESS RATINGS BY MAJOR SUBJECT GROUPS

	Item type[a]					
	Short story jokes					
Subject group	Funny	Unfunny	Puns	Tricks	Puzzles	Foils
Right hemisphere ($N = 16$)	2.0	1.1	2.2	1.7	1.7	.8
Normal control ($N = 16$)	1.8	.3	1.3	1.2	1.3	.3

[a]The funny–unfunny variable was manipulated for the short story jokes only.

other than short story jokes. These stimuli included puns, tricks, puzzles, and foils. There was a large effect of item type; puns were rated relatively high and foils relatively low. As can be seen in Table 9.4, the profiles of perceived funniness across the types of items were roughly the same in the two subject groups. Thus, even in the face of the discrepant humor responses discussed earlier, right hemisphere patients were sensitive to distinctions among classes of items.

A further analysis carried out on these same data confirmed that although right hemisphere subjects appeared normal in their ability to distinguish among types of stimulus items (e.g., puns versus foils), they were abnormal in their appreciation of humor per se. In this study, there were eight examples of each type, and these examples within each type were rank ordered according to how funny the normals rated them. Surprisingly, the right hemisphere subjects' data did not contain the same rank ordering; in fact, unlike the normal subjects, the right hemisphere group data contained almost no consistent variation of funniness within each type. This contrast between distinctions in rated funniness across- versus within-types suggests that the right hemisphere patients were able to appreciate some linguistically defined variation in humor (i.e., that puns as a kind of linguistic unit or class are funnier than are foils) but were unable to appreciate variations in funniness within type (i.e., variations that rest solely on evaluation of humorous *content* rather than *form*, cf. Gardner *et al.*, 1975).

When the right hemisphere patients' data were broken down by subgroups (see Table 9.5), other patterns emerge. First, the anterior patients showed an elevated level of response across all conditions. It is worth conjecturing that this extreme humor response to linguistic stimuli is related to a euphoria sometimes exhibited by these patients, including perhaps an

Table 9.5
MEAN FUNNINESS RATINGS BY RIGHT HEMISPHERE SUBGROUPS

	Item type[a]					
	Short story jokes					
Right hemisphere subgroup	Funny	Unfunny	Puns	Tricks	Puzzles	Foils
Right anterior (*N* = 2)	4.6	3.4	3.5	3.8	3.9	2.8
Right posterior (*N* = 2)	.8	.0	1.3	.6	1.9	.0
Right central (*N* = 8)	1.5	.4	2.0	1.4	1.0	.3
Right extensive (*N* = 2)	2.4	1.8	2.4	2.0	2.3	1.3

[a]The funny–unfunny variable was manipulated for the short story jokes only.

inappropriate lack of concern for, or denial of, one's illness. In contrast to the anterior patients, the two subjects with posterior lesions gave very low overall ratings indicating an inappropriately flat humor response. This result suggests a possible relationship between the effects of posterior right hemisphere lesions and symptoms accompanying depression. These contrasting results from two right hemisphere groups provide another reason for concluding that the right hemisphere plays a particularly important role in modulating emotional responses, a role which would be manifest in dealing with humorous materials.

CONCLUSIONS

The general picture of right hemisphere patients gleaned from earlier studies, from clinical observations, and from the behavior of public figures such as Justice Douglas, or President Woodrow Wilson (Weinstein, 1982), has been supported by the current results. Overall, the patients exhibit a striking amount of difficulty in handling complex linguistic materials. Although their ability to remember isolated details and wordings is often preserved, they exhibit clear difficulties in inhibiting tangential and confabulatory responses, in ordering and integrating specific information, in abstracting morals, and in assessing the appropriateness of various facts, situations, and characterizations. Furthermore, these patients lack a normal metric for evaluating humor.

Evidence of spared capacities was also observed. The patients were more successful than had been hypothesized in handling specific contents—spatial and emotional, in particular—possibly because these contents can be handled exclusively on the lexical level and do not require the access of special imagery. Nonetheless, the patients often demonstrated difficulty in making the proper inferences about certain kinds of information, particularly emotional contents. This difficulty seems due less to a deficit in logical inference per se—answers often reflected what *could* have happened—than to a dampened appreciation of the kind of emotion in fact experienced by the individual in question. Similarly, the patients' apparent insensitivity to incongruities reflected, at least in some cases, a compulsion to justify the bizarre incongruity rather than a total insensitivity to the incongruity. Patients seem at least tangentially aware that something does not fit and yet are either unwilling or unable to frankly label the anomalous element as such.

An alternative way of conceptualizing many of the present findings is to attribute the results to a difficulty in handling complex ideational materials, rather than to deficits in the processing of complex linguistic materials. To some extent, this characterization hinges on definitional factors; one certainly can characterize many of the defects in terms of ideational or conceptual factors, rather than in terms of linguistic ones. Indeed, it would require the construction and administration of a lengthy set of tests in order to cleave apart from specifically linguistic deficits the contributions of general conceptual impairments to the present symptom picture. Nonetheless, the characterization in terms of linguistic deficits seems justifiable, both because of the current tendency to incorporate issues of discourse and narration into the realms of linguistics proper, and because of the putative existence of integrative capacities which are particularly appropriate to narrational-linguistic materials (Rumelhart, 1975). Finally, the ability of many aphasic patients to infer the moral of stories presented linguistically and to process other narrative features (Engel, 1977; Engel-Ortlieb, 1980; Stachowiak, Huber, Poeck, & Kerschensteiner, 1977) documents that, at least in this patient group, basic language deficits (e.g., syntactic or lexical semantic impairments) do not necessarily entail narrative difficulties.

A definitive description of the underlying disorders which give rise to the observed profile of responses must await further testing. Nonetheless, the findings summarized here suggest some tentative formulations about difficulties exhibited by right hemisphere patients as a group. One way of conceptualizing the difficulties of these patients is to invoke the notion of a "plausibility metric." Normal individuals appear able to assess, with reference to a given element, whether that element is appropriate to a given context. It is precisely this ability to assess plausibility that seems vitiated in many right hemisphere patients. Thus, even as a patient may challenge a statement which normal controls consider to be perfectly plausible, the same patient may accept, or even strive to justify, that noncanonical element which is immediately challenged or ignored by a normal control. Bereft of a structure into which to place the element, unaware of (or insensitive to) the rules that generally govern discourse, the patient must make an assessment based only on the element itself. And so, when a patient's individual answer or remark is examined without respect to context, it generally seems appropriate.

Moreover, the patients may have a preserved sense of the usual value of two linguistic entities: Hence he can judge that a pun should be funnier than a foil. But when specific contents (one pun vis-à-vis another) or wider contexts (the general setting, the purpose of the interchange, previous and successive events, etc.) are taken into account, the patient's inappropriateness stands out. In keeping with this result is the fact that the right hemisphere patients virtually never respond "I don't know" to an open-ended question, but instead generally contrive an answer—confabulating if necessary—in seeming indifference to its inappropriateness.

Another related but somewhat more abstract way of characterizing the difficulties of these patients is to stress their problems in acquiring a sense of the overall gestalt of linguistic entities. Patients seem unable to appreciate the relations among the key points of the story or the joke. The basic schema—the major episodes organized in an appropriate manner—seems disturbed, if not totally destroyed, whereas it may well be spared even in linguistically compromised left hemisphere patients (cf. Stachowiak *et al.*, 1977). To be sure, when memory is sufficiently acute, or cues sufficiently abundant, subjects may well mention all the major points. But their inability to negotiate noncanonical elements, their frequent confabulations and injections of personal details, all suggest that the basic scaffolding of the story has not been apprehended. Without an organizing principle, the patients are consigned to undirected rambling, unable to judge which details matter, and what overarching points they yield.

In closing, we must stress that this portrait of the linguistic capacities of the right hemisphere patient is still highly tentative. It is not known, for example, to what extent specific characteristics apply to all right hemisphere patients, or only to patients with lesions in a certain site, or of a certain size. Many of the results reported here have also been cited with reference to frontal lobe pathology, and it will be important in future studies to determine which of the response patterns seem better attributed to frontal pathology (irrespective of hemisphere), which to parietal or temporal disease, and which seem an accompaniment of any significant right hemisphere pathology. Also, though the right hemisphere patients seem to differ in certain respects from the normally aging individual, the precise profile of performance characterizing both groups has yet to be ascertained. The foregoing analyses suggest a fairly coherent, if still preliminary, picture of linguistic abnormalities in significantly impaired right hemisphere patients. Confronted with complex linguistic entities, such patients exhibit clear and recurring difficulties relating to the abilities to conceptualize the unit as a whole, to appreciate its purpose and its form, and to integrate specific elements appropriately within these forms. Correlatively, many of the patients seem insensitive to the context in which these linguistic entities are produced and utilized. Finally, they seem unable to honor the world of the fictive, the imaginary, the humorous—they seem uncertain how to relate to these entities and, in fact, sometimes appear as if they are unaware altogether of their existence as separate, specifiable, and bounded forms of language (Winner & Gardner, 1979).

It is possible to conceptualize the emerging picture in terms of two orthogonal axes. On the horizontal axis, which represents purely linguistic competence, are arrayed at one end certain canonical or "basic" aspects of language: phonology, syntax, literal lexical entities, whose processing may depend solely on relatively "cognitively impenetrable" computational capacities. At the other end of this horizontal axis are arrayed more complex linguistic entities, ones that involve redundant information, nonliteral information, and information that requires integration across the boundary of the clause (e.g., jokes, stories, adages). Right hemisphere patients consistently perform better with the more canonical aspects, worse with the more complex (even as left hemisphere patients may exhibit an opposite pattern—cf. Dennis, 1980; Eisenson, 1962; Stachowiak *et al.*, 1977; Winner & Gardner, 1977).

The vertical axis maps the extent to which pragmatic and paralinguistic features contribute to the comprehension of a linguistic entity. At one end of this axis, one can place the ideal "content-free" situation: a simple assessment of whether a word is spelled or defined correctly, whether a sentence is syntactically acceptable, whether one is dealing with a pun or a puzzle. Contextual information plays a minimal role here. At the opposite end of the axis are situations in which contextual information is wholly or largely determinant—understanding the underlying intention of a question or comment, judging the plausibility of a particular fact within an adventure story or a fairy tale, evaluating which of two jokes is funnier. Once again, it is on these contextualized linguistic assignments that right hemisphere patients are disproportionately impaired. It is as if the left hemisphere is a highly efficient, but narrowly programmed linguistic computer; in contrast, the right hemisphere constitutes a suitable audience for a humorous silent film. Whereas the left hemisphere might appreciate some of Groucho's puns, and the right hemisphere might be entertained by the antics of Harpo, only the two hemispheres unified can appreciate an entire Marx Brother's routine.

We have depicted the left hemisphere as a context-free language machine, and, accordingly, the right hemisphere patient as an individual who is largely dependent upon that machine as he attempts to negotiate his way around the world. To a point, this simplification may be justified. However, in conclusion, we must stress our own belief (along with that of most neuropsychologists) that no functions are housed solely in a particular region of the brain, that all important human capacities have wide cortical representation. Moreover, in pathology, one never receives a direct read-out of what a certain portion of the brain normally governs, but rather an impression of how an impaired brain (and an impaired person) attempts to compensate for deficits.

Finally, in attempting to account for profiles of cognition, we must never lose sight of the many important functions that are pertinent—functions which go far beyond language *simpliciter* to include emotional sensitivity, motivation, attentional mechanisms, goals and defenses, imaginative powers, and an individual's previous personality. Neuropsychologists still know little about how to study each of these functions, let alone how they may interact in the normal and the diseased individual. We must remember too, that, despite brain injury, our patients continue to carry out numerous complex functions and remain in many ways the same people. Whatever modest inroads have been made by the program of research described here, we have far to go before we account for the behavior of a single individual, let alone the behaviors of the numerous individuals who have the misfortune to suffer damage to one half of the brain.

ACKNOWLEDGMENTS

Among the colleagues who have worked with us on the research reported here, we wish to thank Michael Cicone, Dean Delis, Murray Grossman, Suzanne Hamby, John Powelson, Barbara Shapiro, and Edgar Zurif for their collaboration on various aspects of the studies. Dee Michel deserves special thanks for his major role in the design and execution of the study of humor; this study has been reported more fully in a separate publication. We are also grateful to Lillian Gray and Nancy Lefkowitz of the Massachusetts Rehabilitation Hospital, Dr. Anna Pomfret of the New England Rehabilitation Hospital, and Drs. Michael Alexander and James Liljestrand of Braintree Hospital for their help and support in carrying out the research reported here.

REFERENCES

Ajuriaguerra, J. de, & Hécaen, H. *Le cortex cerebral*. Paris: Masson et Cie, 1964.
Albert, M. S., & Kaplan, E. Organic implications of neuropsychological deficits in the elderly. In L. W. Poon, J. L. Fozard, L. S. Cermak, D. Ehrenberg, & L. W. Thompson (Eds.), *New directions in memory and aging: Proceedings of the George Talland Memorial Conference*. Hillsdale, N.J.: Erlbaum Associates, 1980.
Bates, E. *Language and context: The acquisition of pragmatics*. New York: Academic Press, 1976.
Bever, T. G., & Chiarello, R. J. Cerebral dominance in musicians and non-musicians. *Science*, 1974, *185*, 137–139.
Bogen, J. E. The other side of the brain, I: Dysgraphia and dyscopia following cerebral commissurotomy. *Bulletin of Los Angeles Neurological Societies*, 1969, *34*, 73–105. (a)

Bogen, J. E. The other side of the brain, II: An appositional mind. *Bulletin of the Los Angeles Neurological Societies*, 1969, *34*, 135–162. (b)

Bogen, J. E. The other side of the brain, III: The corpus callosum and creativity. *Bulletin of the Los Angeles Neurological Societies*, 1969, *34*, 191–220. (c)

Broca, P. Perte de la parole. Ramollissement chronique et destruction partielle du lobe antérieur gauche du cerveau. *Bulletin de la Societé Anatomique de Paris* (Paris), 1861, *2*, 219.

Caramazza, A., Gordon, J., Zurif, E. B., & DeLuca, D. Right-hemispheric damage and verbal problem solving behavior. *Brain and Language*, 1976, *3*, 41–46.

Cicone, M., Wapner, W., & Gardner, H. Sensitivity to emotional expressions and situations in organic patients. *Cortex*, 1980, *16*, 145–158.

Critchley, M. *The parietal lobes*. London: Arnold, 1953.

Delis, D. *Hemispheric processing of discourse*. Unpublished Ph.D. dissertation, University of Wyoming, 1980.

Dennis, M. Language acquisition in the single hemisphere: Semantic organization. In D. Caplan (Ed.), *Biological studies of mental processes*. Cambridge, Mass. MIT Press, 1980.

de Reuck, A. V. S., & O'Connor, M. (Eds.). *Disorders of language*. London: Churchill, 1964.

Eisenson, J. Language and intellectual modifications associated with right cerebral damage. *Language and Speech*, 1962, *5*, 49–53.

Engel, D. *Text experimente mit aphatikern*. Tübingen: T B L Verlag Gunter Nair, 1977.

Engel-Ortlieb, D. *Discourse processing in aphasics*. Unpublished manuscript, 1980.

Foldi, N. S. *Sensitivity to indirect commands by right and left hemisphere brain-damaged patients*. Unpublished Ph.D. dissertation, Clark University, 1982.

Galin, D. Implications for psychiatry of left and right cerebral specialization. *Archives of General Psychiatry*, 1974, *31*, 572–583.

Gardner, H. *The shattered mind*. New York: Knopf, 1975.

Gardner, H., & Denes, G. Connotative judgements by aphasic patients on a pictorial adaptation of the semantic differential. *Cortex*, 1973, *9*, 183–196.

Gardner, H., Ling, K., Flamm, L., & Silverman, J. Comprehension and appreciation of humor in brain-damaged patients. *Brain*, 1975, *93*, 399–412.

Gardner, H., Silverman, J., Wapner, W., & Zurif, E. The appreciation of antonymic contrasts in aphasia. *Brain and Language*, 1978, *6*, 301–317.

Geschwind, N. *Approach to a theory of localization of emotion in the human brain*. Paper presented at the International Neuropsychological Symposium, Roc-Amadour, France, 1976.

Goodglass, H., & Kaplan, E. *Assessment of aphasia and related disorders*. Philadelphia: Lea and Febiger, 1972.

Head, H. *Aphasia and kindred disorders of speech*. Cambridge: Cambridge University Press, 1926.

Hécaen, H. Clinical symptomatology in right and left hemisphere lesions. In V. B. Mountcastle (Ed.), *Interhemispheric relations and cerebral dominance*. Baltimore: Johns Hopkins University Press, 1962.

Heeschen, C., & Reischies, F. *On the ability of brain-damaged patients to understand indirect speech acts*. Paper presented at the German–Dutch Colloquium in Aphasia, Aachen, Germany, September 1979.

Lebrun, Y., & Hoops, R. (Eds.). *Intelligence and aphasia*. Holland: Swets Publication Service, 1974.

Lezak, M. D. *Behavioral concomitants of configurational disorganization in right hemisphere damaged patients.* Unpublished manuscript, 1979.

Luria, A. R. *Higher cortical functions in man.* New York: Basic Books, 1966.

Luria, A. R. *Traumatic aphasia.* The Hague: Mouton, 1970.

Michelow, D., Brownell, H., Masson, L., Wapner, W., & Gardner, H. *On the sequencing of emotional and non-emotional verbal materials by organic patients.* Unpublished manuscript, 1982.

Milner, B. Laterality effects in audition. In V. B. Mountcastle (Ed.), *Interhemispheric relations and cerebral dominance.* Baltimore: Johns Hopkins University Press, 1962.

Ornstein, R. *The psychology of consciousness.* New York: Viking Press, 1972.

Piercy, M. The effects of cerebral lesions on intellectual functions: A review of current research trends. *British Journal of Psychiatry,* 1964, *110,* 310–352.

Ross, E. D. The aprosodias: Functional–anatomical organization of the affective components of language in the right hemisphere. *Archives of Neurology,* 1981, *38,* 561–569.

Ross, E. D., & Mesulam, M. M. Dominant language functions of the right hemisphere: Prosody and emotional gesturing. *Archives of Neurology,* 1979, *36,* 144–148.

Rumelhart, D. E. Notes on a schema for stories. In D. G. Bobrow & A. M. Collins (Eds.), *Representation and understanding.* New York: Academic Press, 1975.

Sadock, J. *Toward a linguistic theory of speech acts.* New York: Academic Press, 1974.

Searle, J. *Speech acts.* Cambridge: Cambridge University Press, 1969.

Stachowiak, F. J., Huber, W., Poeck, K., & Kerschensteiner, M. Text comprehension in aphasia. *Brain and Language,* 1977, *4,* 177–195.

Tucker, D. M., Watson, R. T., & Heilman, K. M. Affective discrimination and evocation in patients with right parietal disease. *Neurology,* 1977, *27,* 947–950.

Veroff, A. E. A structural determinant of hemispheric processing of pictorial material. *Brain and Language,* 1978, *5,* 139–148.

Wapner, W., Hamby, S., & Gardner, H. The role of the right hemisphere in the apprehension of complex linguistic materials. *Brain and Language,* 1981, *14,* 15–33.

Weinstein, E. A. Linguistic aspects of amnesia and confabulation. *Journal of Psychiatric Research,* 1971, *8,* 1–7.

Weinstein, E. A. *Woodrow Wilson: A medical and psychological biography.* Princeton: Princeton University Press, 1981.

Weinstein, E. A., & Kahn, R. C. *Denial of illness, symbolic and physiological aspects.* Springfield, Ill.: Charles C Thomas, 1955.

Wertheim, N., & Botez, M. I. Receptive amusia: A clinical analysis. *Brain,* 1961, *84,* 19–30.

Winner, E., & Gardner, H. The comprehension of metaphor in brain-damaged patients. *Brain,* 1977, *100,* 719–727.

Winner, E., & Gardner, H. (Eds.). Fact, fiction and fantasy in childhood. *New Directions in Child Development,* 1979, *6.*

Woodward, R., & Armstrong, S. *The brethren.* New York: Simon and Schuster, 1979.

Zangwill, O. *Cerebral dominance and its relation to psychological function.* Edinburgh: Oliver and Boyd, 1960.

10

Negative Evidence for Language Capacity in the Right Hemisphere: Reversed Lateralization of Cerebral Function

MARGARET HAN
SUN-HOO FOO

Since the nineteenth century, it has been known that almost all patients who lose speech following brain damage have had pathology involving the left hemisphere. Early studies on linguistic deficits subsequent to brain damage were based on war wounds of the first and the second world wars, which presumably involved bilateral lesions. Observations of patients with brain pathology, mainly cerebral vascular accidents, have generally shown that aphasia is caused by lesion in the left hemisphere.

However, there have been documented exceptions to this rule. Ever since Bramwell originated the term *crossed aphasia* in 1899, clinical investigators of patients with cerebral lesions have noted the rare phenomenon of language disturbance following cerebral lesion ipsilateral to the dominant hand (Boller, 1973; Gloning, Gloning, Haub, & Quatember, 1969; Kennedy, 1916; Roberts, 1969). Boller's review of the published cases of crossed aphasia raised some questions about the justification of making such a diagnosis in certain cases. Some cases lacked careful physical or language examination, some cases had lesion site inferred from a hemiplegia, and in some, even handedness was uncertain.

Using the 89 cases reviewed by Roberts (1969), Boller (1973) found that

COGNITIVE PROCESSING IN
THE RIGHT HEMISPHERE

only 23% of the crossed aphasia cases had an etiology of a vascular origin, the rest of the cases being caused by trauma or tumor. This is quite different from the low percentage of a trauma or a tumor origin in aphasia in dextrals. Boller reported that trauma often causes bilateral lesions and tumor tends to produce distance effects. He therefore cautioned of correlating lesion site and language dysfunction in these trauma and tumor cases.

These problems certainly have made the study of incidence of crossed aphasia difficult. Most researchers, however, do agree that crossed aphasia is rare. Zangwill (1967) reported an incidence of 1.8% in dextral adults, while Gloning *et al.* (1969) and Roberts (1969) reported the incident rate of 1.0% and 2.6% respectively.

More recently, investigators have generally adopted the criteria proposed by Brown and Wilson (1973) in diagnosing crossed aphasia. These include absence of personal or family history of left-handedness, absence of childhood brain injury, lateralized lesion, and specific language deficits. There have been several reports on crossed aphasia lately, but only four cases met these criteria: April and Han (1980), April and Tse (1977), Denes and Caviezel (1981), and Wechsler (1976).

HANDEDNESS

According to several studies (Zangwill, 1960; Subirana, 1969), only one-quarter of all people are completely right-handed and slightly more than one-third show marked dominance of the right hand, whereas the rest are distinguished by relatively slight dominance of the right hand, with the exception of one-tenth of all cases, in which there is a left-hand dominance. Subirana (1969) reported that the pure left-hander is extremely rare, and must always be suspected of pathological origin.

The relationship between sinistrality and language lateralization is thus an unresolved one. Numerous clinical and experimental studies have suggested that a positive history of familial sinistrality is associated with reduced left hemisphere language dependence. Nevertheless, other studies have found familial sinistrality to be unrelated to language lateralization (Briggs & Nebes, 1976; Bryden, 1973). Several studies even suggested that familial sinistrality may be indicative of more, not less, dependence upon the left hemisphere for language processing (Bryden, 1965; McKeever & Van Deventer, 1977; Satz, Achenbach, & Fennell, 1967).

Using the technique of injecting sodium amytal into the right intracarotid artery, Wada and Rasmussen (1960) found an appreciable incidence of transient aphasia (5 out of 50 cases) in right-handed patients.

Penfield and Roberts (Roberts, 1951) performed cortical excision on patients to relieve focal epilepsy. Roberts (1951) reported that right hemisphere cortical excision resulted in aphasia in 2 out of 258 right-handed patients, and in 3 out of 23 left-handed patients. Of course, one must bear in mind that the long-standing nature of epilepsy in these patients certainly confounds the picture, yet one cannot but ponder the presence, though low (less than 1%) incidence, of aphasia in dextrals.

THEORIES OF CROSSED APHASIA

There have been numerous explanations for crossed aphasia. Bramwell's original use of the term "crossed aphasia" was in reporting in 1899 the case of a 36-year-old left-handed man with sudden onset of right hemiplegia and aphasia. This patient used his left hand for everything except for writing, which he had been forced to learn with his right hand. Bramwell proposed that it is the act of learning to write and the practice of writing with his right hand that determined the location of the "leading" speech centers in the left hemisphere in this patient.

In referring to a case he reported the previous year (Bramwell, 1898), Bramwell further hypothesized a "highly specialized" nondominant hemisphere theory in explaining crossed aphasia. The case involved a right-handed man in whom acute and complete destruction of the left motor–vocal speech center merely produced a temporary motor aphasia with persistent naming difficulty. Bramwell proposed that the motor aphasia was only transient in this patient because the nondominant hemisphere was "highly specialized" and therefore could independently carry on the speech function when the normal leading speech center was acutely destroyed.

In 1916, Kennedy explained crossed aphasia on the basis of "stock-brainedness," that is, the independent genetic origin of handedness and "brainedness" in a small group of people. The "brainedness" of these people, either left or right brained occurring idiosyncratically in a right- or left-handed stock respectively, was determined by the trend of the stock, rather than by the individual's own peculiar handedness. Kennedy postulated speech and hand preference as having separate genetic origins: Despite their tendency to be related in the dextral individual, some 90% of the time the two preferences were based upon completely independent mechanisms.

The most widely accepted notion in explaining crossed aphasia, however, is that of bilateral representation of language (Brown, 1982).

Botez and Wertheim (1959) reported a 26-year-old man who developed transitory aphasia and a persistent amusia after the removal of a glioma in the right frontal lobe. They attributed the mildness of the aphasia and its rapid recovery to a bilateral representation of language. The hypothesis that music function is mediated by the right hemisphere seems to be confirmed by the amusia in this case. Though Botez and Wertheim discussed the possible effects of edema and distant vascular troubles in other cases they did not consider these factors in discussing their own case. Rather than attributing the transitory aphasia to edema, these investigators were more willing to accept the idea that because there was a familial history of sinistrality (one out of seven siblings was left-handed) one could easily assume a bilateral representation of language.

Wechsler (1976) rejected the notion of bilateralization of language on the grounds that had this been the case one would always expect a greater recovery of speech function than one usually observes in aphasic patients, just as what was not observed in his 83-year-old patient. Good recovery was also not evident in some other published reports (see Table 10.1).

Others claim that destruction of either the left cortical area or the right subcortical nuclei could result in aphasia. In the case described by Holmes and Sadoff (1966), the patient, a 65-year-old right-handed man with no history of familial sinistrality, suffered from glioblastoma in the right hemisphere, which involved the internal capsule and lenticular nucleus but which

Table 10.1
REVIEW OF PUBLISHED CASE REPORTS OF CROSSED APHASIA

Author	Initial mutism	Aphasia type	Agram-matism	Naming	Compre-hension	Recovery
Wechsler (1976)		Nonfluent	+	Good	Fair	
April and Tse (1977)		Nonfluent	+	Good	Good	
Zangwill (1979)						
Case 1		Fluent	+	Fair	Fair	Poor
Case 2		Fluent		Poor	Fair	Fair
April and Han (1980)	+	Nonfluent	+	Poor	Good	Fair
Trajanowski, Green,						
and Levine (1980)	+	Nonfluent			Fair	Fair
Assal, Perentes,						
and Deruaz (1981)		Nonfluent	+	Poor	Poor	Good
Denes and Caviezel						
(1981)		Nonfluent	+	Poor	Good	Good

did not extend through the cortex. The tumor in this case was extensive, which posed difficulty for the claim that aphasia was caused only by destruction of "subcortical nuclei in the right hemisphere [Holmes & Sadoff, 1966, p. 396]." The patient's dominant hemisphere could be the right hemisphere; however, the authors, did not consider the possibility that the diffuse cerebral dysfunction induced by edema and increased intracranial pressure could also interfere with left cerebral functions.

There were two reported cases of crossed aphasia that demonstrated a dissociation between speech and writing, such that the former was much affected but the latter preserved (Brown & Wilson, 1973; Zangwill, 1979). Zangwill (1979) hypothesized that speech and writing were controlled by opposite hemispheres, in this case.

BILINGUALISM AND MULTILINGUALISM

Albert and Obler (1978) reported a higher percentage of crossed aphasia in bilinguals than in monolinguals. Similarly, as reported by Albert and Obler (1978), Gloning and Gloning (1965) had reported that of the 4 left-handed subjects among the 11 polyglot aphasics whose cases they reviewed, 3 had exclusively right-sided lesions. This led them to postulate a high incidence of bilateral language representation, at least in bilingual left-handers.

Albert and Obler (1978) postulated further that some polyglots may have what they called asymmetrical lateralization, that is, a different lateralization pattern for each of their languages. Asymmetrical lateralization may explain cases like those reported by Pitres (1895) in which one language recovers to some extent but the other does not: In such cases, the recovering language may have been more bilaterally represented than the nonrecovering language. One of Albert and Obler's cases displayed a different aphasic syndrome in each of several languages in question.

However, this asymmetrical lateralization was not observed in some other published crossed aphasia cases. The cases reported by April and Han (1980, Chinese–English), Wechsler (1976, Yiddish–English), and Zangwill (1979, Case 1, French–English) all had equal impairment in both languages.

The two Chinese–English cases reported by April and Tse (1977) and April and Han (1980) posed some interesting questions. The authors hypothesized that because of the ideographic orthography and the tonal inflection of the spoken language in Chinese, Chinese is processed to a greater extent by the right hemisphere than an alphabetic nontonal language and there is therefore a higher incidence of crossed aphasia among Chinese speakers. This hypothesis, however, has not been substantiated.

CHARACTERISTICS OF APHASIA
IN CROSSED APHASIA

As described by Brown and Wilson (1973), most crossed aphasia cases demonstrated initial mutism, agrammatism, fairly well preserved naming skills, moderately impaired comprehension, and good recovery. However, an analysis of some recently published cases (Table 10.1) revealed that the range of poor to good naming skills in these cases and the lack of a consensus on their recovery certainly deserve further study.

ABSENCE OF APHASIA DESPITE
APPROPRIATE LESION

The case reported by Bramwell in 1898, involved a 70-year-old right-handed man whose lesion in the left frontal lobe completely destroyed Broca's area and resulted in temporary motor aphasia, with persistent anomia, agraphia, and difficulty in oral reading.

Boller (1973) described a case with a left hemisphere lesion in a dextral without any language disturbance. As this was a retrospective study, there was no detailed analysis of the patient's speech and language performance except the report that the family was not aware of any speech disturbance.

More recently, Selnes, Rubens, Risse, and Levy (1982) reported another such case, in which massive damage to the anterior and posterior suprasylvian language zones produced only transient aphasia and hemiparesis although with persistent ideomotor apraxia and agraphia. Even the severity of the initial aphasia was reportedly far less than one would have predicted given the size of the lesion. These investigators proposed that the absence of aphasia in their case was the result of a mixed dominance, rather than bilateral language representation. They hypothesized that the patient had "right-hemisphere dominance for expressive language and visuo-spatial function and . . . left-hemisphere dominance for praxis, writing, and spelling [p. 126]."

We have observed a similar case with a massive left cerebral infarct but no aphasia. This is further "negative" evidence suggesting a right hemisphere dominance for language in cases of crossed aphasia.

CASE REPORT

M.S., a 55-year-old right-handed male, was a high school graduate and worked as a salesman for an electronics firm. His medical history included hypertension for about 6 years, and he was treated with Inderal and Diazide. He had an anteroseptal myocardiac infarction in 1980. There was no history of neurological or language disorders.

The patient woke up on July 7, 1981 with transient right-sided weakness lasting for a few minutes. He went to see his physician. The examination was negative. This included an EKG which showed only the previous anteroseptal myocardiac infarction. He drove home, but was unable to get out of his car. During a period of 5–10 minutes, he developed progressive right-sided weakness, greater in the upper extremity than in the lower. He also complained of ipsilateral numbness. He was rushed to the hospital where he experienced some headache and vomited a few times. He denied any seizures, speech difficulty, visual defect, or loss of consciousness.

A Computerized Axial Tomography (CT) scan performed during the initial stage of hospitalization revealed a decreased enhancement in the left middle cerebral artery distribution. However, there was ipsilateral ventricular compression compatible with an acute massive infarction without evidence of blood.

Three months after onset the patient was admitted to the Institute of Rehabilitation Medicine at New York University Medical Center, where the current study was conducted.

Neurological Examination

The patient was alert, oriented, and cooperative. Cranial nerve examination revealed a complete right homonymous hemianopsia, and a partial right central facial palsy. There was no Hollenhorst plaque in the retina. Other cranial nerve functions were within normal limits. Neck was supple. There was no carotid bruits. Motor examination revealed a complete flaccid paralysis of the right extremities. Sensory examination was markedly suppressed in the right extremities and the facial area. Patient could experience pain and deep pressure sensation; however, vibration, touch, and position sense were absent. Reflexes were $1+/5$ on right biceps, triceps, knee, and ankle and $2+/5$ in the left side. There was a positive right Babinski.

Neurometric tests were performed using microprocessor computer analysis of brain electrical activity. Spectral analysis of 1 minute of the resting awake EEG as shown in Table 10.2 indicated marked increase of delta ac-

Table 10.2
RESTING EEG: NUMERIC RESULTS OF SPECTRAL ANALYSIS OVER 56.76 SECONDS OF
EDITED DATA

	Central		Temporal		Parieto-occ.		Front.-temp.	
	Left	Right	Left	Right	Left	Right	Left	Right
Absolute power								
Low Delta	5.00	3.41	5.41	2.86	6.12	2.06	10.17	3.33
High Delta	3.07	2.92	2.54	1.84	5.07	1.93	2.47	1.74
Theta	5.21	6.00	2.25	4.51	4.80	4.22	1.67	3.29
Alpha	4.19	13.58	1.32	17.55	3.19	10.67	.71	13.32
Beta	5.06	9.27	.97	4.72	1.50	3.65	.87	6.04
Percentage power								
Delta	17.53	9.18	35.93	6.42	34.86	9.40	43.14	7.14
Theta	29.72	18.89	31.77	15.76	32.97	20.62	29.19	13.47
Alpha	23.88	42.75	18.64	61.33	21.89	52.13	12.49	54.62
Beta	28.87	29.18	13.66	16.48	10.28	17.84	15.19	24.77
EEG ratios, total (mean μV^2)								
Low = d + t	47.25	28.08	67.70	22.19	67.83	30.03	72.33	20.61
m = t/a	1.24	.44	1.70	.26	1.51	.40	2.34	.25
w = low/high	.90	.39	2.10	.29	2.11	.43	2.61	.26
Total	17.53	31.76	7.08	28.62	14.56	20.47	5.73	24.39

tivity in the left temporal area (35.93% delta wave versus 6.42% of the right side), left parieto-occipital area (34.86% versus 9.40%), and left front-otemporal area (43.14% versus 7.14%).

An average of 50 auditory evoked potential responses (Figure 10.1) from a random "click" presentation, and 50 visual evoked potential responses (Figure 10.2) from flashing of the letter *b* likewise indicate poor responses in the left parietal and temporal areas. These results demonstrate a remarkable disturbance of function of the left cerebral hemisphere.

Hospital Course

The patient developed grand mal seizures several days after admission. A CT scan performed at this time revealed an old massive infarction involving the entire left middle cerebral artery distribution (Figure 10.3). Ophthal-pneumoplethysmography (OPG) showed a 10-mm Hg decrease in the ophthalmic systolic pressure on the left, suggesting stenosis of the left carotid artery. He was placed on a 300 mg dosage of Dilantin, 300 mg qd. Two weeks later he developed a right femoral artery occlusion. Surgery revealed an embolus sitting in the right femoral and iliac artery. An electro-

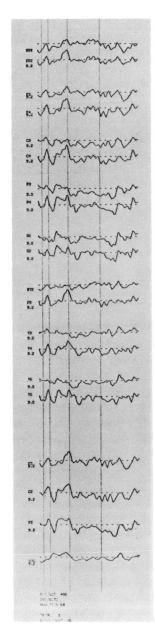

Figure 10.1. Auditory evoked potential showing decreased responses in the left cerebral hemisphere, especially T_3, T_5.

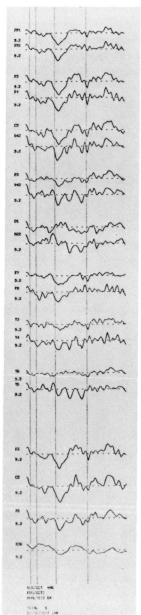

Figure 10.2. Visual evoked potential showing decreased responses in the left cerebral hemisphere.

cardiogram revealed infrequent VPC and APC without atrial fibrillation. Echo cardiogram was negative. He was then maintained on Coumadin after embolectomy. His neurological condition remained the same for the last 3 months during the rehabilitation stay.

Handedness

The patient's handedness was tested by means of the Edinburgh Inventory (Oldfield, 1971), which revealed an exclusive use of the right hand for all 12 activities. The patient reported that he had always been right-handed. His parents were right-handed. However, one of his two sisters was left-handed. There was no environmental pressure for transfer of handedness.

Assessment of Speech and Language

Comprehension. The Boston Diagnostic Aphasia Examination (Goodglass & Kaplan, 1972) was administered. The patient displayed no difficulty in carrying out commands or in understanding spoken complex materials.

Auditory comprehension was further assessed through the shortened version of the Token Test (De Renzi & Faglioni, 1978), a powerful tool for distinguishing between normals and aphasics. The test yielded a score of 33/36 indicating no comprehension deficit. The patient used verbal rehearsal throughout the test.

Expression. The patient's uttering of automatic sequences and repetition of words and phrases were within normal limits. His naming skill was adequate except during a timed task when he was asked to name as many animals as he could within a 1-minute period. His response of eight animals was below the average for normal adults. However, this appeared to be a consequence of his overall reduced rate of responding, rather than an indication of word-finding difficulty, as word retrieval difficulty was absent from the sample of conversation and narrative speech.

Speech. Examination of the peripheral speech mechanism revealed grossly intact structures at rest with the exception of a slight facial droop on the right side. The patient was able to purse his lips but retraction was asymmetrical with reduced range on the right. Range and strength of tongue movement were grossly intact. There were no other signs of weakness, incoordination, or asymmetry. Overall rate of articulatory movement was slow. The patient performed alternate repetitive movements with reduced rate.

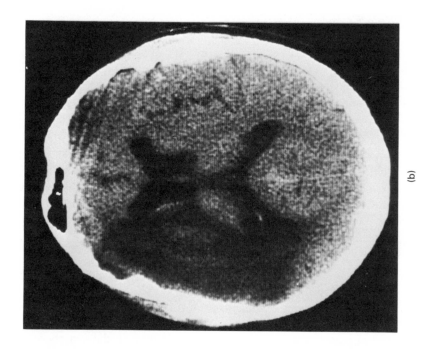

(b)

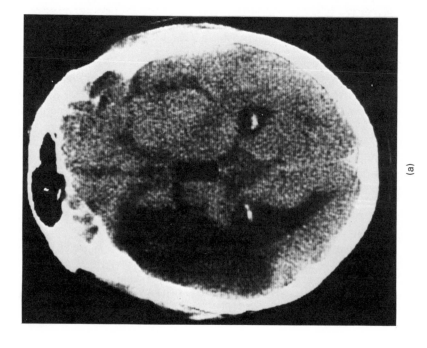

(a)

204

(d)

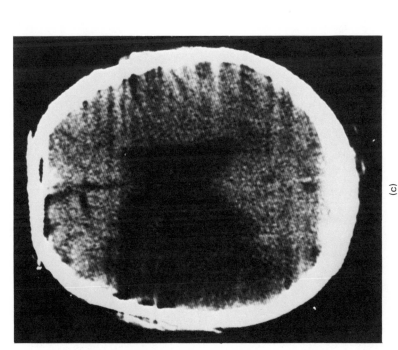

(c)

Figure 10.3. CT scan revealing an infarction involving the entire left middle cerebral artery distribution, including both Broca's and Wernicke's areas.

No chewing difficulty was reported. The patient experienced some difficulty with swallowing during the initial stage of hospitalization. During the present evaluation swallowing for solid food was intact, but there was slight choking while drinking from a cup.

Voice was slightly hypernasal and breathy. Pitch range was unremarkable; however, it was monotonous, lacking the modulation for emotional affect.

Reading.   Both oral and silent reading were affected by a right visual neglect. However, once an anchor point was established for him, M.S. managed to read with good comprehension.

Writing.   Initial attempts to write with the unaffected left hand resulted in almost illegible script (Figure 10.4). During the course of the hospitalization, the mechanics of writing improved such that when he printed his writing was recognizable, although not when he attempted cursive writing. Both spontaneous writing and writing to dictation displayed errors of deletion of word endings, especially morphological inflections such as *ing*

Figure 10.4. Patient's handwriting, using the unaffected left hand.

and *s*, even though these inflections were present in his verbalization of what he was writing. Misspellings were also noted for words of low frequency of occurrence. These errors usually occurred in the latter half of the word, indicating either a lapse of focusing or limited auditory retention.

Arithmetic calculations were intact for simple addition, subtraction, and multiplication. The patient often reported "I lost my place," when solving complicated calculations, and there was indeed confusion of columns. Also, he had to be reminded frequently to look at the right side of the page which otherwise would be left unanswered.

His visual problem-solving skills were further examined by means of the Raven's Coloured Progressive Matrices (Raven, 1965). His score of 24 was significantly higher than the mean score for left-brain-damaged adults (13.31 as reported by Kertesz & McCabe, 1975). An error analysis uncovered some interesting points: M.S. had more difficulty appreciating differences in patterns and closure function than with analogous reasoning, as demonstrated by his poor performance on Sections A & A_B (6/12 and 7/12 respectively), and his almost perfect score (11/12) on Section B. It also took him more time to solve matrices involving pattern matching or pattern completion than those involving analogous reasoning.

M.S. displayed no constructional apraxia. He was able to copy from memory matchstick designs, though he did have occasional directional disorientation. His drawing of a human figure was symmetrical but lacked detail, his clock face had dots rather than numerals (Figure 10.5).

A single digit dichotic listening task was administered. The patient had

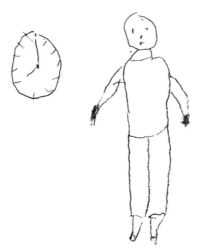

Figure 10.5. Patient's drawings.

total right ear extinction under dichotic conditions. Monaural listening disclosed accurate scores in both ears.

M.S. stands out as a unique case of reversed lateralization of cerebral functions. It seems that the huge infarction in the left hemisphere has resulted in symptoms one generally observes in patients with a right hemisphere lesion: visuospatial deficit and a lack of facial and verbal affect with intact language functioning. The visual field defect, on the other hand, is probably due to destruction of the optic radiation pathway. Reports have indicated that patients with right hemisphere lesions have a disturbance in the affective component of prosody (Ross & Mesulam, 1979; Tucker, Watson, & Heilman, 1977). Our patient's inability to impart affective tone to his speech or to his facial expression seems to indicate a reversed lateralization of these functions. This may partially, of course, be the consequence of massive brain destruction.

Though M.S. recognized his right visual field neglect verbally, 6 months after onset he still needs constant reminding. There was no intrapersonal neglect of the right side of the body, nor was such neglect indicated in his drawing of a person.

The complete extinction on the right in the dichotic listening task is more likely a result of the lesion than an indication of right hemisphere dominance. As reported by Damasio and Damasio (1979), deep suprasylvian lesions in the parietal or parieto-occipital region in either the left or the right hemisphere can block the interhemispheric auditory pathway traveling from the nondominant hemisphere to the posterior temporal region of the dominant one.

The CT examination (Figure 10.3) showed complete destruction of the brain in the left middle cerebral artery distribution. This includes not only the motor and sensory cortex, but also Broca's and Wernicke's areas, plus the subcortical connection. Functional study of cerebral activity with computerized EEG reading and auditory and visual evoked potential studies also indicate severe left cerebral dysfunction. These results correspond to clinical observations of complete right hemiplegia, hemisensory loss, and hemianopsia. Should patient's dominant hemisphere be the left hemisphere, severe speech disturbance would certainly be expected. One has to infer, then, in this particular case, that the speech center is in the right hemisphere.

Our case is similar to the one reported by Selnes *et al.* (1982) in terms of extensive cerebral damage (CT scan). However, our patient differs in that he showed no speech difficulty, even early on, and has complete hemiplegia. We could not, of course, test our patient for apraxia or agraphia because of the motor deficit on the right side. We could not prove or disprove a mixed dominance in this case such as was hypothesized by Selnes *et al.* (1982) for theirs. However, given the absence of any initial difficulty in speech, as witnessed by family, referring physician, and patient himself, one could argue that most of the speech function, if not all, resides in the right hemisphere.

Our observation provides further "negative" support for the notion of crossed cerebral dominance. Prior to the CT era, one could easily have disregarded a dextral with right hemiparesis and no speech difficulty as having a capsular infarction. With the growing use of the CT scan, one can expect an increase in reports of crossed aphasia and cases similar in nature to ours.

ACKNOWLEDGMENTS

We gratefully acknowledge the assistance of Sanders Davis and Emile Hiesiger in referring and examining the patient; Han Sook Ahn in performing the evoked potential tests and EEG; Joseph Lin in interpreting CT scan; and Lucia Kellar in administering the dichotic test.

REFERENCES

Albert, M. L., & Obler, L. K. *The bilingual brain.* New York: Academic Press, 1978.

April, R. S., & Han, M. Crossed aphasia in a right-handed bilingual Chinese man. *Archives of Neurology*, 1980, *37*, 342–346.

April, R. S., & Tse, P. Crossed aphasia in a Chinese bilingual dextral. *Archives of Neurology*, 1977, *34*, 766–770.

Assal, G., Perentes, E., & Deruaz, J. P. Crossed aphasia in a right-handed patient. *Archives of Neurology*, 1981, *38*, 455–458.

Boller, F. Destruction of Wernicke's area without language disturbance. A fresh look at crossed aphasia. *Neuropsychologia*, 1973, *11*, 243–246.

Botez, M. I., & Wertheim, N. Expressive aphasia and apraxia following right frontal lesion in a right-handed man. *Brain*, 1959, *82*, 186–202.

Bramwell, B. A remarkable case of aphasia. *Brain*, 1898, *21*, 343–373.

Bramwell, B. On "crossed" aphasia. *Lancet*, 1899, *1*, 1473–1479.

Briggs, G. G., & Nebes, R. D. The effects of handedness, family history and sex on the performance of a dichotic listening task. *Neuropsychologia*, 1976, *4*, 129–133.

Brown, J. W. Heirarchy and evolution in neurolinguistics. In M. Arbib, D. Caplan, & J. Marshall (Eds.), *Neural models of language processes.* New York: Academic Press, 1982.

Brown, J. W., & Hécaen, H. Lateralization and language representation. *Neurology*, 1976, *26*, 183–189.

Brown, J. W., & Wilson, F. Crossed aphasia in a dextral. *Neurology*, 1973, *23*, 907–911.

Bryden, M. P. Tachistoscopic recognition, handedness, and cerebral dominance. *Neuropsychologia*, 1965, *3*, 1–8.

Bryden, M. P. Perceptual asymmetry in vision: Relation to handedness, eyedness, and speech lateralization. *Cortex*, 1973, *9*, 418–432.

Damasio, H., & Damasio, A. R. "Paradoxic" ear extinction in dichotic listening: Possible anatomic significance. *Neurology*, 1979, *29*, 644–653.

Denes, G., & Caviezel, F. Dichotic listening in crossed aphasia: "Paradoxical" ipsilateral suppression. *Archives of Neurology*, 1981, *38*, 182–185.

De Renzi, E., & Faglioni, P. Normative data and screening power of a shortened version of the Token Test. *Cortex*, 1978, *14*, 41–49.

Gloning, I., & Gloning, K. Aphasien bei polyglotten. *Wiener Zeitschrift fuer Nervenheilkunde*, 1965, *22*, 362–397.

Gloning, I., Gloning, K., Haub, C., & Quatember, R. Comparison of verbal behavior in right-handed and non-right-handed patients with anatomically verified lesion of one hemisphere. *Cortex*, 1969, *5*, 43–52.

Goodglass, H., & Kaplan, E. *Boston Diagnostic Aphasia Examination*. Philadelphia: Lea & Febiger, 1972.

Holmes, J. E., & Sadoff, R. L. Aphasia due to a right hemisphere tumor in a right-handed man. *Neurology*, 1966, *16*, 392–397.

Kennedy, F. Stock-brainedness, the causative factor in the so-called "crossed aphasics." *American Journal of Medical Science*, 1916, *152*, 849–859.

Kertesz, A., & McCabe, P. Intelligence and aphasia: Performance of aphasics on Raven's Coloured Progressive Matrices (RCPM). *Brain and Language*, 1975, *2*, 387–395.

Kinsbourne, M. The control of attention by interaction between the cerebral hemispheres. In S. Kornblum (Ed.), *Attention and performance* (Vol. 4). New York: Academic Press, 1973.

McKeever, W. F., & Van Deventer, A. D. Visual and auditory language processing asymmetries: Influences of handedness, familial sinistrality, and sex. *Cortex*, 1977, *13*, 225–241.

Moscovitch, M. On the representation of language in the right hemisphere of right-handed people. *Brain and Language*, 1976, *3*, 47–71.

Oldfield, R. C. The assessment and analysis of handedness: The Edinburgh Inventory. *Neuropsychologia*, 1971, *9*, 97–113.

Pitres, A. Etude sur l'aphasie. *Revue de Medicine*, 1895, *15*, 873–899.

Raven, J. C. *Guide to Using the Coloured Progressive Matrices*. London: H. K. Lewis, 1965.

Roberts, L. Localization of speech in the cerebral cortex. *Trans America Neurological Association*, 1951, *76*, 43–50.

Roberts, L. Aphasia, apraxia, and agnosia in abnormal states of cerebral dominance. In P. J. Vinken, & F. W. Bruyn (Eds.), *Handbook of clinical neurology* (Vol. 4). Amsterdam: Elsevier/North-Holland, 1969.

Ross, E. D., & Mesulam, M.-M. Dominant language functions of the right hemisphere: Prosody and emotional gesturing. *Archives of Neurology*, 1979, *36*, 144–148.

Satz, P., Achenbach, K., & Fennell, E. Correlations between assessed manual laterality and predicted speech laterality in a normal population. *Neuropsychologia*, 1967, *5*, 295–310.

Searleman, A. Subject variables and cerebral organization for language. *Cortex*, 1980, *16*, 239–254.

Selnes, O. A., Rubens, A. B., Risse, G. I., & Levy, R. S. Transient aphasia with persistent apraxia. *Archives of Neurology*, 1982, *39*, 122–126.

Sperry, R. W., Gazzaniga, M. S., & Bogen, J. E. Interhemispheric relationships: The neocortical commissures: Syndromes of hemispheric disconnection. In P. J. Vinken & F. W.

Bruyn (Eds.), *Handbook of clinical neurology* (Vol. 4). Amsterdam: Elsevier/North-Holland, 1969.

Subirana, A. Handedness and cerebral dominance. In P. J. Vinken & F. W. Bruyn (Eds.), *Handbook of clinical neurology* (Vol. 4). Amsterdam: Elsevier/North-Holland, 1969.

Trajanowski, J. Q., Green, R. C., & Levine, D. N. Crossed aphasia in a dextral: A clinico-pathological study. *Neurology*, 1980, *30*, 709–713.

Tucker, D. M., Watson, R. T., & Heilman, K. M. Discrimination and evocation of affectively intoned speech in patients with right parietal disease. *Neurology*, 1977, *27*, 947–950.

Wada, J., & Rasmussen, T. Intracarotid injection of sodium amytal for the lateralization of cerebral speech dominance. *Journal of Neurosurgery*, 1960, *17*, 266–282.

Wechsler, A. Crossed aphasia in an illiterate dextral. *Brain and Language*, 1976, *3*, 164–172.

Zangwill, O. L. *Cerebral dominance in relation to psychological function*. Edinburgh: Oliver and Boyd, 1960.

Zangwill, O. L. Speech and the minor hemisphere. *Acta Neurologica et Psychiatrica*, 1967, *67*, 1013–1020.

Zangwill, O. L. Two cases of crossed aphasia in dextrals. *Neuropsychologia*, 1979, *17*, 167–172.

PART IV

LANGUAGE REHABILITATION VIA THE RIGHT HEMISPHERE

11

Heightening Visual Imagery:
A New Approach to Aphasia Therapy

JOYCE FITCH-WEST

Two major cognitive strategies have long been associated with human cognition: the analytic, or serial, and the synthetic, or holistic. Neuropsychological research suggests that analytic processing is primarily a left hemisphere function, whereas the right hemisphere deals with stimuli in a more holistic manner, experiencing more than one sensory modality simultaneously, grasping the gestalt, yet not being particularly aware of detail. Both processes operate most of the time in most people to varying degrees, depending upon the nature of the stimulus presented or the response expected; both processes may continue to be available following brain damage. For many aphasic patients, however, the cognitive strategies that remain after brain damage seem to be those associated with the intact right hemisphere: holistic, global processing. A dependence on these strategies might explain why patients with no verbal output except very limited stereotypes are able, within the context of a conversational setting, to convey with facial expression, intonation variation, and limited gesture, their communicative intent and comprehension of the intent of others participating in the conversation. Indeed, it is not unusual to find the family of a patient reporting

COGNITIVE PROCESSING IN
THE RIGHT HEMISPHERE

Copyright © 1983 by Academic Press, Inc.
All rights of reproduction in any form reserved.
ISBN 0-12-550680-5

that he or she "understands everything" while standardized aphasia tests indicate remarkably global deficits across language modalities.

We have in our clinic a videotape of a patient whose verbal output was limited primarily to one sterotypy, "thrill–thrill–thrill." On the standard test batteries that we routinely administer, he was unable to successfully complete virtually any item. When asked to point to pictures or objects, or perform other tasks of a similar nature, comprehension seemed almost nil. And yet playing this sequenced videotape to audiences produces remarkable agreement as to the meaning of what this patient is trying to convey. With vivid facial expression, limited gestures, and widely varied vocal intonation of only "thrill–thrill–thrill," he answers our questions about how he spends his day, then tells us that he is tired of being in the hospital. By mimicking the tone people use in talking to him, he shows us how disgusted he is with being treated as if he were a child and points out (painstakingly writing $40) that he, after all, was once a viable professional writer who made $40,000 a year. My experience in playing the videotape is that audiences invariably become defensive if I make the claim that in fact this patient's comprehension is very limited. How can they be so certain that they know what he meant to convey, when, in fact, all he objectively said was "thrill–thrill–thrill"? But, of course, the intent of the videotape is just that: to demonstrate the kind of global, overall grasp and comprehension that such a patient can have. In support of the claim that these are strategies associated with the right hemisphere, note that much of this patient's left hemisphere was removed due to a massive hematoma following a fall down a flight of stairs. One could speculate that what such a patient is doing is calling upon the cognitive strategies that remain available to him: He grasps the whole, sees and conveys the gestalt, deduces meaning from the situation at hand, and is very effective at setting up his listener to do the same.

Patients with such limited linguistic ability have suffered severe and/or extensive left hemisphere damage and might of necessity automatically fall back on right hemisphere processing strategies. It could be argued that no one has to "teach" such a patient to use these strategies. But, obviously, not all globally impaired patients communicate as effectively as the patient described here.

What accounts for the difference in performance? And can the implementation of an appropriate program of language therapy "heighten" the cognitive processing strategies that remain available in the intact hemisphere?

This chapter proposes that when brain damage has severely dampened the processing strategies associated with the left hemisphere, emphasizing strategies associated with the right hemisphere is a more viable therapeutic goal than stressing linguistic recovery per se.

How does one facilitate this? How would one go about "heightening" right hemisphere functioning even in an undamaged brain? The answer suggested by the preceding example is to use naturalistic, conversational settings that are highly redundant and have rich contexts so that the patient is able to extract as much as possible from the nonlinguistic context itself. Information in such a setting need not be processed sequentially. Rather, the patient can call upon holistic processing strategies which will help him gain an intuitive grasp of what is happening. As this is the hemisphere that can recognize melodic contours, facial expressions, emotions, and the like, it would be helpful to be extraordinarily expressive vocally and facially in this naturalistic setting. Slower presentation rates are also said to enhance the right hemisphere's participation (Paivio, 1960). Finally, it should be kept in mind that placing minimal demands on oral output and allowing for maximal "nonverbal" responses would circumvent the verbal output limitations of the right hemisphere. In fact, one could argue that the pointing so frequently used in aphasia test batteries and in treatment programs induces a bias against right hemisphere participation, for these tasks so frequently require the patient to decode each lexical unit as it occurs in time, hold each in memory until the entire message or command is given, analyze the meaning, and then respond by pointing in sequential order—all skills associated with left hemisphere processing.

All of this may sound rather vague and imprecise as a therapeutic or diagnostic concept. Certainly the notion of heightening right hemisphere functioning seems to be difficult to define, both qualitatively and quantitatively. The holistic nature of the processing associated with the right hemisphere may make it impervious to discrete analytic measurement. Yet one cognitive strategy associated with right hemisphere functioning that *has* received extensive study and quantification is visual imagery.

The use of visual imagery as a mnemonic device has been known in Western civilization since ancient Greek times (Bower, 1970). When normal subjects have been instructed to use imagery as a learning strategy, recall has greatly exceeded that of subjects not so instructed (Paivio, 1969, 1971, 1975).

Allen Paivio, a major theorist and researcher in visual imagery, views images and verbal processes as alternative coding systems, or modes of symbolic representation. Paivio (1971) argues that:

> Imagery develops as a symbolic capacity or mode of thought through the individual's perceptual–motor experiences with concrete objects and events, and remains particularly

functional in dealing symbolically with the more concrete aspects of situations. Verbal processes develop through language experience....Verbal thought remains functional in coping with concrete situations but surpasses imagery in its capacity to deal with abstract tasks requiring the integration and manipulation of spatially and temporally remote objects or events, or tasks involving abstract reasoning [p. 18].

As visual imagery seems to be largely a consequence of right hemisphere processing (Seamon & Gazzaniga, 1973), retention of this important aspect of thinking may well remain when verbal symbolic processes are damaged, as in aphasia. Indeed, if nonverbal imagery and verbal symbolic processes can be viewed as two major components of thinking, it seems reasonable that if one component is damaged, the other may serve either as an alternative means of cognitive processing, or as a means of stimulating retrieval of the process damaged. On the other hand, as visual and verbal coding processes are so interwined in their developmental acquisition (Paivio, 1975), both may be lost at the onset of aphasia. A more intermediate position would follow from Paivio and his associates' (Paivio, 1969, 1971; Paivio & Csapo, 1971) assumption that the two coding systems are independent and yet interconnected.

Although research on the function of imagery as a facilitator of learning in adult aphasics is sparse, the early literature on aphasia placed great emphasis on the critical role played by the loss of images (Brain, 1965).

Jackson (1874/1958) believed that the aphasic "has words which can be automatically revived so as to place images of objects in order. Although he has but one side for verbalising—the automatic side—he has, according to my hypothesis, *two* sides for the revival of images, and thus, he can still think, can still have certain relations of likeness and unlikeness [p. 141]." He also felt that "the left is the side for the automatic revival of images, and the right the side for their voluntary revival—for recognition [p. 142]." Further, the aphasic "can bring two images into coexistence—existence in one unit of time—but cannot, without speech, organize the connection, if it be one of difficulty [p. 142]." Marie and Vaschide (1903/1971), on the other hand, reported that aphasics are unable to associate images with words or to chain images in response to a word, syllable, or fact. Head (1926/1963) believed that vivid images stand in place of words and as such tend to be affected by aphasia. He felt that in aphasia visual images can frequently "be evoked spontaneously and used for direct reference; but they are employed with difficulty as symbols or substitute signs [p. 523]." Weisenburg and McBride (1935) were of the opinion that the relative prominence of one type of imagery or another must play a part in determining the severity and extent of the aphasic disturbance as it appears clinically (p.

436). For example, if auditory imagery has been predominant in mental functioning, pathological changes in and around the auditory area would lead to greater disturbances in mental functioning than when visual imagery has been relatively more prominent.

Experimental work on the role of imagery in language processing provides support for an aphasic therapy based on enhancing imaging techniques. In order to study the effect of visual imagery on a variety of learning tasks, Paivio and his associates conducted a series of experiments (see Paivio, Yuille, & Madigan, 1968) in which they had subjects rate 925 nouns of varying Thorndike–Lorge frequencies for concreteness, imagery, and meaningfulness. A subject was asked to rate each of the words presented for its capacity to evoke images of the event referred to by the word. Each word was rated on a 7-point abstract–concrete scale, on a 7-point low imagery–high imagery scale, and on a similar scale for meaningfulness. According to Paivio (1969), "the availability of imagery is assumed to vary directly with item concreteness or image-evoking (I) value, whereas verbal processes are presumably independent of concreteness but functionally linked to meaningfulness (M) and codability [p. 241]." The higher the concreteness of a stimulus item, the more likely it is to evoke sensory images that can function as mediators of associative learning and memory.

Cannezzio (1977) used Paivio's lists to look at whether reaction time could serve as a measure of the effectiveness of imagery on a word-matching task that was virtually error free for the 16 aphasic subjects involved. Meaningfulness and word length were held relatively constant across four lists. Imageability and frequency were systematically varied, while concreteness covaried with imageability. Table 11.1 presents samples from each list. The aphasic subjects were shown a word for study. Following this controlled exposure on a small viewing screen, a second word was shown. The patient's task was to decide whether the second word was the same or different from the first. Reaction time was measured from the off-time of the second word to the time that the patient pressed a button indicating "yes" the two words were the same, or "no" they were not. The hypothesis that words of high imageability would be more quickly matched than those of low imageability held true. Paivio and his associates (Atwood, 1971; Bower, 1970; Jorgenson & Kintsch, 1973; Paivio, 1969; Rohwer, 1970) concluded that imagery is one of the most influential variables in such learning tasks for normal subjects; these data suggest that the same may hold true for an aphasic population. Concreteness–imagery may be viewed as a major dimension of word meaning and one of the most potent yet identified among familiar words.

Instructions to image enhance imagery coding, improving recognition of

Table 11.1

SAMPLES FROM TWELVE-ITEM WORD LISTS WHICH SYSTEMATICALLY VARY IMAGERY (I), CONCRETENESS (C), AND FREQUENCY (F), WHILE MEANINGFULNESS (M) AND LENGTH (L) ARE HELD RELATIVELY CONSTANT

A. High imageability–high frequency nouns					
Noun	I	C	F	M	L
1. *Wife*	6.53	6.52	AA	6.48	4
2. *Iron*	6.07	6.87	AA	6.12	4
3. *Chief*	6.07	5.87	AA	6.08	5
4. *Engine*	6.33	6.76	A	6.08	6
B. High imageability–low frequency nouns					
Noun	I	C	F	M	L
1. *Nun*	6.67	6.76	9	6.60	3
2. *Tank*	6.23	6.87	19	6.48	4
3. *Skull*	6.47	6.96	13	6.64	5
4. *Cigar*	6.80	6.96	16	6.22	5
C. Low imageability–high frequency nouns					
Noun	I	C	F	M	L
1. *Law*	3.73	3.23	AA	6.32	3
2. *Cost*	3.57	3.41	AA	6.24	4
3. *Duty*	3.17	2.32	AA	5.60	4
4. *Moral*	3.17	1.39	A	6.44	5
D. Low imageability–low frequency nouns					
Noun	I	C	F	M	L
1. *Ego*	2.90	1.93	0	5.72	3
2. *Pact*	3.50	3.77	4	5.12	4
3. *Greed*	3.53	1.73	3	5.52	5
4. *Irony*	2.83	2.10	4	5.24	5

concrete words and pictures to a greater extent than instructions to use verbal mediation (Morris & Stevens, 1974). Paivio and Foth (1970) asked 40 subjects to generate mediaters for 30 concrete or 30 abstract noun pairs, in each case half the pairs being linked by nonverbal images and half by verbal mediators, and found that imagery improved recall better than did verbal mediation in the case of concrete pairs whereas the reverse occurred with abstract pairs. Snodgrass and McClure's research (1975) indicated that both imagery and verbal instructions significantly improved recognition memory for highly imageable words, and for their corresponding pictures. Picture memory under verbal and imaginal instructions was superior to that of word memory under the same instructions.

Edelstein (1976) conducted a study which tested, with 16 aphasic male subjects, whether providing instructions to image and an oral description of a picture or word would help facilitate imagery and hence enhance recognition memory. Aphasics were shown lists of 10 highly imageable words which were balanced for frequency of occurrence and length.

Instructions to image were followed by a study trial, in which the patient sat in a carrel wearing headphones. During the study trial, slides of pictures and words or words alone were presented on a small screen via rear projection and the patient simultaneously heard a verbal description of the item being shown on the screen. For each item, two descriptions were composed: One was highly relevant and could enhance the imageability of the item; the other was neutral in its ability to arouse an image. There were thus four study conditions: RW (relevant description–word alone), RP (relevant description—word plus picture), NW (neutral description–word alone), and NP (neutral description–word plus picture). Both the relevant and neutral types of descriptions contained two sentences, totaling 7–10 words, with a mean of 8.0 words for each list. In neither type of description was the item specifically named.

Thus, in the RP condition, the word *snake*, for example, appeared together with a picture of a snake and the accompanying relevant oral description was "See the long body. It appears slimy." In the RW condition, the word *flag* was shown without a picture and was paired with the oral description "See the many colors. Look how it waves." Neutral descriptions included, "Some people have one. It looks like that." and "I've seen one. That's what it is." Counterbalancing assured that each of the items chosen as study trial stimuli was shown to an equal number of subjects in the picture–word and in the word conditions and was paired with both the relevant and the neutral descriptions.

Each study trial was followed by a test trial. The test trial consisted of 20 words—10 words from among the stimulus items previously seen (under condition RP, RW, NP, or NW) and 10 additional words of similar frequency of occurrence, imageability, and length characteristics. The 20 items in this list were randomized and shown to the subject one by one. The patient had only to answer "yes" he had seen the word previously during the study trial, or "no" he had not.

Performance in the picture–word conditions was consistently better than performance on words alone in the content of a neutral verbal description, but regardless of whether a word appeared with or without a picture, the relevant verbal descriptions written to heighten visual imagery produced the best recall (Table 11.2).

Table 11.2
T SCORES FOR RAW SCORE DATA

Experimental variable	T	Significance
Conditions RP versus RW	30	.05
Conditions NP versus NW	18*	.05
Picture versus word effects	106	.025
Conditions RW versus NW	31	n.s.
Conditions RP versus NP	23	n.s.
Imagery versus neutral description	91.5	.01

*Two-tailed Wilcoxen.

Normal subjects have been found to have superior recognition memory for pictures as opposed to words (Paivio & Csapo, 1969), presumably because pictures elicit an image with greater ease than do their word equivalents. Paivio (1969) assumes, therefore, that normal subjects can benefit more from the facilitating effects of imagery with pictures than they do with their word equivalents. This assumption seems to hold true for the aphasic subjects. In the Edelstein (1976) study pictures, as expected, produced recognition memory that was superior to that of words: Under instructions to image during the study trials, words paired with their picture equivalents (condition RP) were later recalled better than words presented alone (condition RW). Increasing the imageability of a stimulus enhances recognition by heightening coding in the imaginal symbolic mode (Paivio, 1971). Accordingly, with instructions to image, aphasic's performance on a memory recognition tasks improves when pictures are used to strengthen imagery coding.

The hypothesis that language is dually coded, or is stored, organized, and retrieved via two coding systems, is supported by the research of Bower (1970), Paivio (1971), Seamon (1974), and many others. These two coding systems—the nonverbal imagery process and the verbal symbolic process—can function either independently or in connection with each other (Paivio & Csapo, 1971). In normal populations, pictures and highly imageable words are most likely to be dually coded and consequently stored in and retrieved from memory more readily than other stimuli (Katz & Paivio, 1975; Paivio, 1965, 1966; Paivio & Csapo, 1969). If this were true for an aphasic population, it would suggest that the visual imagery system could continue to function even though retrieval from the verbal system is impaired. According to the theory, since both codes can function independently, either code can be activated depending upon the stimulus attributes of the recall or recognition task. The connection between the two codes assumes that one code can be changed into the other, that is, words can arouse nonverbal images as well as their verbal labels. However, evocation of verbal labels is a process secondary to evocation of images; a transformation is necessary. The pictorial image must first be aroused, then the verbal label, followed by retrieval of the label. Pictorial learning can activate both codes more readily. Hypothetically, if access to one code, that is, the verbal, is damaged as in the case of aphasia, the imaginal code may still be available. Recall of this code may trigger recall of the verbal code. On the other hand, retrieval of the verbal code directly may be impossible due to extensive aphasia. If such were the case, at least the imaginal code should be available (West, 1977).

The facilitating effects of imagery in coding, storing, and retrieval is perhaps best exemplified in paired-associate learning (PAL) tasks. Imagery aids PAL by linking the stimulus and response members of the pair in an imaginal associative chain during the study trial. During the recall or test trial, the stimulus member elicits the appropriate referential or associative image, which acts as a "peg" in arousing the corresponding response item.

Research on PAL has been extensive (see Paivio, 1969; Rohwer, 1970; and Levin, 1976, for comprehensive reviews). The following summarizes its salient features:

1. Nouns rated high in their capacity for arousing imagery (high imagery nouns) are easier to learn as paired associates than those rated low in their capacity for arousing imagery.
2. Concrete noun pairs are easier to learn than abstract noun pairs.
3. Concrete nouns are higher in imagery value than abstract nouns.
4. The image-evoking value of nouns correlates more highly with PAL than any other known attribute.
5. Even when a subject is given explicit instructions to use verbal mediation, there is a high correlation between PAL and the imagery value of the stimuli.
6. Imaginal mediators predominate when both members of a pair are concrete.
7. Verbal mediators predominate when both members are abstract.
8. Pairs reported by subjects to be linked by imagery are more frequently recalled than pairs associated by verbal mediation.
9. The rated subjective vividness of an image-mediated association correlates directly with the probability of recall.
10. Subjects recall associations better when instructed to imagine scenes in which the parts are linked by actions and spatial relations into

easily visualized wholes than when instructed to imagine the parts as separated in space and noninteracting.

11. A positive effect of noun imagery is greater on the stimulus side than on the response side of pairs.
12. Action imagery is more memorable than static imagery.
13. Locational static imagery is more memorable than coincidental imagery.
14. The ability to profit from the stored images is contingent upon the subject's ability to store an appropriate verbal representation of the object along with its image.
15. Imagery instructions produce more facilitation than sentence instructions.
16. The capacity for deriving profit from imagery representations develops later than the capacity for deriving profit from verbal representations.

Paired-associate learning seems particularly useful as a paradigm to test the dual coding hypothesis, for the image-evoking capability of the stimulus or the response items can be easily manipulated as can the instructions given to the subject about how to link the two items together in memory. If PAL is enhanced in aphasics under imagery conditions, it could lend support to the hypothesis that visual imagery might serve as an alternative coding device.

Altman (1977) conducted a study that compared the effects of highly imageable pictures and words, this time looking at the differential effect of pictures versus words in a PAL task. Subjects were given instructions to remember the pairs, but no emphasis was placed on using an imagery strategy. The picture–word contrast was manipulated independently for stimulus and response positions, so that four different lists were used: picture–picture (P–P) pairs, picture–noun (P–N) pairs, noun–picture (N–P) pairs, and noun–noun (N–N) pairs. On the assumption that aphasics might well remember an association but be unable to report the response when shown the stimulus, a recall trial with response alternatives was provided after every fourth study pair. For example, if the fourth study pair had been the noun–noun combination *table-queen*, during the recall trial the patient would see the word *table* followed immediately by the response alternatives slide for that pair, *flower-queen-candy-snake*. Thus, in all cases the patient had only to point to the item that correctly completed the pair; no oral response was required. This raises an important point because Dilley and Paivio (1968) found that although pictures are more likely to evoke imagery than words, the requirement that a response be given verbally entails a transformation of information if it is stored visually. Therefore, the picture–noun pairs were superior to all others in children because the word was provided. Rohwer and his associates (cf. Rohwer, 1970), however, suggest that the capacity for deriving benefit from pictorial modes of representation develops later than the capacity for deriving benefit from verbal modes.

Altman found (Figure 11.1) that learning under the picture–picture condition was better than learning under the other conditions, although a statistical difference between the picture–picture and the noun–picture conditions emerged only when 1 of the 16 subjects studied was eliminated. This was the one subject—a fluent, very impaired patient—whose scores went in the reverse direction: Discarding his performance resulted in the picture–picture condition always being superior.

We see in this figure the extremely strong effect of pictures. Whenever the patient made the direct match between picture and picture, performance was better. When the study trial involved pictures in the response position, and the patient had to choose his response from picture choices, he always did better.

Altman also obtained a correlation between subjects' performance on the PAL task and performance on Parts A and B of the Minnesota Test for Differential Diagnosis of Aphasia (MTDDA) (Schuell, 1965). The correlation between the number of errors made on the MTDDA and the number of items correct under PAL was significant at the .01 level. That is, the better the subject did on the MTDDA, the better his performance on PAL. These results substantiate Paivio's dual coding hypothesis: When the verbal code was more available, as it presumably is in the case of the less severely im-

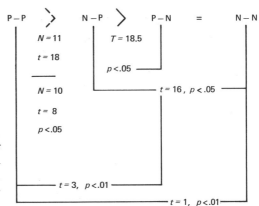

Figure 11.1. Performance of 16 aphasics under four conditions of paired-associate learning: picture–picture (P–P), noun–picture (N–P), picture–noun (P–N), and noun–noun (N–N).

paired patients, PAL was better. The patients with the less severe aphasia perhaps had two codes available.

The Altman study, of course, involved recognition memory, and the results from studies with normal subjects are similar to those found here: Recognition scores are higher for concrete than for abstract nouns (Gorman, 1961), and pictures, in turn, are easier to recognize than are their names or words generally (Jenkins, Neale, & Deno, 1967; Shepard, 1967). Taken together, these findings suggest that recognition memory increases from abstract words to concrete words to pictures, and lead to the conclusion that such a hierarchy of difficulty has application in the treatment and diagnosis of aphasia.

Paivio (1969) argues that image arousal to words is slower than verbal coding of words or familiar pictures, providing the following ranking of the availability or arousal probability of verbal versus visual image code for the different stimuli: Image arousal in the case of pictures and verbal coding in the case of words rank first, the verbal code in response to pictures ranks second, imagery in response to concrete words third, and images in response to abstract words fourth. Thus, he says, the cumulative availability of *both* codes is highest in the case of pictures, intermediate for concrete nouns, and lowest for abstract nouns. Paivio interprets his results in terms of his "dual coding" hypothesis that both the verbal and the visual imagery code become available when pictures are being processed. "The effect of concreteness on memory is hypothesized to be direct function of the availability of each code in that the appropriate verbal response can be retrieved from either [p. 257]."

The experimental work on the role of imagery in language processing bears upon the problem of treatment of language disturbance in the following way: If one uses concrete pictures as treatment stimuli, then both the verbal and imagery code may be aroused. In aphasics, the capacity to arouse the verbal code is depressed, if not absent. But these stimuli still hold the potential to arouse the visual code, which is presumably unimpaired.

Furthermore, if one code is able to assist in indirectly arousing the other, then arousal of the visual code may in some cases facilitate arousal of the verbal code. In other words, the chances of arousing the verbal code are increased by using pictures. On the other hand, if the naming impairment, for example, or the aphasia in general is so dense that no verbal code is aroused, at least the visual imagery code will have been aroused. Something presumably has happened to affect coding. Using visual imagery to its fullest extent can serve as an effective mediator between what is visualized and

to this process. Albert and Bear (1974) hypothesized that after left hemisphere damage the right hemisphere learns to process materials presented slowly. In melodic intonation therapy the patient not only listens to slowed auditory stimuli, but slowed stimuli that are intoned musically. Theoretically, this combination of variables should maximize the potential for right hemisphere comprehension.

MELODIC INTONATION THERAPY AND CT SCAN LESION LOCALIZATION

In 1980 we reported a retrospective study in which lesion localization sites identified by CT scan were correlated with good or poor response to melodic intonation therapy (Helm-Estabrooks, Naeser, & Kleefield, 1980). Both CT scans and Boston Diagnostic Aphasia Examination (BDAE) scores (Goodglass & Kaplan, 1972) were studied for eight right-handed patients who received MIT. Particular attention was given to changes in verbal expression as measured by conversational phrase length, articulatory agility, and grammatical form. Four good response cases and four poor response cases were selected on the basis of changes on these parameters. Pre-MIT phrase length scores ranged from 1 to 4. Articulatory agility scores ranged from 1 (always impaired) to 7 (never impaired). Grammatical form was rated from 1 (none available) to 4 (limited to simple declaratives and stereotypes).

Although five of the eight patients initially had little or no ability to produce speech, none were judged to have global aphasia because overall auditory comprehension ranged from -1 to $+1$ standard deviation on the BDAE Z-score profile.

Following MIT, the four ''good response'' patients showed improved conversational phrase length. Of these four, three also improved in articulatory agility and grammatical form.

The four ''poor response'' patients failed to show change in phrase length or grammatical form. Three of these four likewise showed no change in articulatory agility.

Examination of CT scans obtained for all eight patients showed that the four good response cases had lesions confined to the left hemisphere whereas two of the four poor response cases were found to have small right hemisphere lesions in addition to larger left hemisphere lesions. The remaining two poor response cases had unilateral brain damage but distinguished themselves from the good responders and from the two bilaterally involved poor responders by earning better pre-MIT articulatory agility scores. One had normal articulation in familiar words and phrases, and the other had normal articulatory agility for all speech tasks. These findings led us to conclude that melodic intonation therapy facilitates the motor speech aspects of verbal output in aphasic patients, if the patient has poorly articulated speech associated with exclusively left brain damage.

That MIT has a positive effect on articulatory agility is not surprising. Speech pathologists have long used paced speech or syllabication approaches to the management of neuromotor articulatory problems (Rosenbek & LaPointe, 1978). It has never been suggested before, however, that an intact right hemisphere may be required for melodic pacing to have a rehabilitative effect on articulation. But, in addition to improving articulation in the good response cases, a course of MIT resulted in improved conversational phrase length and grammatical form. In this respect the method has to be regarded as an aphasia treatment and not merely a speech treatment.

THE RIGHT HEMISPHERE AND RECOVERY FROM APHASIA

Although damage to the left hemisphere is more likely to cause language disturbances than is damage to the right hemisphere, if left brain damage occurs in childhood recovery may be dramatic and virtually complete. The recovery in these cases is thought to be the result of rapid assumption of language processing by the right hemisphere (Moscovitch, 1981). When aphasia is associated with a stroke in adulthood, recovery is often a slow and incomplete process. Aphasiologists question whether this form of recovery is the result of gradual left to right switch in language dominance, or rather the reorganization of the left hemisphere. Some evidence in favor of the former hypothesis is offered in the following studies.

In 1960 Tikofsky, Kool, and Thomas studied EEG patterns of 33 adult aphasic patients who received an unspecified form of therapy. A high correlation was found to exist between poor response to treatment and bilaterally slow EEG patterns. To the investigators this suggested a possible role of the nondominant hemisphere in language recovery.

Subsequently, Smith (1966) reported the case of a 47-year-old right-handed man who had a left hemispherectomy for a glioma. During the first 7 months following surgery, the patient showed slow recovery of language function. Smith concluded that the minor or right hemisphere has considerable capacity, even in adults, to organize language.

Smith's conclusion is supported by the study of Kinsbourne (1971) who staged serial unilateral intracarotid amobarbital injections on two right-handed aphasic patients. A third patient had a left side injection only. Left-side injections did not result in speech arrest, but arrest of all vocalization occurred with the right-side injections. For Kinsbourne the results indicate that in these cases dominance for residual language had shifted to the right.

Further evidence of left to right shift of language in adult aphasia is found in the 1979 study of CT scan lesion localization by Mazzocchi and Vignolo. Their Case 8 had a first stroke in July 1971, which resulted in a severe aphasia. The patient had 6 months of aphasia therapy and was not aphasic in March 1977. A second stroke occurred in July 1977 and, like the first, resulted in a severe aphasia. A CT scan performed 21 days following the second stroke showed an older left hemisphere lesion and a second, newer right hemisphere lesion. The authors conclude that the finding "strongly suggests that recovery of language after the left hemisphere lesion was due to functional compensation by the right hemisphere [p. 635]."

The role of traditional therapies in facilitating right hemisphere language is uncertain. Although Mazzocchi and Vignolo's patient received treatment, a case described by Cummings, Benson, Walsh, and Levine (1979) did not. This right-handed patient had severe aphasia associated with a large left lesion involving the entire middle cerebral artery distribution. The classical language areas were totally destroyed. The patient was discharged after resisting treatment. Upon readmission more than 2 years later he showed improvement on the Boston Diagnostic Aphasia Examination, although he still displayed distinct symptoms of aphasia. The authors concluded that given the severity of his language zone lesion, right hemisphere function may underlie much of the recovery from aphasia.

One might speculate as to how much more recovery this patient may have experienced had he accepted treatment. For example, one of the good response cases studied by Helm-Estabrooks, Naeser, & Kleefield (1980) and described in Albert, Goodglass, Helm, Rubens, and Alexander (1981) had two left hemisphere lesion sites. The first involved the inferior temporal lobe and Broca's area (cortical and deep) with extension up the precentral gyrus and superior frontal lobe. A second lesion involved the supramarginal and angular gyri in the parietal lobe. At 10 months post onset this patient's BDAE auditory comprehension Z-score was $-.5$ SD and his verbal output was restricted to a few consonant–vowel combinations such as *goo-go, doe-kah* for all tasks. He had severe buccofacial apraxia. Following approximately 120 sessions of melodic intonation therapy over a 4-month period, the patient's auditory comprehension had improved a full standard deviation and his verbal output had improved in every sphere. Most notably, confrontation naming had progressed from 0/105 to 58/105 and he had functional communication skills (e.g., "Dis week-end, we go home"). This is just one of several cases where melodic intonation therapy has been successful with patients having a persistent history of producing restricted phonemic stereotypies despite traditional (nonintoned) therapy approaches.

Recently we saw a patient with the most severe form of buccofacial apraxia who produced only the stereotypy *dee-oh-ah* for 6 weeks following stroke. Within three sessions of melodic intonation therapy, he spontaneously produced appropriate phrases. His CT scan showed a left subcortical capsular, putaminal lesion with anterior–superior extension. Our clinical experience tells us that no other known method could produce such dramatic results in this type of patient (Naeser, Alexander, Helm, Levine, Laughlin, & Geschwin, 1982).

CONCLUSION

There is a growing body of evidence that the right hemisphere plays a major role in producing and processing melody and intonational contours. It is reasonable, therefore, to hypothesize that melodic intonation therapy facilitates recovery from aphasia by way of the right hemisphere. In support of this hypothesis it was found that two patients who appeared to be, but were not, good candidates for melodic intonation therapy had bilateral brain lesions.

In 1969 Geschwind stated, "It is my belief that the major hope for the eventual effective rehabilitation of the type of aphasic for whom we can do so little now lies in the possibility that language is present but inaccessible in the minor hemisphere [p. 123]." Melodic intonation therapy, I maintain, appears to be one approach to gaining access to right hemisphere language.

ACKNOWLEDGMENTS

Lorraine Obler provided helpful suggestions for this chapter.

REFERENCES

Albert, M., & Bear, D. Time to understand. A case study of word deafness with reference to the role of time in auditory comprehension. *Brain*, 1974, 97, 373–384.

Albert, M., Goodglass, H., Helm, N., Rubens, A., & Alexander, M. *Clinical aspects of dysphasia*. New York: Springer-Verlag, 1981.

Albert, M., Sparks, R., & Helm, N. Melodic intonation therapy for aphasia. *Archives of Neurology*, 1973, *29*, 130–131.

Benton, A. L., & Joynt, R. J. Early descriptions of aphasia. *Archives of Neurology*, 1960, *3*, 205–222.

Blumstein, S., & Cooper, W. Hemispheric processing of intonation contours. *Cortex*, 1974, *10*, 146–158.

Bogen, J., & Gordon, H. Musical tests for functional localization with intracarotid amobarbital. *Nature*, 1971, *230*, 524–525.

Cummings, J. L., Benson, D. F., Walsh, M. J., & Levine, H. L. Left to right transfer of language dominance: A case study. *Neurology*, 1979, *29*, 1547–1550.

Gardner, H., Albert, M., & Weintraub, S. Comprehending a word: The influence of speed and redundancy on auditory comprehension in aphasia. *Cortex*, 1975, *11*, 155–162.

Geschwind, N. Anatomical understanding of the aphasias. In A. L. Benton (Ed.), *Contribution to clinical neuropsychology*. Chicago: Aldine, 1969.

Goldstein, K. *After-effects of brain injuries in war: Their evaluation and treatment*. New York: Grune and Stratton, 1942.

Goodglass, H., & Kaplan, E. *Boston Diagnostic Aphasia Examination*. Philadelphia: Lea and Febiger, 1972.

Helm, N. A. *Criteria for selecting aphasia patients for melodic intonation therapy*. Paper presented at the symposium Language Rehabilitation in Aphasia, annual meeting of the American Academy for the Advancement of Science, Washington, D.C.: 1978.

Helm, N. A. *The gestural behavior of aphasic patients during confrontation naming*. Doctoral dissertation, Boston University, 1979.

Helm-Estabrooks, N., & McGillivray, C. *The influence of melodic intonation therapy on auditory comprehension skills of aphasic patients*. Paper in preparation.

Helm-Estabrooks, N., Naeser, M. A., & Kleefield, J. *CT scan lesion localization and response to melodic intonation therapy*. Paper presented at the annual meeting of the Academy of Aphasia, Bass River, Mass., 1980.

Kimura, D. Left–right differences in the perception of melodies. *Quarterly Journal of Experimental Psychology*, 1964, *15*, 355–358.

Kinsbourne, M. The minor cerebral hemisphere as a source of aphasic speech. *Archives of Neurology*, 1971, *25*, 302–306.

Lasky, E., Weidner, W., & Johnson, J. Influence of linguistic complexity, rate of presentation and interphrase pause time on auditory verbal comprehension in aphasia. *Brain and Language*, 1976, *3*, 386–395.

Mazzocchi, R., & Vignolo, L. H. Localization of lesion in aphasia: Clinical CT scan correlations in stroke patients. *Cortex*. 1979, *15*, 627–654.

Mills, C. K. Treatment of aphasia by training. *Journal of the American Medical Association*, 1904, *43*, 1940–1949.

Milner, B. Lateral effects in audition. In V. B. Mountcastle (Ed.), *Interhemispheric relations and cerebral dominance*. Baltimore: Johns Hopkins University Press, 1962.

Monrad-Krohn, G. Prosody and its disorders. In L. Halpern (Ed.), *Problems of dynamic neurology*. Jerusalem: Jerusalem Post Press, 1963.

Moscovitch, M. Right hemisphere language. *Topics in Language Disorder*, September, 1981, 41–61.

Naeser, M., Alexander, M., Helm, N., Levine, H., Laughlin, S., & Geschwind, N. Aphasia with predominately subcortical lesion sites. Description of three capsular/putaminal syndromes, *Archives of Neurology*, 1982, *39*, 1.

Penfield, W., & Roberts, I. *Speech and brain mechanisms.* Princeton, N.J.: Princeton University Press, 1959.

Rosenbek, J., & LaPointe, L. The dysarthrias: Description, diagnosis and treatment. In D. F. Johns (Ed.), *Clinical management of neurogenic communicative disorders.* Boston: Little, Brown & Co., 1978.

Ross, E. D., & Mesulam, M. Dominant language functions of the right hemisphere? *Archives of Neurology*, 1979, *36*, 144–148.

Smith, A. Speech and other functions after left (dominant) hemispherectomy. *Journal of Neurology, Neurosurgery, and Psychiatry*, 1966, *29*, 467–471.

Sparks, R., Helm, N., & Albert, M. Aphasia rehabilitation resulting from melodic intonation therapy. *Cortex*, 1974, *10*, 303–316.

Tikofsky, R. S., Kooi, K. A., & Thomas, M. H. Electroencephalographic findings and recovery from aphasia. *Neurology*, 1960, *10*, 154–156.

Yamadori, A., Osumi, U., Mashuara, S., & Okuto, M. Preservation of singing in Broca's aphasia. *Journal of Neurology, Neurosurgery, and Psychiatry*, 1977, *40*, 221–224.

Author Index

A

Abstract (versus concrete) language, processing of, 7, 63, 64, 66, 114, 165, 172
Acoustic stimuli, processing of, 27
Acquired skills, 3
Affect, positive versus negative, 113, 118, *see also* emotion
Affective
  responses, 50
  semantic relations, 51
  tone
    comprehension of, 172
    ear advantage for, 112
Affectively loaded (versus neutral) words, 5, 6, 117
Age
  at time of brain injury, 126
  as a variable, 135, 174
Aging, 4, 174, 180, 187
Agraphia, 51

Alzheimer's Disease, 61
Amobarbitol injection, effect on speech, 234
Amplitude asymmetry in electrophysiology, 126, 127, 130, 131, 141
  and cognitive processing, 143, 144
  and IQ, 136, 137, 142
Amusia, 196, 232
Anagrams, sentence, 69
Analytic (versus holistic) processing, 3, 4, 8, 9, 25–29, 41, 48, 78, 86, 171, 172, 215, 217
Anesthetization of right hemisphere, *see* Sodium amytal injection
Anosagnosia, 5, 172
Antonymic contrasts, appreciation of, 69, 172
Aphasia, 48, 50, 51, 58, 150, 173, 180–182, 186, 193–209, 215–227, 229–238
  emotional outburst in, 115
  recovery from, 236–238

PERSPECTIVES IN
NEUROLINGUISTICS, NEUROPSYCHOLOGY, AND
PSYCHOLINGUISTICS: A Series of Monographs and Treatises

Harry A. Whitaker, Series Editor
DEPARTMENT OF HEARING AND SPEECH SCIENCES
UNIVERSITY OF MARYLAND
COLLEGE PARK, MARYLAND 20742

HAIGANOOSH WHITAKER and HARRY A. WHITAKER (Eds.).
Studies in Neurolinguistics, Volumes 1, 2, 3, and 4

NORMAN J. LASS (Ed.). Contemporary Issues in Experimental Phonetics

JASON W. BROWN. Mind, Brain, and Consciousness: The Neuropsychology of Cognition

SIDNEY J. SEGALOWITZ and FREDERIC A. GRUBER (Eds.). Language Development and Neurological Theory

SUSAN CURTISS. Genie: A Psycholinguistic Study of a Modern-Day "Wild Child"

JOHN MACNAMARA (Ed.). Language Learning and Thought

I. M. SCHLESINGER and LILA NAMIR (Eds.). Sign Language of the Deaf: Psychological, Linguistic, and Sociological Perspectives

WILLIAM C. RITCHIE (Ed.). Second Language Acquisition Research: Issues and Implications

PATRICIA SIPLE (Ed.). Understanding Language through Sign Language Research

MARTIN L. ALBERT and LORAINE K. OBLER. The Bilingual Brain: Neuropsychological and Neurolinguistic Aspects of Bilingualism

TALMY GIVÓN. On Understanding Grammar

CHARLES J. FILLMORE, DANIEL KEMPLER, and WILLIAM S-Y. WANG (Eds.). Individual Differences in Language Ability and Language Behavior

JEANNINE HERRON (Ed.). Neuropsychology of Left-Handedness

FRANÇOIS BOLLER and MAUREEN DENNIS (Eds.). Auditory Comprehension: Clinical and Experimental Studies with the Token Test

R. W. RIEBER (Ed.). Language Development and Aphasia in Children: New Essays and a Translation of "Kindersprache und Aphasie" by Emil Fröschels

GRACE H. YENI-KOMSHIAN, JAMES F. KAVANAGH, and CHARLES A. FERGUSON (Eds.). Child Phonology, Volume 1: Production and Volume 2: Perception